D1552957

THE

PRODUCTION

OF

DIFFERENCE

THE
PRODUCTION
OF
DIFFERENCE

RACE AND THE MANAGEMENT
OF LABOR IN U.S. HISTORY

DAVID R. ROEDIGER
ELIZABETH D. ESCH

OXFORD
UNIVERSITY PRESS

OXFORD
UNIVERSITY PRESS

Oxford University Press, Inc., publishes works that further
Oxford University's objective of excellence
in research, scholarship, and education.

Oxford   New York
Auckland   Cape Town   Dar es Salaam   Hong Kong   Karachi
Kuala Lumpur   Madrid   Melbourne   Mexico City   Nairobi
New Delhi   Shanghai   Taipei   Toronto

With offices in
Argentina   Austria   Brazil   Chile   Czech Republic   France   Greece
Guatemala   Hungary   Italy   Japan   Poland   Portugal   Singapore
South Korea   Switzerland   Thailand   Turkey   Ukraine   Vietnam

Published by Oxford University Press, Inc.
198 Madison Avenue, New York, NY 10016

www.oup.com

Oxford is a registered trademark of Oxford University Press

An early treatment of some of the material in this book appeared as Elizabeth Esch and
David Roediger, "Race and the Management of Labor in U.S. History,"
Historical Materialism 17 (2009), 3–43 and is used with the permission of the publisher
Koninklijke Brill NV, The Netherlands.

Library of Congress Cataloging-in-Publication Data
Roediger, David R.
The production of difference: race and the management of labor in U.S. History /
David R. Roediger, Elizabeth D. Esch.
p.   cm.
Includes bibliographical references and index.
ISBN 978-0-19-973975-2 (hardcover: alk. paper)
1. Discrimination in employment—United States—History.
2. Labor—United States—History.
3. Race discrimination—United States—History.
4. United States—Race relations. I. Esch, Elizabeth D. II. Title.
HD4903.5.U58R636   2012
658.30089'00973—dc23   2011038641

1 3 5 7 9 8 6 4 2

Printed in the United States of America
on acid-free paper

In memory of

Derrick Bell
(1930–2011)

Troy Davis
(1968–2011)

Stetson Kennedy
(1916–2011)

Manning Marable
(1950–2011)

David Montgomery
(1927–2011)

CONTENTS

⸻⸻◦∞◦⸻⸻

ACKNOWLEDGMENTS

—⊰⊱—

WE THANK LONG-STANDING mentors, scholars, and activists with whom we have exchanged writings and ideas on the concerns of this book over the years, and people whose examples have taught us. These include Venus Green, Yvette Huginnie, Shelton Stromquist, Peter Rachleff, Susan Porter Benson, Marvin Rosen, Pedro Cabán, Marcus Rediker, Jerry Tucker, Jennie Kassanoff, Herb Sloan, Eric Foner, Danny Widener, Robin Kelley, Michael Lacombe, Margaret George, Peter Linebaugh, Noel Ignatiev, David Montgomery, George Fredrickson, Nikhil Singh, Brent Edwards, Erin Small, Steve Downs, David Levin, Tom Bender, Catherine Sameh, Mike Rosenow, Josh Fraidstern, Rick Halpern, Philip S. Foner, Angela Davis, Lisa Lowe, Fred Thompson, Janet Jacobsen, James Barrett, Paul Garon, Gabriela Arredondo, George Rawick, David Noble, Kimberly Gilmore, George Lipsitz, Josef Barton, Matt Noyes, X Nate Mosley, Penelope Rosemont, Franklin Rosemont, David McNally, Don LaCoss, Blake Schwarzenbach, Karen Brodkin, Herbert Gutman, and Neferti Tadiar. In writing, we have benefitted from criticism, advice, and in some cases very generous sharing of research from Zachary Sell, Nick De Genova, Cheryl Harris, David Schley, Jeremy Wells, Victor Devinatz, Jake Mattox, Julie Greene, Augusto Espiritu, Faranak Miraftab, Robert Zeidel, Thomas Mackaman, Shawn Leigh Alexander, Rebecca Hill, Manu Vimalassery, Jennifer Guglielmo,

Brian Kelly, and Kornel Chang. Martin Smith, Isaac Curtis, and Zachary Sell provided critical research assistance. Susan Ferber's editing greatly improved the book.

We are lucky to have had so many opportunities to present parts of this work over the past several years. We thank audiences, fellow conference participants, and organizers at University of Wisconsin-Milwaukee, Vanderbilt University, the Kirwan Institute at Ohio State University Conference on Structural Racism, Louisiana State University, University of Kentucky, Xavier University, University of Notre Dame, University of Copenhagen, Southern Illinois University, Mississippi State University, University of Maine, California State University at Long Beach, Highline Community College (Seattle) Dr. King Lecture, University of Pittsburgh's E.P. Thompson Memorial Lecture, the Historical Materialism Conference at University of York, the Cordelia Beam Lecture at University of Iowa, University of Toronto, and the New Approaches to Capitalism and Imperialism in US History Conference at Harvard University. An early version of some arguments in the book appeared in *Historical Materialism*, which provided valuable editorial advice. We especially thank Jeff Webber and Sebastian Budgen for their roles in that process. Research leave was provided by the Center on Democracy in a Multiracial Society and the Center for Advanced Study at University of Illinois and the Special Assistant Professor Leave at Barnard College.

We thank librarians at University of Illinois, Columbia University, and Barnard College and the archivists and library staff at the Herbert Hoover Presidential Library in West Branch, Iowa, the Benson Ford Research Center at the Henry Ford, Dearborn, Michigan, the Oral History Collection at Columbia University's Butler Library; Special Collections at Tulane University; the John R. Commons Papers, State Historical Society of Wisconsin; and the Minnesota Historical Society.

Finally, as coauthors we also very much thank one other. The ideas that shaped this project emerged from many conversations over time and genuine collaboration. The emphasis on transnational work and capital and on taking the history of management seriously emerges from Elizabeth Esch's work, while that on slavery and on whiteness from David Roediger's. Neither of our initial emphases emerged unchanged, perhaps nowhere more clearly than in the necessity to think through the ways in which the choice of emphasis on a "white" identity by many workers was tragically conditioned by the coercions of capital.

THE

PRODUCTION

OF

DIFFERENCE

Introduction

Race in the History of U.S. Management

MR. BLOCK, THE CARTOONISH ANTIHERO of radical comics in the early twentieth century, had plenty of troubles. The thick-headed Block suffered constant indignities based on his mistaken belief in the good intentions of capitalists, politicians, cops, conservative union leaders, and labor contractors. Ernest Riebe, cartoonist and member of the Industrial Workers of the World (IWW), created Block to be stupid in an instructive sort of way, the prototypical unthinking white worker who had to learn about class to survive. But in supporting an organizing drive among Louisiana timber workers, Riebe not only had to make Mr. Block learn about race but also had to imagine that the antihero might not always be white. In the 1913 Mr. Block strip "He Meets Others," Riebe shows workers in the Louisiana Piney Woods region as a most diverse group, a fact not lost on the boss. A suit-wearing manager circulates among a group of workers, drawn with slight variations to identify them as being of varied races and nationalities—Anglo-Saxon, Irish, German, Italian, Chinese, Polish, and black. These various others are easily set against one another by the manager. The boss threatens and cajoles them to compete by appealing to masculinity, to fears of joblessness, and especially to their willingness to believe in racial and national differences among themselves. Management-by-race proceeds individual by individual in the comic,

3

Ernest Riebe, MR. BLOCK: HE MEETS OTHERS. Originally published in Ernest Riebe, *Twenty-Four Cartoons of Mr. Block* (Minneapolis, MN: Block Supply Company, 1913), n.p.

suggesting that the idea is is to keep competition alive by putting each individual worker on trial, racially and personally. By the last frame in Riebe's strip, the manager is reclining serenely, successful in getting the men to work frantically while swapping racial slurs among themselves.[1] Riebe shows race management to be crucial not only to the undermining of trade union unity and the lowering of wages but also to the very extraction of production from day to day. The cartoonist hopes that the high-stakes game will end favorably for labor when workers see through the strategy of the boss, but in the short run results are tragic.

Within a left tradition accustomed to simplifying organizing problems by asserting that all workers shared one common experience of exploitation, Riebe pictured management's purposeful use of difference-within-commonality at the point of production. In the Louisiana woods Riebe had in mind in "He Meets Others," another IWW supporter educated workers toward unity as follows: "Trees don't care who fells them. . . . They make as good a lumber when felled by the hand of a negro [or] a Hindoo . . . as when coming from the hand of a white American citizen. The interests of all who work in the woods . . . are the same."[2] For Riebe, such generalizations captured some truths while missing others. He portrayed the manager's insistence on exploiting racial difference as being central to capitalist production and, in the later frames, showed that the perils faced by black and Asian workers carried more dire consequences than those faced by Europeans.

The same acute awareness of the role of race in management found in "He Meets Others" appeared in the more scholarly work of John R. Commons, the labor economist and founder of academic labor history in the United States. In 1907 Commons's *Races and Immigrants in America* argued that U.S. management had shown just one "symptom of originality," namely "playing one race against the other." Commons took a leading part in progressive movements that often celebrated the advances in efficiency made by Frederick Winslow Taylor's system of scientific management. That Commons could pronounce management-by-race as the nation's paramount managerial innovation at the very time when scientific management was most lavishly publicized is no small matter, especially as his judgment was intimately tied to direct investigations of factory conditions.[3] Commons's striking connection of the cutting edge of management with the bloody history of race contrasts sharply with the bloodless efficiency of stopwatches and assembly lines that dominate histories of U.S. managerial contributions to history. Indeed, it is Commons's later glowing assessment of Taylor and of scientific management as "the most productive invention in the history of modern industry" that has prevailed rather than his insights on race management.[4]

Riebe and Commons highlight a historical drama that has until recently remained little investigated, scarcely theorized, and too often unnamed. The Marxist tradition exemplified by Riebe, the studies of labor history begun by Commons, and academic histories of management each have different reasons for letting race management pass almost unnoticed. From *The Communist Manifesto* forward, capitalism has for more than 160 years received credit from the mainstream of Marxism for introducing a "cosmopolitan character to production and consumption in every country." Marx later argued, "As against capital, labor is the merely abstract form, the mere possibility of value-positing activity, which exists only as a capacity, as a resource in the bodiliness of the worker." The body, so central to Riebe's images of management's manipulation of racial difference, is not absent in Marx, but the emphasis lies on its particularities being overcome by reducing it to standardized movements, on its race yielding to its class. Value arises from making labor abstract, not from accentuating differences among workers. Appreciation of the ability of capital to create a homogenized "world after its own image" has meant that the major Marxist studies of management in the United States have emphasized only the common experience of oppression visible in Riebe's cartoon. Even such major works on U.S. management as those of Antonio Gramsci, Harry Braverman, and C. L. R. James either ignore racial and national differences or see them as being effaced by the goals of progressive management to Americanize and homogenize workers.[5] Nor does split-labor market theory, effective in showing racial differences among workers and in some ways usefully derived from Marxism, consistently root racial divisions in production, rather than wages.[6]

Within standard academic studies of labor and management other barriers prevented scholars from seeing and naming race management. Among the foundational group of labor historians brought together by Commons, the belief that "labor" was white and that race was a natural reality rather than a difference made in the world of production cut against any ambitious attempts to pursue Commons's own insights. When Commons and his associates wrote their multivolume history of labor in the United States, they told the story of Chinese labor under the heading "class struggle versus race struggle." The infamous Chinese Exclusion Act of 1882 became in this view the turning point in all American working-class history, an alleged achievement without which "Mongolian labour" might have "overrun" the country. The assumption that the working class was white informed praise for Chinese exclusion, which was said to have prevented the history of labor from becoming a "conflict of races instead of one of classes." Such inapt dichotomizing of race and class impoverished serious treatment of both and particularly prevented studies that actually considered how management produced and then relied on differences among workers in an ongoing way.[7] Mainstream histories of U.S. management fix on its origins during the rise of large-scale industry, and with the advent of a formal literature in which experts describe their empirically based industrial management strategies in the early twentieth century. A southern and western extractive industry like that pictured by Riebe scarcely fits in such a framework, nor do the multiple connections of "He Meets Others" to Southern systems of Jim Crow, to Chinese exclusion in the Far West, and to the brutalities of the plantation and the frontier as foundational sites of race management.[8]

Although our world has not in any simple way become a more cosmopolitan place with less divided working classes, it is now possible to name race management and to tell its story boldly and broadly. Over the past decades, labor historians have begun to examine systematically the managerial use of race to divide workers, especially in Hawaii, in the deep and border South in the late nineteenth and early twentieth centuries, and within Asian American history. Where critical theory is concerned, what Grace Hong has called the "ruptures of capital"—strategies to make differences among workers pay—now often seem as impressive, calculated, and productive as capital's universalism.[9] Such universalism itself has come to be presented as less a truth about modern life than as one strand within capitalist modernity. The economist Michael Lebowitz finds difference so missing from Marx's *Capital* that he offers a name for what is absent: An "x-factor" has to be introduced as a new variable to help account for capital's behavior. "X" constitutes "the tendency to divide workers," an imperative so powerful that pursuit of it potentially leads to the sacrifice of profits in the short term.[10]

The most urgent calls for giving race management a name have come from feminist and antiracist scholars working at the boundaries of postcolonial studies and Marxism. Literary historian and theorist Lisa Lowe's *Immigrant Acts* insists both on the centrality of class and on the necessity of transcending any tendency within Marxism to isolate analyses of work from the specifically racialized bodies and histories of those performing it. Lowe powerfully demonstrates why Marxism is both indispensable and has been slow to apprehend the "specific history of the United States" where race, capital, and class are concerned. She argues that Marxism has too often stopped at viewing race-making processes like the slave trade and the seizure of indigenous lands as existing only in an early period of the "primitive" accumulation of capital. In the world's most developed capitalist nation, Lowe maintains, the connection of race and exploitation persisted, driving the accumulation of capital and shaping subsequent strategies of rule. "In the history of the United States," Lowe writes, "capital has maximized its profits not through rendering labor 'abstract' but precisely through the social productions of 'difference,'. . . marked by race, nation, geographical origins, and gender."[11]

The Production of Difference borrows from Lowe in its conceptualization as well as its title, and attempts to present a history of what Lebowitz calls the x-factor. The dynamics that Riebe portrayed suggest that the history of race management will be elusive at times even in the clearest of studies. The problems in this connection are several. If capital's goal has been to produce difference and division on the one hand, and interchangeable, standardized motions of labor performed by all workers on the other, the history of race management must include significant emphases on contradictions. Moreover, imagining themselves able to preside over such contradictions required that managers pretend to possess a knowledge of race and of human behavior that they could never have had. Thus much of what *The Production of Difference* describes as emerging in managerial literature is an imagination of control and wisdom by management, an imagination powerfully believed in and acted upon.

Furthermore, the fostering of competition among the races that Riebe and Commons identify as the key to U.S. management strategy turns out to be only one moment in a process that also emphasized the "race development" of allegedly inferior people. Such approaches gave strategies of racial domination a humanitarian spin, for example, during settlement, slavery, and certain phases in the Americanization of European immigrants. Thus not only the content but even the tone of managerial writing about race varied wildly from page to page, from slavery onward. In addition, neither "race" nor "management" refers in the sources for this book to something stable and easily defined. Bosses and academic experts in the nineteenth and early twentieth centuries defined race in myriad ways. Sometimes they posited a handful of races according to broad "color" groupings, and sometimes they named dozens of hierarchically arranged Europeans races, distinguishing among groups we would now call nationalities. Sometimes race seemed a matter of biology, and sometimes of culture, apprehended through religion, dress, accent, names, and place of residence.[12]

Multiple levels of management were all representative of capital. But they were structured in such a way that conflict among managers and sometimes between managers and the owners of the enterprise was inevitable, especially as managerial hierarchies expanded in large-scale units of production. In Riebe's comic strip, it is not possible to tell if the boss is meant to represent an upper manager or even owner—after all he wears a pretty nice suit—or the foreman providing hands-on belligerence at the lowest level of the managerial hierarchy. While it is true that capital made management as a whole develop a "personality" over and against labor, specific layers of management and individual managers retained their distinct personalities as well.[13] As Marx described this hierarchy, "An industrial army of workmen, under the command of a capitalist, requires, like a real army, officers (managers), and sergeants (foremen, overlookers), who, while the work is being done, command in the name of the capitalist."[14] Even those layers do not exhaust the varieties of management. White managers in this study include planters, plantation mistresses, overseers, women supervising domestic hired help, military occupation forces, foremen, guards of convicts providing forced labor, outside consultants, engineers, captains of industry, and of ships, and more.

Such complexities also provide opportunities to tell the story of race management. Indeed, the conflict between layers of management regarding whose racial knowledge was to be acted upon turns out to be a telling illustration of the drama of how race management proceeded, from overseers and masters in slavery to foremen and scientific managers in factories. Moments of group-based and individualized race baiting as well as those of collective racial development are not randomly distributed occurrences but instead are highly interesting in their timing and their ability to exist alongside each other. Shifts in the definition of racial categorization help to trace how emerging policies, like immigration restriction, impacted what managers saw as their project, given the workers available to them.

In discussing changes over time, this book emphasizes broad geographical coverage through case studies. It focuses on a one hundred year period, roughly from 1830 until 1930. The former date marks the decade of the first appearance of Southern journals that ambitiously discussed agricultural development in relation to the management of slaves. It also coincides with the boom in cotton production made possible by the full opening of lands in the Old Southwest. Beginning not with the northern factory but with antebellum studies on managing slaves underscores how quickly and thoroughly racial and managerial knowledge became entwined. Managers were never outside of the U.S. racial system and in many ways made that system. Further, the degree to which factory management, at various levels, understood itself as possessing racial knowledge connects it to, rather than distinguishes it from, the management of work under slavery.[15]

The closing date derives from the implementation of sharp restriction of immigration of the racialized European poor in 1924, giving time for the effects of such restriction to register in managerial thought and practice, but not moving far into the new and very different era of Depression and industrial unionism. Nevertheless, patterns set in these decades reverberate in our time. During World War I and the two decades that followed, management became unable to imagine itself as enduringly able to focus on playing European "races" against each other. It began to "concentrate" race management onto African Americans and recently arrived immigrants of color, especially Mexicans, which muted the discussion of intra-European "race" differences. In 1830, the United States was a second-tier nation in terms of economic power. By 1930, the nation was the world's unrivalled leader in production. Race management helped to engineer this tremendous shift.

Choosing these chronological parameters is not to suggest that race management did not have a history before 1830. While the management literature produced by slaveholders in the 1830s marks an important change, management of course occurs without being elaborated in journals. In the case of the United States, and the colonies antedating it, such management reflected the processes of settlement, dispossession of Indians, and adoption of slave labor in ways directly and powerfully connecting to race. To understand the habit of managing labor in terms of tribe and race, and of easily accepting that whites should do such managing, necessitates some appreciation of foundational processes.

As members of white settler colonies and often of slaveholding societies, Americans developed a sense of themselves in large measure by casting their racial and national heritage as making them uniquely suited to manage land and work, and to evaluate how other races might best labor under white managerial direction. Dispossession of Indians, and the "changes in the land" that it entailed and celebrated, were justified by the supposed inability of indigenous people to "husband," or manage, the resources at their command and conversely by "white" male claims to do so effectively.[16] The "doctrine of discovery" that made colonial projects "legal," which would be fully elaborated as an example for the world in the U.S. law, decisively linked conquest with management of nature. Thus what legal scholar Cheryl Harris describes as an emergent colonial notion of "whiteness as property" might also be considered "whiteness as management" from its founding impulses forward.[17]

Early American management decisions regarding labor likewise centered on what sort (and then on what "race") of coerced labor was most economical, skilled, durable, efficient, and tractable. After a period in which Indian slavery seemed a possibility, the last century of the colonial period featured cycles of favoring white indentured servants or African slaves. The turn in the late seventeenth century in Virginia to the mass use of slave labor and to laws dividing what came to be called "races," responded to repeated crises in and conflicts over the management of tobacco production and to the security of the colony. The most intense such conflict, Bacon's Rebellion in 1676, spurred the transition to African labor and to highly gendered elaborations of race as a means of social control, even as it aided the legitimation of cross-class European claims to Indian land.[18]

The choice of a slave labor force and the elaboration of ideologies eventually basing such a choice in allegedly racial group differences made for harsh judgments on the culture and abilities of Africans. Such white supremacist evaluations, though fierce, were mitigated by the manifest value of African labor. Combining the unfamiliarity and degradation of imported Africans with a long-standing British contempt for the labor and reason of the poor, planters soon supposed that the Africans they so zealously sought to acquire suffered from "gross bestiality and rudeness of their manners [and] the weakness and shallowness of their minds."[19] At the same time, the turn by profit-seekers to African labor represented and made concrete a confidence in African workers and their abilities. As assets in slaves accumulated, the tendency of planters to see and realize value in black labor never lost its logic even as theories of African inferiority came to be centerpieces of the defense of slavery.[20]

Just as whites began to make racial claims to a special capacity to manage other races, and/or the lands they occupied, the exigencies of securing labor in a colonial setting also encouraged managerial decisions that hinged on knowing the difference between nationalities within "races." Management-by-nationality and ethnicity led slave traders and owners to attempt to discern putative group propensities in Africans to survive and to resist, making such matters measurable and marketable according to the "tribe" of those imported. Recent scholars have elaborated on the planters' sharp awareness and valuation of skills that slaves brought from particular areas of West Africa. But the practice was also familiar to U. B. Phillips, who a century ago included in his documentary history eighteenth-century evidence of South Carolinians' preference for imported "windward and gold coast negroes, who have been accustomed to the planting of rice." Phillips also featured an 1803 guide for sugar planters that, for example, reported (and imagined) Senegalese imports as a "handsome race . . . in features resembling the whites . . . and excellent for the care of cattle and horses," if useless in field labor. The "Congos" "captivate the eye by their appearance and the ear by their humor." Iboes, the guide judged, were truculent, stubborn, and "much addicted to suicide" but withal "hardy and susceptible to labour, the women in particular." Often this claimed wisdom barely rose, as historians Ira Berlin and Philip Morgan remark, even to the level of "shallow stereotypes," and experts in Brazil, Jamaica, and the American South reached different and changing judgments about the same groups. Nonetheless, this alleged racial knowledge was rehearsed, acted upon, and connected to the management of plantations over long stretches of time. Sometimes it could claim to make "choices on long experience and a considered understanding . . . of various African nations." Planters also cultivated and shared knowledge on how to specifically manage the newly arrived African.[21]

To some extent, the need to people the vast landscape being "scoured," as Benjamin Franklin put it, also energized debates over which "races" of Europeans should be attracted to the colonies. Franklin himself was capable of diatribes against the "swarthy" peoples of Europe, among whom he included the Spanish and Italians, but also at times the Germans and even the Swedes. The threat of domination by German immigrants to Pennsylvania particularly preoccupied Franklin, who feared they would bring changes in language and culture but also in "complexion." However, Franklin balanced such judgments against a commitment to settler colonialism and economic development. He added that the Germans "have their Virtues, their industry and frugality is exemplary; they are excellent husbandmen and contribute to the improvement of a Country," and he therefore could not countenance "refusing to admit them entirely to our Colonies."[22]

The founding industry of the colonies—transport—anticipated the modern workplaces in which an astonishing variety of the world's peoples, in various degrees of unfreedom and statelessness, performed hard and drudging labor. By the end of the colonial period, one sailor in six was African or African American, with even the crews on slave ships including Africans as labor as well as cargo. Demand for maritime workers, military and otherwise, made the seagoing proletariat likewise include large numbers of other non-European hands and of European workers on board as a result of having been kidnapped or "impressed" into service. Black sailors existed in rough, if diminishing, equality with other shipboard workers, but they were also heavily slotted into service jobs and kept out of positions of authority. After the American Revolution, nationalist, mercantilist, and racialist regulations further made the sea a place of restriction as well as opportunity for workers of color.[23]

With the need to manage successful military and commercial alliances with some Indians against others, a similar tendency to make discriminating, if shifting, judgments about the merits of various native groups also appeared. Within the fur trade, assessing the abilities and fostering the willingness of specific Indian tribes and individuals to organize and defend the gathering and transport of vast quantities of product defined successful management. The skills of mountain men in such trade hinged as much on their knowledge of, and networks of relations with, specific Indian groups as on any other attribute.[24]

In the early national period, such racial judgments coalesced into the idea that a small group of "civilized tribes" might develop racially as they proved their capacity to husband the land (and sometimes to manage African slaves) in settled agriculture. But a blanket urge to see Indian people generally as impediments to progress and to remove them to beyond the Mississippi was increasingly grounded in race. The focus of early national debates over Indian civilization, and then over the brutalities of Indian removal, emerged most dramatically in the slaveholding Southwest. As historian Daniel Usner reminds us, fantasies of a primitive male-dominated "hunter state" among Indians allowed elites to regard the attempts by white mountain and backwoods people to resist commercial agriculture through hunting as reverting to "the temptations of savagery." Thus "whiteness-as-management" implied the need for poor whites to manage themselves and for men to manage women in ways allegedly setting white "civilization" apart from the supposed gender brutalities of the imagined "hunter state." To be fully white was to manage, intimately and expansively, before 1830.[25]

In tracing the further history of whiteness-as-management, and of the production of difference, the book's first part elaborates the detailed ways that slave masters described race and plantation management in antebellum journals such as *De Bow's Review* and *Southern Cultivator*, in debates over whether to use "white" (often Irish) wage labor or enslaved African labor, and in day-to-day plantation management. Three themes of consequence for this book emerge in the discussion of slavery. First is the extent to which masters and overseers made different and competing claims to racial knowledge they insisted was crucial to managing. The second theme concerns how race was sometimes used, especially in industry, as a way to "play" groups of workers against each other. It also served to justify the entire labor regime, by promising that it was the best, or even only, way to effect the racial development and uplift of the African workers involved. This bifurcation of "race management" into racial competition, on the one hand, and race development on the other, recurs in other places and times, making an irrational system also flexible and enduring. Finally, a persistent obsession with constructing ratios of productivity of workers of one race versus those of others appears during slavery and recurs consistently after it.

The second of the book's parts moves the story to the postbellum period and to the west. It analyzes the management of labor involved in building the infrastructures of U.S. expansion both continentally and beyond, and it shows how fully transnational the U.S. "symptom of originality" proved to be. Not only were racialized laborers imported into the U.S. West but also American managers and engineers claiming to possess racial knowledge moved into the Pacific Rim and the world. The construction of the Transcontinental Railroad is a story of intense racial competition. Race management in this instance not only enabled management to drive laborers in some of the most dangerous working conditions in U.S. history but also informed the engineering calculations regarding safety, especially for Chinese workers. The second case study of this section focuses on transnational mining engineers who conquered the world for informal U.S. empire after 1890. These men marketed internationally a presumed knowledge of race they had gained in managing mines in the U.S. West. Herbert Hoover, in particular, made racialized ratios of productivity a hallmark of his engineering work. He combined attention to the efficacy of racial competition and the possibility of "race development," and explicitly discussed the savings on safety measures that could occur when nonwhite labor was employed. Material on management of labor and management in the occupied Philippines and in Panama reveals the racial-strategies preoccupation of those managing formal U.S. empire.

The book's third section treats the coexistence within factory management in the late nineteenth and early twentieth centuries of highly rationalized and seemingly "raceless" scientific time-and-motion studies with a sharp awareness of racial competition in the managerial literature. The absence of much actual close study of race and labor by outside experts left much of the "foreman's empire," resting as it did on presumed knowledge of the immigrant "races," intact. Racial managerial knowledge was often tantalizingly close to being systematized, but it remained more effective if informally wielded by lower managers who hurried and pushed workers, and often hired and fired them. At the same time, racial development of eastern and southern European immigrants was sometimes trumpeted.

The immigration declines after 1915, culminating in immigration restriction in 1924, ended the possibility of playing European races against each other by the dozens. Management so feared the rebellious immigrant working-class militancy that erupted during and after World War I that it questioned the wisdom of such a wholesale system of race management and largely acquiesced in the restriction of immigration. Race management narrowed its sights to focus at times on consideration of blacks and Mexicans coming in unprecedented numbers to factories and to "factories in the fields." Foremen still managed existing European nationalities but in smaller numbers and, by the 1930s, in the face of strong countervailing powers of industrial unions. Thus race management came to be both narrower and more concentrated against workers of color, surviving to see a renaissance of mass immigration in our time.

PART I

FACING SOUTH

I

The Antebellum South and the Origins of Race Management

African Slavery, Indian Removal, and Irish Labor

IN AN INTRODUCTORY CHAPTER on "The Planter" that framed his *Black Reconstruction in America*, W. E. B. Du Bois made the lies and truths masters told to each other and to the world about their knowledge of managing Africans the key to their wealth, power, and limitations. For Du Bois, while planters necessarily "insisted on the efficiency of Negro labor for ordinary toil" and on its "essential equality of physical condition with the labor of Europe," the South's "pedantic periodicals" screamed that "higher intelligence" was impossible for "Negro labor." Such a stance justified the managerial authority masters assumed. Grand claims of racial knowledge born of management ramified tragically. What began in the South and in "industry" proved "singularly disastrous for modern civilization in science and religion, in art and government." To the "watching world" a racism designed to supervise what Du Bois called "slave industry" seemed "the carefully thought-out result of experience and reason," even as planters contradictorily obsessed over facing "sullen labor" determined to do as little work as possible.[1]

If Du Bois identified the management periodicals produced by the planter class as ponderous and pernicious, his contemporary, the celebrated proslavery historian U. B. Phillips, at times verged on

denying their existence. The Georgia-born Phillips posited the absence
of writings by slave masters on managing labor in his epic 1918 study
American Negro Slavery. Phillips began a chapter titled "Plantation
Management" with: "Typical planters though facile in conversation
seldom resorted to their pens. Few of them put their standards into
writing except in the form of instructions to their stewards and overseers." He informed readers that these writings amounted to little
more than "counsels of perfection, drafted in widely separated periods
[and] localities, and varying much in detail."² Such a view comfortably
coexisted with Phillips's notions of the planter class as premodern and
as laudably concerned with white racial rule over slaves rather than
productivity—with developing Africans rather than exploiting them.

However, it proved hard for Phillips to sustain such a view.
Elsewhere he portrayed a master class voluble about its own expertise in
management. Economist John R. Commons chose Phillips as editor of
the first two volumes of *A Documentary History of American Industrial
Society*. When those volumes appeared in 1909, Phillips led off with
a generous sampling of primary sources on "plantation management"
as structurally central to what would become industrial America.³ In
American Negro Slavery, Phillips once allowed, "On the generality of
the plantations the tone of the management was too much like that in
most modern factories." In this view slavery was all-too-modern, "The
laborers were considered more as work-units than as men, women and
children. Kindliness and comfort, cruelty and hardship, were rated at
balance-sheet value; births and deaths were reckoned in profit and loss,
and the expense of rearing children was balanced against the cost of
new Africans."⁴ For Phillips, slavery hinged either on the extraeconomic
attempts of masters to manage and develop another race, or on cold
calculations of profit.

This chapter, on the maturation of slave management alongside
settler expansion and Irish immigration, and the next on the day-to-day
dynamics of race management under slavery, take advantage of the rich
sources Du Bois identified. The chapters argue that the planters' cold
economic logic and their fully modern attempts to "develop" Africans
cannot be separated. The South's "pedantic periodicals" of the late antebellum period inaugurated management theory in the United States and
specifically set out to manage "the negro." From the legendary Southern

nationalist Edmund Ruffin's *Farmers' Register* forward, flagship agricultural journals like *Southern Cultivator*, *American Cotton Planter*, and *De Bow's Review* achieved huge circulation and engaged the leading intellectuals of the region during slavery's last three decades. Reflecting the dynamism of expansion into the Southwest, Noah Cloud's *American Cotton Planter*, printed in Montgomery, reached ten thousand homes in 1858, but still did not surpass the sweeping influence of the mostly New Orleans–based *De Bow's Review* and may not have matched the circulation of the Georgia-published *Southern Cultivator*.[5] Again and again, antebellum Southern journals offered extended disquisitions on management of black labor. In the sixty-nine examined volumes, each covering one year, of *Farmer's Register*, *Southern Planter*, *Southern Cultivator*, *American Cotton Planter*, and *De Bow's Review*, "management of slaves" came up for substantial discussion sixty-five times and "management of negroes" ninety times.[6] Managerial issues very often received discussion under other headings, but the term "negro" seems to have been preferred to "slave" in describing who was being managed. Inevitably, such accounts praised the managerial virtues of white masters, and indeed of whites as a race, so that the broad idea of "whiteness-as-management" received emphasis.[7]

In the frequent and contentious articles on the "management of negroes" produced by planter intellectuals in the twenty years before the Civil War, the claim for the vital import of race management was earnestly remade. Planter J. W. Pitts wrote of the "best method of managing negroes" as a "grave subject, and one that is not only always in order, but a subject that imperiously demands our instant and unremitted thoughts and our most devout consideration." When *De Bow's Review* announced that a group in Georgia was offering a one-hundred-dollar prize for the best essay on managing slaves, it took the contest and an attendant fair as evidence of the "great industrial reputation" of that state. For a *Southern Cultivator* correspondent writing as the war loomed, in the universe of possible subjects there was "none other more interesting in the planter's mind" than the "Management of Negroes." When another writer praised the same journal for lingering over "the 'almighty nigger' question" he defined the crux of that question as "The Negro and His Management." The *American Cotton Planter* itself featured the industrious black worker, the screw press for packing cotton, the steamboat, and the railroad on its mast-head, which also declared the publication's commitment to "plantation economy."[8]

The guide to best practices expressed in slave management journals reflected elitism and ideology at every turn. Editors, cor-respondents, and readers represented a relatively literate, leisured group of slaveholders who described how the large plantation ought to work. The very idea of "gang labor," much dissected by wealthy planters, implied a productive unit of substantial size. Masters on the smaller units that provided the setting for the typical slavehold-er's experience, though not that of most slaves, could not directly apply managerial lessons from the journals. Moreover, as with any prescriptive literature, the gap between ideal practices being debated and actual practice loomed potentially large. Day-to-day man-agement often fell to white overseers, who seldom wrote in the journals, and black drivers, who never did. The managerial prescrip-tions offered by masters might as easily be taken as evidence of their lack of control, and consequent desire to invent in a biomanagerial discourse what could not really exist. Even so, the race-saturated discourse of management represented a way to frame the extraction of production that large slaveholders insisted upon. From day to day some of the prescriptive measures did surely find application in the master's efforts to produce what one antebellum management writer called "accountability among the negroes." Blank forms for measuring productivity, included in *Affleck's Southern Rural Almanac and Plantation and Garden Calendar*, for example, can be found filled out in varying degrees of detail in many archives of plantation records.[9]

The writers tackling issues arising from the management of slaves knew that their words could be thrown back at them during debates over sectional political conflicts of the South with the North and North-west. With the antislavery world watching, particularly harsh variants of managerial practice doubtless found less expression than paternalistic ones. As an agricultural reformer, management editor, and Southern partisan Ruffin openly worried about how "the enemies of the insti-tution of slavery might cite [his] opinions."[10] One result was that the fears of African American revolt, and the measures taken to militarily manage slaveholding, tended to be raised obliquely in the major journals. Thus in the volumes of leading Southern management journals examined for this study, the U.S. slave patrol, a cross-class mobilization of whites policing slaves' behavior and movements at night, received only one brief mention. Debates over such a key institution of military plantation management could scarcely be aired in print, although the issue of slave resistance and its connections to race surfaced in articles not discussing patrols.[11] This chapter uses master-class management journals, along with other sources, to situate slavery within the history of management. It does so by adopting the broad usages of the term "management" that the masters themselves preferred. It first expansively considers management of military matters and especially of nature and Indians. It then turns to a much more focused antebellum literature comparing African productivity to poor white, and especially Irish immigrant, labor, particularly in dangerous and deadly work.

The Origins of U.S. Management in Slaveholding and Settlement

Slave labor and race management were central to how workers came to be bossed. The factory, so often seen as the site of management innovation, long coexisted with the plantation as the main site for the management of large groups of workers in the Americas. If anything, the latter ran ahead of the former in generating thought about management. As historian Robin Blackburn has written, "By gathering the workers under one roof, and subordinating them to one discipline, the new industrial employers were . . . adapting the plantation model."[12] The words "overseer," meaning the manager surveilling and speeding up the labor of slaves, and "supervisor," meaning the manager performing the same roles in industry, are synonyms. Similarly, the word "factories" was used for the West African staging areas gathering laboring bodies for the slave trade, and then for the production of the cotton that made possible the textile "factories" of England and of New England. More broadly, as the anthropologist Karen Brodkin has memorably written, "although race was initially invented to justify a brutal regime of slave labor . . . race making [became] a key process by which the United States continue[d] to organize and understand labor and national belonging."[13]

Antebellum U.S. politics, as well as economics, often turned on the relative merits of free versus slave labor. Such discussions easily devolved into considerations of the (dis)abilities of African American labor, in the fields and especially in manufacturing, as opposed to those of "white" labor or of work done by the "Irish race." Far from simply arraying the industrial North against the agrarian South, this issue saw capitalists in the two regions debate not only the relative merits of slavery and free labor but also the productivity of "black" versus "white" workers. Even as the Civil War raged, the *Richmond Examiner* broached the possibility that the South could rectify its mistake in employing black labor too overwhelmingly in agriculture. It argued that a refurbished system of bondage based on an "elaborate . . . subdivision of labor" could respond to both the "advanced intelligence" and the "thievish propensities" of African slaves, and therefore constituted the key to "the management of the race."[14]

Calculations leading to the replacement of free black workers in service and seaports in the North by desperately poor Irish immigrants hinged on the willingness of the Irish to compete with African Americans by accepting low wages. But the transition in employer preferences from one group to the other, and the threat that other reversals could occur, also featured broad discussions of whether the African or the Irish "race" was more tractable and efficient. For example, the wealthy New York City lawyer and diarist George Templeton Strong believed the Irish had "prehensile paws," instead of hands and judged from watching labor on his own home that "Southern Cuffee seems of a higher social grade than Northern Paddy."[15] The antebellum replacement of white American-born "helps" in domestic labor with "servants" of the Irish "race" likewise brought scrutiny and comparison, as did the turn from native-born to Irish women in northern textile mills.[16]

It was nevertheless the slave South where management was most insistently concerned with race. While the antebellum South featured gaping inequalities of wealth and power, the idea that whites managed blacks collectively, and individually succeeded by knowing how to do so, had broad material foundations. In no state did a majority of white families own slaves, and therefore manage them as property, at the time of secession, but in the entire Deep South substantial pluralities did. In South Carolina just less than half did so and in Mississippi 48 percent. Even in Texas, where Mexico had abolished slavery in 1830, more than 28 percent of white families owned slaves on the eve of the Civil War and Florida, Alabama, Georgia, and Louisiana all exceeded 30 percent. For the entire Confederacy nearly one white family in three owned slaves. Families moved in and out of slaveholding, and many hoped to save to buy slaves or to marry into the master class, making the experience of and aspiration to white managerial control still more widespread. At least one slave in twenty—and perhaps one in seven— was hired out in a typical year, and these practices led to deeply layered calculations about how best to manage black labor. What the literary and labor scholar Lisa Lowe has called the "social productions of 'difference'" undergirded the production of Southern crops first and foremost by producing whites who felt themselves superior to Africans and fit to manage them.[17]

Whole categories of employment hinged on the claims of racial knowledge. Slave traders needed to know, and be seen as knowing, how slaves would produce and reproduce. "Young or old, wise or foolish, ambitious or plodding, dour or debonair, harsh or indulgent," U. B. Phillips wrote of overseers, "they were alike only in their weather-beaten complexions and their habituation to the daily control of Negro slaves as a daily routine." As one observer wrote, overseers were "experts in the art of farming and managing negroes."[18] Even Southern medicine, requiring expertise not only in treating "slave diseases" but specifically in differentiating illness from avoidance of work, intersected with race management. Doctors sought greater sway over slave care and frequently testified in court regarding the contested soundness of slaves who had been exchanged in the marketplace. Most important, the slave patrol, militias, and networks devoted to catching runaways offered poor whites opportunities to earn small amounts of cash and elites opportunities to secure property and exercise leadership. If the virtual "declaration of war against the slaves" that John Hope Franklin's *The Militant South* describes as central to plantation management's project were to work, it needed "the cooperation of the entire community" in a patrol system designed to keep slaves from being out all night and therefore working wearily by day. White unity in policing slaves in what historian Peter Wood aptly calls the "slave labor camp" of the plantation goes far to explaining why a writer in *American Cotton*

Planter could maintain that "this species of property [the slave] has the tendency to produce among us who are living in its midst, and are interested in its management, an identity of interests" even though class differences within the white South were vast.[19]

While holding Africans as slaves informed whiteness-as-management as a set of ideas and practices, such "management" had many meanings, some of them intimately linking land use to settler colonial dispossessions of Indians. In 1840, *Farmer's Register* approvingly reprinted the 1818 edition of *Arator*, John Taylor of Caroline's series of agricultural essays, as a contribution to discussions of plantation management. Introducing management of Africans after a long analysis of "managing" fertilizers, Taylor apologized: "Perhaps this subject ought to have preceded that of manuring, as it is idle even to think of a good system of agriculture in any point of view, if the labor on which it depends is convulsed by infusions the most inimical to its utility; and if those who direct it, are to live in a constant dread of its loss, and a doubt of their own safety." Within a few lines, the subject had become military management, specifically during the Haitian Revolution and the need to prevent its imitation on U.S. soil. Soon Indian corn, cider, and sheep came up as objects whose management interested Taylor and the *Register*. Weymouth Jordan's study of the *American Cotton Planter* finds a similar range of concerns running through its pages: "It crusaded for railroads, manufacturing, direct trade with Europe, diversification of crops, horizontal plowing, crop rotation, use of fertilizers [and] Negro management." An early correspondent further laid out agricultural reform as "planting more corn, potatoes, peas; sowing more wheat, oats, rye; raising more mules, horses, hogs, cattle; and have better milch cows." He then stressed a need to "take better care of our negroes, especially our negro children; beautify and improve our plantations, make more manure, plant less land, and make heavier crops, and improve the comforts of our slaves, horses and mules." In advertisements for the plantation management guidebook featured repeatedly in *Southern Planter*, "Rules for the Discipline and Government of the Negroes" existed alongside sections on "Rural Economy, Sheep, Steam Engines [and] Tools &c. used by the Negroes."[20]

In its inaugural 1833 volume, *Farmers' Register* featured "On the Management of Negroes," which offered few details beyond the belief that "discipline is just as necessary on a plantation as in the navy or army." By 1840, the subject of managing black labor had developed into a central concern of the journal with characteristic and fruitful complications. After hundreds of references over previous years to "management" as equaling the efficient care of bees, cows, soil, silk-worms, sheep, hay, and other aspects of nature, Ruffin reprinted an article from the *Carolina Planter* in which Dr. R. W. Gibbes gingerly backed into the subject of the "management of slaves":

> While others, abundantly more competent than myself, are discussing the more weighty matters, and . . . in elevating the character of the tillers of the soil, the mainspring of all occupations— I feel a disposition to throw in my mite upon a subject too much neglected, but one of infinite magnitude, and pregnant with evil; so much so, that inadequate as I may feel myself to be I have no doubt but that I may cause the guilty to blush—I mean a proper regard to, and management of slaves.

Gibbes quickly clarified what was at stake by connecting management with security, given the "alarming" lack of "a proper, close, uncom-promising discipline over negroes, keeping in mind at all times the line of distinction between master and servant, and prohibiting entirely the association of any and all white persons from intercourse with [the slaves] who do not observe the same rule rigidly." As Phillips later wrote in describing the contradictions raised by "capable slaves," it was "masterfulness on the part of the whites" that made security possible. Management was thus military and biological as well as directed toward production by slaves.[21]

Similar strains in early writings on slave management complicate the claim that antebellum Southerners originated modern management solely through the race management of Africans. "Management" clearly meant many different things in the proliferation of Southern writings using the term. Through the 1830s, the term was decidedly more likely to apply to managing land and crops than to labor, and this tendency did not disappear at the height of managerial writings in the 1840s and 1850s. The leading modern collection of Edward Ruffin's writings aptly carries the title *Nature's Management.*[22] In describing his own system of management and what he did for slaves, one planter-expert wrote of acting on the conviction "that man is as much duty bound to improve and cultivate his fellow-men as . . . to cultivate and improve the ground."[23] Given such realities and the overwhelming importance of the slave as an asset, when management of labor was broached, experts tended to discuss black workers in conjunction with managing and improving land and animals. The alignment of alleged white managerial genius vis à vis slaves with a general ability to husband and develop nature makes the connections to race more profound; it also puts proslavery arguments in the context of the dispossession of indigenous people by settler colonialism. The antebellum South, and especially the Southwest, was not only the site of slavery but also of brutal dispossession, dislocation, and decimation of Indians. Some of the same political forces later calling for abolition of slavery also vigorously protested the removal of Southern Cherokees, Creeks, and Choctaws to trans-Mississippi territories in the 1830s.[24]

Justifications of dispossession connected expansion to the ability of white settlers to manage nature's gifts, including slaves. In C. C. Clay's 1853 homage to Alabama in the *American Cotton Planter*, frontier and plantation merged:

> Alabama . . . may truly triumph over her compeers as most worthy to bear the banner of Agriculture. . . . she is a child in years, but yesterday reclaimed from the Indian, whose footprints are still visible in her virgin forests, how marvelous her past progress! How incalculable her future attainments! And yet, the plenitude of her riches, the magnitude of her power, and the brightness of her glory, are attributable to a single production of her soil—the cotton plant![25]

The Indians, the Southern intellectual George Fitzhugh argued in a proslavery tract, were "*feroe naturæ*" as "wild as those who met Columbus on the beach." In a riposte to antiremoval forces, he added "[the Indian] is doomed to extermination, and those who most sympathize with his fate would be the first to shoot him if they lived on the frontier." In a particularly fractured 1853 account, William S. Price wrote, "The Indians have had ample opportunity for improvement in the . . . moral government of civilization; the protection of our government is and has been thrown around them . . . sums of money have been appropriated to their use . . ., without any valuable consideration . . . from them in return." Aid to Indians, Price significantly added, came out of "the properly directed labour of the African heathen," but "the result of all these efforts is that they [Indians] are Indians yet, and are likely to continue such."[26]

The offerings of proslavery theorists, often in plantation management journals, continually found ways to bring African and Indian histories together and to keep them apart. Writers fabricated megahistories naturalizing and aggrandizing supposed white abilities to manage nature, humans, and human property. Fitzhugh began with the Bible in order to defend both Indian "extermination" and African slavery. The former group would vanish "like the races of Canaan," but Africans might survive since "God did not direct his chosen people to exterminate all races; such as were fit for slaves they were ordered to make slaves of." Fitzhugh brought history's long arc to the present: "Despite the mawkish sensibility of the age, practical men are . . . pursuing the same course; they slay the Indians hip and thigh, as in the days of Moses and Joshua, and enslave the negroes."[27] Price strikingly connected proslavery arguments to supposed white abilities to husband nature and to civilize Africans. "Now if it is the . . . desire and ambition of civilized man to bring the things of the earth to a state of usefulness," he held, "how much more is it his duty to bring persons bearing his own physical (and probably mental) image purported to have descended from the same common stock, who are by millions roaming the earth's surface, as wild as beasts of the forest, without any . . . usefulness, a terror to civilized men." The Alabama mixed-race Creek slaveholder Alexander McGillivray anticipated this connection of whiteness with management of things human and inhuman in his everyday practices. As historian David Chang has observed, "Just as McGillivray hired white drovers to drive his animals, he hired a white overseer to command his slaves."[28]

The notorious 1857 Supreme Court decision in *Dred Scott v. Sandford* is rightly remembered as a nadir of proslavery and antiblack opinion, but it also elaborately affirmed what legal historian Aziz Rana calls "frontier settler rights." Settler-slavemasters resisted federal controls on expansion often said to amount to tyranny or even slavery. In deciding the *Scott* case, the court accelerated splits between advocates of taking Indian land on behalf of free white labor and taking it in favor of slavery, thereby speeding the coming of the Civil War. The short-lived decision summed up proslavery arguments that powerfully drew on settler colonial ones.[29]

Danger, Ditching, and the Production of Racial Comparisons

Labor remained critical as settler colonial "improvements" to the land hinged on the management of African and white workers. At its core, plantation management was race management. In his 1856 travel account *A Journey in the Seaboard Slave States*, landscape architect Frederick Law Olmsted interviewed a Maryland slaveholder whose large estate lay just outside of Washington, D.C. The topic quickly turned to Irish versus "negro" labor. The master, whom Olmsted called Mr. C., "employed several Irishmen for ditching, and for this work, and this alone, he thought he could use them to better advantage than negroes." On the other hand, he "would not think of using Irishmen for common farm-labor, and made light of their coming in competition with slaves." Negroes, in Mr. C.'s view, would "do two to their one" in comparison to the Irish in "any steady field-work." The Irish also were "dishonest, would not obey explicit directions about their work, and required more personal supervision than negroes." A Virginia planter soon explained to Olmsted why the Irish might suffer under such stereotypes but still were hired for ditching and draining: The Virginian "thought a negro could do twice as much work, in a day, as an Irishman" and complained of the latter's "sprees and quarrels." The explanation for continued use of the Irish was simple: "It's dangerous work . . . and a negro's life is too valuable to be risked at it. If a negro dies, it's a considerable loss, you know." In Alabama, the same logic became the key to Olmsted understanding the "reckless" way that cotton was being loaded with bales careening downward, often onto workers. "Negro hands were sent to the top of the bank, to roll the bales to the side, and Irishmen were kept below to remove them, and stow them," Olmsted reported. The mate in charge explained, "The niggers are worth too much to be risked here; if the Paddies are knocked overboard, or get their backs broke, nobody loses anything!"[30]

The supposed connection of the Irish, but not slaves, with draining, ditching, and danger in Southern workplaces has caught the attention of historians who agree on little else and has circulated widely. The stories appeal across ideological divisions. U. B. Phillips thought such examples showed that "that the planters cherished the lives of their slaves." The Marxist writer Bernard Mandel, on the other hand, stressed Irish victimization in a bitter pun making Irish workers exposed to plummeting into water and drowning the "fall guys" for the rich.[31]

While the occasional connections in antebellum Southern sources of the Irish to dangerous tasks holds interest, the weight of evidence shows no overriding preference for immigrant labor in risky and debilitating work. Indeed, the historian Kenneth Stampp rightly regarded a blanket preference for putting Irish workers in danger as "legend."[32] Variety was great. There was a national market in labor on large infrastructural projects, and contractors often hired Irish workers in the North and West as well as the South, playing them against each other along lines of county and clan of origin. A preference in some Southern places for skilled and experienced Irish workers, "who travel about the country under contractors," as noted in William H. Russell's memoirs, suggests that it was canal-building experience among Irish workers, rather than concern for the occupational health and safety of slaves, that shaped the choice to hire them.[33] Limits on the use of slaves were also set by the fact that it was particularly risky for masters to hire them out to be controlled by another master to perform potentially killing jobs, for example in mines or on the "mudmachine" dredging Baltimore's harbor.[34]

Even so, immigrant labor and local black labor often worked on the same infrastructural projects, including building major canals. When, for example, the British antislavery plantation mistress Fanny Kemble explained the "utter impossibility" of mixing slave and Irish labor on the construction of Georgia's Brunswick canal, her logic did not turn on a need to protect capital invested in slaves. The danger feared was instead disorder among workers, with the Irish seen as especially given to being "despisers of niggers," but also potentially willing "with a right mixture of ardent spirits" to act in solidarity with Africans. That one could allegedly "manage them with whiskey" in the Irish case underwrote some preferences for them, indicating the impossibility of separating racial types and cultural practice in making employment decisions. Competition was highly prized by some managers. In supervising construction of the turnpike through the Shenandoah Valley in 1840, Joseph R. Anderson remarked, "We don't want to rely on white labor." He made this the watchword for "heavy construction work" and soon applied it in managing the South's most important iron works.[35]

All that said, most dangerous and unhealthy work fell to slaves. There can be little doubt in cotton, rice, tobacco, and sugar that "most planters used their own field-hands for ditching and for clearing new ground," as Kenneth Stampp put it. Prideful memories of such labor sometimes persisted long after slavery, as when Gabe Lance recalled the reshaping of the Sandy Island, South Carolina, land where he had been enslaved: "All dem rice field been nothing but swamp. Slavery people cut kennel [canal] and cut down woods—and dig ditch through raw woods. All been clear up for plant rice by slavery people."[36] One form of dangerous labor became so attached to slaves that it continued to be connected with them even in the free state of Illinois, which early in its history excepted the large salt mines at Shawneetown from the state's ban on slavery because slave miners were seen as more racially suited for the perilous work. On the Couper family's Hopeton plantation in Georgia, "none but the primest male" slaves did ditching labor, and in both sugar and cotton production in the Southwest such gendered division of labor obtained. But elsewhere slave women, despite a closely calculating concern for their reproductive capacity, also performed such tasks.[37]

Masters regularly engaged in protracted reconsiderations of race and labor, tempered by the fact of their own massive investments in slaves and by the "truths" their own managerial practices were bringing into existence. Olmsted, whose own interest in what kind of labor was cheapest derived from his profession as a designer of parks, offers the richest evidence. Again and again, he recorded comparisons of African and immigrant, or sometimes black and white, labor in the South. Just after being told in a Virginia interview early in his travels that African productivity doubled that of the Irish in field labor, he spoke to an ex-slaveholder farming in the region. The farmer, moved to change labor systems by moral considerations, employed a mixed group of immigrant workers, free blacks, and poor southern whites. As Olmsted recounted, "He has had white and black Virginians, sometimes Germans, and latterly Irish. Of all of these, he has found the Irish on the whole the best. The poorest have been the native white Virginians; next, the free blacks." On the hard and dangerous jobs "such as carting and spreading dung, and all work with the fork, spade, or shovel, at which his Irishmen will do, he thinks, over fifty per cent more in a day than any negroes he has ever known." The farmer was careful at other junctures to make individual and cultural distinctions within groups. He paid sober Irish workers more and notably regarded slaves as outproducing free blacks. His conversations with the sympathetic Olmsted focused squarely on the superiority of free labor, even when plagued by the presence of allegedly "demoralizing" slave labor, which somehow spread low norms of productivity from adjacent plantations. And yet the discourse ended with a flat " 'negro' versus Irish" comparison that Olmsted would have understood as racial on both sides. Indeed, Olmsted later registered surprise at seeing his first "white man" managed by a black man at work, but added that he had of course seen "Irishmen" taking such direction.[38]

That two of Olmsted's informants, separated by a few miles, could conclude both that "negroes" out-produced the Irish by a factor of two, and underproduced them by a ratio of two-thirds might suggest that race management ciphered sloppily. Such differences in conclusions cannot be ignored, but claims of racial knowledge were nevertheless critical to plantation management. In some instances, especially where black and white workers did similar jobs outside agriculture, precision was claimed. When white skilled workers protested to the federal government over their replacement by slaves in the Norfolk Dry Dock in 1830, management's response showed how thoroughly difference could be quantified and how easily distinctions between slave and free slipped to become those between black and white. Stones "hammered by White Men" cost precisely $4.05 more than those "hammered by blacks" in one sample. An 1854 study meticulously argued that "slaves belonging to a company can excavate earth for less than half—can excavate rock for about one-fourth—and can construct culverts, bridges, abatements, locks, dams and &c. at about one-seventh" the cost of white labor. Because textile mills were seen at times as expressions of Southern political power, and even nationalism, conclusions of their managers regarding race and labor were eagerly reported. A Lowell weaver imported to oversee production in a Carolina mill reported that "there is full as much work done by the blacks," who also were supposedly "much more attentive to the looms" than northern white workers. A Pensacola newspaper gloried in the conclusion of mill management there that for "ingenuity of mere labor . . . the negro is just as richly endowed as the white." A textile factory outside Columbia, South Carolina, advertised itself as operating on the "anti free-soil system"—that is, with slave labor, which it found to produce "with equal efficiency, and great superiority in many respects" compared to free labor. The conclusion followed a two-year experiment that began in spinning and moved to weaving, in which slave labor was found to be able to achieve the same production at 30 percent less cost.[39]

Moving people and goods brought service, race, and nationality together in powerful combinations. On the Mississippi black and white crews worked alongside each other—though they lived separately—in closely monitored competition. Even as black workers lost places in northern service jobs, their slavery-derived connections to service work fit them for jobs catering to travelers on the Mississippi, particularly where women workers were concerned. In a protracted battle in Baltimore over whether hundreds of free black carters should be removed by law from their trade, the issue seemed to hinge on whether organized white workers had enough organizational clout to secure such an exclusion, which would improve their own bargaining positions. However, as thousands of citizens weighed in on both sides in petitions, nationality among whites and the connection of Africans to service prominently entered the debate. As one supporter of onerous regulations directed at black carters put it, "When this matter first came up, I heard much said of the degraded character of the IRISH." He defended the honesty, industry, and citizenship rights of that group—it was unnecessary to do so for whites in general—against any "man who seeks to degrade them to the level of a negro." It was, he argued, Irish manliness, as opposed to black servility, that was at issue: "[the Irish] are not 'so polite and obliging' as the blacks. Aye there is the rub. . . . The black man will take off his hat, call his employer master, and bend to the dust before him." The most forceful defense of black workers, nicely signed as "Wilberforce," after the British antislavery leader, concluded, "The black drivers [that is, cartmen] of our city, taken in the aggregate, are as respectable and as worthy of confidence as the white ones, and by far the more polite and obliging."[40]

At times urban employers weighed the choice between using slaves or free blacks, introducing a direct consideration of whether color or condition mattered most in determining productivity, and thus potentially undermining the idea that race was what was being managed. However, as historian Ira Berlin's work has shown, discussions of this matter were insufficiently clear and sustained to act as solvents of racial ideology. The supply and cost of slave labor so fluctuated in response to changes in demand in the agricultural sector that categorical preference for slaves or free blacks by urban employers risked excessive rigidity. Moreover, by the 1830s the influx of poor Irish and Germans into Southern cities made the central story one in which "with white workers available in growing numbers, white employers exercised their racial preference," replacing black workers in many trades and even in domestic service. White workers, often immigrants, supported this framing of matters in their unevenly successful campaigns to institute color bars in various occupations. "Petitions that began with complaints against black competition," Berlin observes, "almost always ended with an attack on the free Negro" specifically.[41]

Similarly, where mixed-race slaves were concerned, judgments of value and productivity that masters and traders made within the population that they regarded as "negro" led to a greater, and more horrific, spread of race management. Lighter-skinned women, who often embodied European standards of beauty and were the products of sexual exploitation by masters, attracted higher prices than darker-skinned "African" women. The value attached itself, as historian Edward Baptist's scholarship shows, not to productivity in a traditional sense but rather to a supposed incapacity of mixed-race "fancy girls" to produce, outside of sex work, or to biologically reproduce. One inventory of slaves made partly in the context of the trade in fancy girls included only four variables: name, age, amount of value, and "color"—the last divided into black, brown, copper, and yellow. But among male slaves, a light skin generally decreased value as managerial "common sense" dictated that mixed-race slaves were less capable of withstanding hot and backbreaking labor in sugar production and were more likely to be unmanageable workers prone to running away. On the other hand, the leading study of drivers suggests a preference for mixed-race slaves in such managerial positions and a belief at times that such slaves excelled because they were racially mixed; one driver drew praise as someone who "bore a striking resemblance to a well-formed man."[42]

Iron production, in which subtle skills mattered, saw some nuanced judgments by those managing African American labor and even some ratios of productivity broken down by race indicating a preference for black labor. In 1812, management in one Virginia iron works reckoned slave laborers worked "ten times" better than free ones. David Ross, at the Oxford Iron Works, was not atypical in recognizing that, as the historian Charles Dew put it, "the institution of slavery" and not "innate talents and abilities" created his managerial problems with African workers. Ironmasters meticulously calculated work produced, at times in elaborate "negro books," reaching conclusions favorable to the efficiency of black labor. Management in iron worried that slaves wasted more pig iron and charcoal in the production process, but also at times found white workers "don't like work and won't do it unless they are compelled to. . . . You can't drive 'em like you can a nigger."[43]

Of course, the not directly calculable benefits of slave labor, and of free black workers lacking civil rights, included undermining the ability of white, often immigrant, workers to effectively make demands for better wages and conditions. Hired slaves afforded a reserve army of labor, providing "strike insurance" and the threat of replacing workers who refused hot and dangerous work. White workers frequently took concerted action to respond to such coercion by campaigning to keep slave and free black workers out of factories and of trades such as carting. At the Tredegar Iron Works in 1847 the increased use of slave labor, especially in the skilled work of puddling, led to a walkout by white workers. Strikers protested against hard-won craft knowledge being taught to slaves who could replace them, but also registered a fear of seeing the work associated with "a degraded race." With strikers fired and replaced by slaves, the *Richmond Enquirer* could glory that a "direct attack on slave property" was defeated and hope that "nothing having even the appearance of a combination" by workers would ever recur.

However, establishing an example, not full replacement of one group of workers by another, was what was sought. As Tredegar vastly expanded in the 1850s, it did so without increasing slave labor. On the eve of the Civil War its labor force was overwhelmingly northern-born or immigrant and workers were slotted into departments by nationality: Irish puddlers, Welsh heaters, English rollers, and the common labor mostly done by Irish and German workers. Meanwhile, at the major Buffalo Forge in Virginia, it was slave forgemen who were seen as causing production bottlenecks in the context of the coming of the Civil War, not because of lack of skill but because of a sense of power growing from their indispensability: they were chronically "at [the] forge but not at work."[44]

On large plantations in the Deep South field labor was so overwhelmingly enslaved that ratios of white (or Irish) to African productivity were made up almost out of whole cloth. This scarcely prevented sweeping and contradictory racial comparisons. The occasional use of Cajun, Irish, and Creole labor in some marginal Louisiana fields drew "unfavorable" assessments of the results. However, in the German enclave of New Braufels, Texas, Olmsted learned of a German immigrant woman who allegedly "in the first year she had ever seen a cotton field, picked more cotton in a day than any slave in the county." Immigrant-picked cotton, reputedly cleaner of impurities, at least briefly was sold for slightly more than slave-picked cotton, though Olmsted carefully observed that it was not German labor that was shown to be superior but rather "the free labor of Germans."[45] Negative judgments of immigrant free labor did at times find grounding in political economy rather than race, as in a widely circulated story of a Louisiana planter who faced a harvest-time strike after attempting to use immigrant field labor.[46]

Expert accounts reflected a cheerful determinism regarding climate and race validating the choice to purchase black field labor. Writers held that a preference for "slave labour" over "free labour" made sense on racial grounds, maintaining that whites "cannot endure heat and labour so well as the negro" or more particularly that slaves "thrive" when faced with "marsh miasma" and hot sun while "a white man particularly foreigners would sink under their influence." A physician observing the ravages wrought by yellow fever among whites in the

Savannah area regarded this destruction as demonstrating "how utterly impossible it is for the white race to do outdoor work in this hot climate," expressing what amounted to an epidemiological defense of slavery.[47] Timothy Flint's estimate from 1834 put well-managed slave productivity at double that of free labor on a unit of one hundred workers. Even so, the ratios of superiority claimed for slave over free labor were sometimes carefully couched as showing the superiority not so much of Africans but of white plantation management and the "advanced stage of our agriculture."[48]

Many ratios, rationales, and rules of thumb regarding race continued to trade in images of the inferior and lazy African in ways that emphasized the importance and the difficulty of the white manager's work. The traveler Harriet Martineau "learned" that it took two white men to get one African to work. One New Yorker transplanted to Louisiana reckoned that he himself had "worked through the very hottest weather, steadily, day after day, and done more work than any three niggers in the State."[49] In 1852 the *New York Times* championed the idea of following Cuba's example in turning away from African labor, preferring the allegedly greater efficiency of Chinese "coolie" contract labor as against slaves. Chinese workers were in this view "a more intelligent grade of labor" available at less expense to replace "the reckless indolent abandon, and passion for amusement, characteristic of the African." Otherwise, the "enterprising Spaniard" would dominate the hemisphere's sugar production. Planter proslavery theorist George Fitzhugh and the planter-diplomat Thomas Marshall broadly agreed with the *Times*, though Fitzhugh fretted that the coolie trade threatened to ruin the prospects of inferior Africans by undercutting masters' paternalistic interest in racial development of the vulnerable "negro" race.[50]

Perhaps most indicative of the contradictions that made both positive assessments of slave labor and their opposites imperativewas the notion that proximity to enslaved African labor would lead to a "sliding into" bad slave habits by poor whites nearby. As Olmsted reported, "Wherever there are slaves, I have found that farmers universally testify that white laborers adopt their careless habits, and that they are even more indifferent than negroes to the interests of their employers."[51] The debates by some Southern nationalists proposing to reopen the slave trade with Africa in the 1850s further show the ways in which a commitment to slaves as an asset, and to "whiteness-as-management" as an ideology, jointly shaped behavior. The campaign eventually garnered impressive support, in part as a way to hold out the possibility that every white could literally own and manage a slave, and in part as an expression of the wisdom of choosing enslaved African labor. Nonetheless proslave trade extremists could not even prevent the constitutional convention of the Confederacy from banning the importation of Africans. Much was at play, including a need not to alienate potential British allies. Nonetheless, the logic that mass importation would decrease the value of existing slaves was central to the calculation, and not only in slave-exporting states like Virginia. Fitzhugh complicated matters by arguing specifically that the value added by white management would suffer if the trade revived. "Slavery with us is becoming milder every day; were the slave trade revived, it would resume its pristine cruelty. The slaves we now hold would become less valuable, and we should take less care of them," he wrote in 1854 before reversing himself on the issue shortly thereafter.[52] Such malleability and contradiction would be equally pronounced in the day-to-day management of African slaves.

2

Managing the Negro

The African Slave as Asset and Animal

THE SOUTH CAROLINA LOW COUNTRY PLANTER John Berkley Grimball confided to his diary in 1832 that "Negro property is certainly the most troublesome in the world." His lament addressed the quandary of the master, who in law and in production faced at once the necessity and the impossibility of making the all-too-human slave into a thing like all other property.[1] In reducing that quandary to the "negro" character of slave property, Grimball replicated the practice of managerial literature that tended to present its articles on plantation efficiency as advice on "managing the negro," not on "managing the slave." Troubles abounded for masters, but for Grimball, the trouble seemed to lie with "the negro," not the master/slave relationship. Sixty years after abolition the historian John Spencer Bassett agreed with Grimball, contending that "an important part of the problem was the negro himself . . . a fundamental part of the slave problem was the negro problem"—the problem of a people "close to savagery."[2] The assumption of white supremacy made by Bassett, Grimball, and most masters fits poorly in a more egalitarian modern world, but when planters wrote about management, race-thinking centrally defined what was modern, scientific, and progressive. It is that worldview that this chapter seeks to delineate where management is concerned.

Insisting that masters thought of themselves as managing not only slaves but also a system of racial slavery underscores how persistent practical problems in antebellum plantation management came to be refracted through prisms of race and biology. The enduring problems deserving attention here include the necessity to manage both the production and the reproduction of slaves, the imperative to define African slaves as at once racially degraded and as excellent investments capable of being dramatically developed, the balancing of the roles of reward and punishment, and the tensions between managing individual workers and controlling the black population as a whole. In examining each tension, the broad pattern emerges that masters claimed understanding of the "negro race" as a key to addressing class-based tensions arising from slavery. Regarding the African both as a working asset and as an animal, planters combined the use of incentives and acts of revenge so that essential to a paternal attitude among masters was the threat of breaking up families through slave sales. At every turn a purported knowledge of "the negro" underwrote an incredible hubris that made an increasingly bold managerial literature possible. Conversely, as extended treatment of the exemplary figure of the professional-managerial slaveholder Dr. Samuel Cartwright shows, claims of managerial knowledge energized outspoken, bizarre, and ruthlessly logical claims of racial knowledge. Those claims, a brief concluding section shows, outlived the emancipation of the slaves.

Paternalism, the Lash, and the Development of the Slave

Grimball's striking phrasing regarding "Negro property" illustrates that slaves were objects of investment and sale before and after they were a productive force. In an antebellum era of most rapid expansion of slavery, in terms of population and area, the market for slaves was as important as the market for cotton. One type of management became a brutal and whip-happy regimen designed to force immediate compliance to the master's or overseer's demand. The force on which it relied was the beating of slaves. The alternative paternalist mode of management arrayed slaves in a broad range of human relationships with each other and especially with masters. It sought to use shame and the threat of sale to enforce discipline in preference to the lash. This paternalism, far from being a hallmark of the premodern nature of a slave system less than tied to market considerations, responded to both cotton markets and slave markets. It claimed that softer exploitation could generate more production and more reproduction among slaves, and could deliver to slave markets workers less scarred by beatings and therefore less likely to be devalued by potential buyers.[3]

Competing claims of differing forms of brutality and manipulation—for production and reproduction, for enforcing discipline and developing talents of slaves, and in the short and long runs—led masters to argue about what moved "the negro." In an 1860 article on both the "management of negroes" and the "duties of masters," N. D. Guerry captured the interplay of race, humanity, and marketplace perfectly. He applauded "all who believe that the moral sensibilities of the negro may be quickened and so improved as to make him obey his master, because he [the slave] loves him [the master] and because it would be wrong to disobey." Guerry equally endorsed all "who believe that the negro, so improved and so elevated, is more contented and profitable" and "will bring more money for sale." A Mississippi planter similarly made "love" the pivot of the "moral management of negroes." Critics of this view equally spoke the language of the marketplace, rejecting "the idea of managing negroes by trying to convince them it is 'wrong to disobey' " by contesting evidence that under such a method the slave "will bring more money when offered for sale." Such views, on both sides, connect paternalism, race management, race development, and the slave market as parts of a whole.[4]

That African slaves came under managerial eyes as both assets to be developed and workers to be driven created tremendous tensions in which both the acknowledgment of African capacities and the most dehumanizing connections of slaves to the animal world occurred as two sides of the same coin. Beyond the fact that planters needed to regard African slaves as valuable in order to validate their own fiscal decisions and social system, the realities of plantation life taught that slaves possessed the technical and managerial knowledge that made the plantation work. Because proslavery argument relied on white supremacy, it could credit the genius of Africans only so much. Notions of racial development through white management thus curiously combined a semiawareness of African contributions to the making of the South with wholesale denials of those contributions. "Whiteness-as-management" had material roots in who bossed and militarily controlled whom, but it was above all ideology covering over large realms in which slaves managed other slaves and performed the skilled labor necessary to production.

The historian C. L. R. James's pronouncement that slaves "ran the plantation" in the Caribbean would have been largely resisted by the planter-experts who wrote in antebellum Southern plantation journals, but the extent of their dependence on Africans consistently crept into their consciousness and even their writings. William H. Russell, an English traveler and diarist, exemplified this tension in recording the views of an overseer of slaves constructing a sugarhouse on a Louisiana sugar plantation. Russell noted the overseer's lavish "praises of the intelligence and skill" of slaves who did "all the work of skilled laborers" on the plantation. Immediately afterward, the same overseer amused Russell by turning to expounding "on the utter helplessness and ignorance of the black race," indeed their "incapacity . . . even to take care of themselves."[5]

The reality of African expertise, long recognized in sugar production, applied elsewhere as well. In sugar, the key skills of "engineer" and "cooper" were transmitted across generations among Africans. Slaves possessing knowledge of those crafts retained value even if they misbehaved.[6] In rice production Charles Manigault contractually required in 1853 that his white overseer "be careful not to interfere too much with the . . . management of the Rice Mill in cases where I am unacquainted with such machinery . . . as the Negroes in charge have much experience therein." When hired out, skilled slaves were frequently allowed to strike their own bargains, returning wages to the owner, but seeing their own expertise in finding a job as well as in doing the work acknowledged. They became, as Frederick Douglass put it, the "master of [their] own time." Even writings on agricultural techniques sometimes credited black expertise, as when a participant in protracted debates on how to provide bedding for cotton plants urged readers to ask "their eldest hand, who was a sensible negro," what worked best. The antebellum plantation reformer who most approximated the later "time studies" and "motion studies" central to industrial management, Georgia's David Dickson, likewise stood as the figure perhaps most eager to identify with the abilities and capacities of African slaves. Expelled from a local agricultural improvement society for openly living with a female slave, he insisted that all his slaves were or were becoming skilled, including the cotton pickers whose work methods he charted, timed, and refined and whose capacity to learn he praised.[7]

Slaves also performed much of the work of management of labor on plantations. Whether James was correct that owners turned away over time from white overseers and toward enslaved African drivers to best solve the "problem of supervision" is questionable, but clearly those whom historian Charles Joyner has called "managerial slaves" smoothed the successful operations of many, probably most, large plantations.[8] Sometimes such slaves were called "overseers," sometimes "head men," and sometimes "foremen," but usually "drivers." In some instances drivers controlled how time was measured in the fields and even carried timepieces as some white overseers did. Often one of them was second in authority in the fields only to the master.[9] Experts in management urged close and frequent consultation with drivers, not only in the interests of "morale" but also to gain "a great deal of valuable experience." In 1854 "A Subscriber" told the *American Cotton Planter* that "generally speaking, employers have more confidence in their negroes than in their overseers. If they wish to know how business progresses, they seldom, if ever, inquire of the white man, but call up some negro, and ask him questions that ought to make any gentleman blush to think of asking a negro."[10]

Far more openly and consistently acknowledged than the African's capability in production and management was her or his value in reproduction and sale. Managerial literature frequently regarded the slave as a product as well as a producer. Noteworthy for its innovations enabling subscribers to systematically study individual labor in cotton picking, *Affleck's Southern Rural Almanac and Plantation and Garden Calendar for 1854* nonetheless held, "As the business of cotton growing is now conducted, a planter's almost sole wealth consists in negroes." Historians of accountancy credit Thomas Affleck, the almanac's editor, with pioneering "depreciation techniques for human property."[11] Affleck insisted that "a fine crop consists first in an increase in the number, and a marked improvement in the condition and value of the negroes."[12] In 1855 Louisiana's S. B. Raby took solace that "any deficiencies in the cane crop" would be more than compensated for by births that increased "our crop of negroes," exemplifying what the historian of sugar and slavery Richard Follett calls the "coldly rational ethos of demographic management." South Carolina's Plowden C. J. Weston emphasized to overseers that they would be judged "first—by the general well-being of the negroes . . . the small amount of punishment; the excess of births over deaths; the small number of persons in hospitals, and the health of children."[13] The Carolina physician W. Fletcher Holmes reasoned that since for up-country planters "the principal value of the negro . . . is his increase," medicine had a particular role to play in the accumulation of wealth.[14]

Concern for slave health, reproduction, and value caused many articles on the "management of negroes" to begin with an emphasis on adequate provisioning that imparts a paternalist and even munificent tone. The "first obligation" was to provide "suitable food and clothing." Presupposing hard work and the need for the young to grow strong, expert masters urged ample meal and meat and sometimes advised readers to provide "nutritious" (and cheap) vegetables such as "cabbage, kale, or mustard for greens . . . squashes, Irish potatoes [and] in fall and winter sweet potatoes, turnips, pumpkins, and peas." Others warned that vegetables ought not be the excuse for "stinting" on other dietary staples. The importance of a good breakfast, in order to have the slave "remain diligently at work," struck a distinctly modern note. James Towns told *Southern Cultivator* readers that the "management of negroes" had to be done "with an eye to their health, their comfort, and their happiness [in] the master's interest." Calculations regarding the "judicious management of the plantation force" factored in the closing of the transatlantic slave trade, and high slave prices, sometimes implying that such limits on the supply of Africans were the preconditions for the emergence of modern slave management. As a correspondent signing himself as P. T. told the *Southern Cultivator*, "The time has been, throwing humanity aside, that the farmer could kill up and wear out one Negro to buy another." But now, he concluded, prices had so risen that "it behooves those who own them to make them last as long as possible."[15]

Often masters cast the tensions that led to high turnover among overseers in terms of the supposed inability of the latter group to take seriously the need to cultivate a "crop of negroes" as well as the crops in the ground. "Overseers are not interested in raising children, or meat [or] in improving land" ran a much-echoed lament in the *American Cotton Planter*. Despite the fact that overseers' pay did not typically include a share of the agricultural commodities produced, they continued to be accused of one-sidedly focusing on maximizing such production. An Alabama report on the "Management of Slaves" complained of overseers, "As they have no property in our slaves, they lack the check of self-interest." Advice literature, overwhelmingly written by masters, provided constant reminders to overseers not to punish "negroes" in anger or with passion. The *American Cotton Planter*'s discussion of the "duties of overseers," for example, stressed, "Never display yourself before [slaves] in a passion; and even if inflicting the severest punishment, do so in a mild, cool manner," using the whip "slowly and deliberately." Indeed, so persistent were these tropes and so slight was the material basis for overseers to behave in such counterproductive ways that it seems possible that hired managers picked up on the fact that planters themselves, whatever their protestations, would fire overseers more quickly when the crop suffered than when the slaves did and perhaps projected their own lack of control in inflicting punishment onto those below. In rejecting an anonymous contribution from "Overseer" in 1855, *American Cotton Planter* demanded that pieces on such fraught subjects needed to be signed. The interaction of masters and overseers with the "negro" was a "subject of great public policy in this country" and therefore no "*ficticious* [*sic*] *signature*" was permissible.[16]

Even as the master-manager's self-interested paternalism has a distinctly modern and therapeutic tone, it consistently cohabited with the most pernicious aspects of white supremacist ideology, especially in comparing slaves to animals. The soft discourse of concern for slaves, sincerely delivered and materially rooted, also served to blunt abolitionist critiques. However, concern with improving the value of "the negro" connected as well to the harshest incarnations of white supremacy where comparing slaves to livestock was concerned. In an important 1855 contribution to *De Bow's Review* on the "Management of Slaves," John A. Calhoun argued that if "it is a matter which pertains to the interest of northern agricultural societies to attend well to the improvement of their lands, and the improvement and comfort of their stock . . . how much more important it is for us to turn our attention to the best means of governing our slaves."[17] Care by the master was necessary, that exemplar of planter paternalism George Fitzhugh wrote, because "not a single negro was ever reclaimed from his savage state till he was caught, tied, tamed and domesticated like the wild ox or the wild horse."[18]

The planter J. W. Pitts strikingly put a softer paternalism and the animality of Africans side by side. "The surest and best method of managing negroes," he held, "is to love them." His reasoning continued, "We know, from a thousand experiments, that if we love our horse . . . he will become gentle, docile and obedient." The "same effect" worked the same magic "upon sheep, cattle, dogs, the lion, the elephant, bird [and] fish." It should, Pitts reasoned, also work with servants. James Towns described the payoff of his managerial liberality as follows: "A negro shows when he is well-fed as readily as a horse; and mine look slick and greasy, and they work lively and are cheerful and happy."[19] Olmsted learned of the practice under which a planter sent "rascally" slaves away from home and loved ones "for the alleviation of their complaint." One would, he was told, similarly get rid of "a horse" seen as troublesome. Such brutality comported fully with paternalism's use of sale, rather than the whip, as its moment of force to secure obedience. When managers talked and wrote about "negroes" and "hogs" together, they did not abandon paternalism.[20]

Of course, making paternalism work was not the only point of such animalizing comparisons. Thus the *Southern Cultivator* praised the new owner of a failing plantation for one day shooting many sickly livestock in order to demonstrate his ruthlessness to workers, while promising to kill 150 underperforming slaves the next day. The master then staged a contrived consultation with an overseer who "persuaded" him to spare the slaves, agreeing to let them live for an eighteen-month probationary period, a strategy that allegedly produced great improvements in productivity. But even this drama was not seen by the author of the account as incompatible with informed, modern paternalist management. He assured readers that such a feigned stay of execution designed to produce "a new spirit of industry" among the slaves did not constitute effective brutality since it rested on managerial knowledge that "the Creator seems to have planted in the negro an innate principle of protection against the abuse of arbitrary power."[21]

Paternalist management intersected most tragically with the animalizing of slaves in the realm of reproduction. The *American Cotton Planter* featured an ad appealing to the desire of masters for the slave woman who could "breed like a cat." Although advertisements for slaves frequently referred to reproduction, propriety and politics kept direct consideration of methods of breeding largely out of public discourse. What was broadcast, as historian U. B. Phillips unapologetically chronicled, was that masters particularly extended their paternalistic "care of negroes" to "breeding wenches." Accounts glorying in the adaptability of "Guinea's" inhabitants for labor in the South specifically referred to reproductive labor as well as agricultural production; African women were said to be "naturally fit" for both.[22]

Balancing reproductive and agricultural labor illustrated how partial, cruel, and sanctimonious paternalism was bound to be. The memories of ex-slaves featured atrocities against pregnant women and mothers of newly born children. Planters only sometimes granted such women a short respite from field labor, allowed them to work in more nearby parts of the fields, avoided their exposure to "low damp tide lands," or placed them together with prepartum women in a special "sucklers' gang." The rules on P. C. Weston's rice estate in 1856, for example, granted every Saturday off for any slave woman "with six children alive at any *one* time." In another case emancipation was promised after a dozen live births, but the woman approaching that reward died while pregnant with her twelfth child. Conversely, "barren" women were frequently sold and faced requirements for more labor, sometimes being held to the standard of men on the plantation. If, as Follett argues, "slave women faced a master class who attempted to manipulate their sexual lives to optimize reproduction," such manipulation was often wrapped up with paternalism. Pregnancy could best be encouraged and coerced, since promiscuity and infecundity were seen as connected, through the policing of slave women's sex lives.[23]

Masters assessed the value of slave births with sound, if awful, logic. Abraham Lincoln told an 1860 audience that the value of U.S. slaves was $2 billion. He may have underestimated by a billion dollars or more, in a year when the value of the cotton crop was just over $250 million.

Indeed, from 1810 on women's reproductive labor probably produced more value than was realized through cotton production, though the value of slaves of course ultimately depended on profitable production.[24] The "increase" continually increased, making what the legal scholar Adrienne Davis has called the "sexual economy of American slavery" the greatest success story in plantation race management.[25]

Managing a Race, Managing Slaves, and Managing Individuals

If the major journals on plantation improvements more frequently focused on the management of "the negro" than on the "management of slaves," both phrasings appeared, registering the reality that planters thought of themselves as managing a race, but within a particular social system. Moreover, like all race managers in U.S. history, the masters faced the necessity of tempering their wholesale judgments about a group with the reality that they bossed individuals. "The negro," however much used as a collective noun, remained distinctly singular as well, a fact creating considerable tension in slave management writings. Thus "Hurricane" wrote to the *Southern Cultivator* in 1860 that "to lay down a set of rules for the management of all negroes would, in my opinion, be a very silly act. . . . One is whipped with the first lick, another with moderate correction, while a third one may require punishment to an extent revolting to the humane man." On the next page, he nevertheless pronounced that "the negro" collectively "cannot and will not exercise the slightest economy of time or labor [and] is naturally filthy." Hurricane concluded his doubled discourse in a way that left no doubt that he sought to manage a race: "So I will sum up in a few words: The African negro is physically a man, mentally a child—treat him as such." But to manage a race required managing individuals.[26]

The difficulties in apprehending differences between "managing slaves" and "managing negroes" emerge in classic histories of slavery. In the primary sources on slavery that U. B. Phillips collected for the *Documentary History of American Industrial Society* a century ago, documents referred to management tasks and problems such as "The Breaking in of Fresh Africans," "Petty Annoyances in Using Negro Labor," and "Negro Labor Slow and Careless." Such master-generated sources tended to use "negro" or "nigger" in preference to "slave," but the pattern seems not to have attracted the notice of Phillips, perhaps because usages so shifted and varied. One document was titled "Discipline and Riddance of Refractory Slaves," but its text used racial and racist language in every case and "slave" not at all. Eugene Genovese's *Roll, Jordan, Roll* framed matters squarely and sometimes usefully in terms of class—the master/slave relationship—but the primary sources he introduced very often spoke in the language of race, suggesting that the "master-negro" relationship also merited emphasis.[27]

When masters spoke of managing "negroes" the constraints and possibilities for managing slaves as a class pervaded their discussions. Planters at times spoke of "the negro" as capable of being driven and conversely noted that "you could never depend on white men . . . and you couldn't drive them any; they wouldn't stand it," as if these were matters of race. But the law and armed force of the slave system made such driving possible. Such choices of racial language may even have served as a defense of slavery in a republican nation and an increasingly antislavery world, places where slavery was defended with increasing difficulty and white supremacy with greater ease. However, at other moments late antebellum Southern thinkers did frankly and proudly defend slavery itself and their managerial writings were mostly directed not to the North and the world, but to each other. That is, in fundamental ways, planters did see themselves as managing and developing "the negro" within a slave system.

When articles' titles referred to slaves, practical issues like housing, rations, supervision, discipline, and diet bulked larger. When the subject was proclaimed to be managing "negroes," broad pronouncements on racial difference more consistently appeared as part of the calculus of how to run an efficient, productive plantation or farm. But the differences were far from absolute, as business knowledge and racial knowledge thoroughly mixed and the major plantation management journals consistently took the supposed racial character of Africans into account. Articles that began as discussions of managing slaves slid into use of "negroes," though the opposite pattern was not as pronounced. John A. Calhoun's 1855 "Management of Slaves," summarizing the views of a committee of slaveholders, ended by enumerating ten commandments for such an enterprise, all couched in terms of "negroes." Even rosters and inventories of those owned, perhaps the sources most likely to use "slave" in their titles, sometimes then moved to listing property under the heading of NEGROES.[28]

Most impressively, even when discussing labor issues like tasking work, maximizing the effectiveness of the overseer, or introducing technology, the language of race obtruded. The ubiquity of literal connections among race, work, and management in the Old South remains singularly impressive. When debating whether to allow and encourage slaves to independently grow crops on small plots for their own consumption and sometimes for sale, an expert weighed in on whether "negro crops" improved morale and health or simply detracted from commodity production in the fields. "Nigger work" famously described whole categories of degraded labor. Medico-managerial problems with slaves appeared to be racial. The Georgia physician H. A. Ramsay found that "the negro is prone to dissemble and feign illness; probably no race of human beings feign themselves ill so frequently, and are so incapable of concealing their duplicity." It was "negro mothers" who endangered valuable slave children.[29] One major ironworks kept "negro books" to describe work, costs, and compensation of its enslaved workers. Plantation rules covered the setting of times "for the negroes to breakfast and dine." Even the naming of the means of production came to be modified by "nigger." "Nigger hoes," manufactured for the hard usage of tools by workers on plantations weighed up to three times more than hoes sold in northern markets. Genovese observes that in this case and others having to do with tools, "the most obvious obstacle to the employment of better equipment was the slave himself"—that is, the slave system provided scant incentive to take care of the master's property. He adds that neglect and abuse of such equipment frequently constituted reasons "for punishing Negroes."[30]

Managing the slave required judging "the negro." The great debates of slave management consistently hinged on racial knowledge and who had it. The constant clashes between overseers and masters, for example, could turn on both whether slaves' criticisms of overseers ought to be credited in the specific instance, but also more broadly on whether such criticisms ever deserved consideration within a universe of racial assumptions. An overseer registering a complaint against masters believing slaves' testimonies argued that "every one conversant with negro character knows well their proclivity for lying and stealing." A particularly harsh master echoed this sentiment in *Southern Cultivator*, casting enslaved workers as both stupid and capable of organizing impressive collective resistance: "Negroes are weak-minded, unprincipled creatures, and at the same time will frequently evince a great deal of shrewdness in fixing up a 'tale' on an overseer they do not like." Attacking all use of "negro evidence" in managing, his "rule" was to "whip any negro that tries to tell me anything about the overseer." A subsequent correspondent disagreed sharply, registering a more widely held view: "It is a very great mistake . . . to assume that the negro is incapable of moral elevation—that he will lie and steal simply because he is a negro."[31]

Assessments of "negro character" shaped general debates over the wisdom of paternalist methods, though the patterns remained quite complex. The argument that Africans were "naturally" docile could lead, for example, to calls for harsher confinement. If, as one master held, there "never was an insurrection . . . which was not instigated by white men," all opportunities for the "negroes" to "run about" had to be policed. Other allegedly "innate" characteristics of Africans absurdly deflected abolitionist charges regarding mistreatment of slaves and ensured that experts could generally align themselves to paternalist methods without abjuring use of the whip. Negroes were a people, so this theory argued, "whose ethnical elements, like the mule, restrict the limits of arbitrary power over [them]." Another expert imagined that "innately" Africans would not respond to force so that "abuse and harsh treatment carries its own antidote," making Africans "unprofitable, unmanageable, a vexation, and a curse."[32]

The assumption that the group of enslaved individuals being managed belonged to an inferior race sometimes shaped the very ways that production was organized and that output was measured among slaves. The central managerial decision, over a wide expanse of place and time, was whether to organize slaves into gangs being pushed collectively to work by pacing from a driver or overseer, or to assign carefully quantified tasks that an individual might perform in less than a full day, leaving time for independent production on small plots slaves controlled. That the "gang system" applied so widely suggests that the ideological assumption that Africans worked best when "driven" was a powerful one, but the "task system" also spoke to how the skill and value of slave labor were seen. Indeed, flexibility necessarily was a hallmark of any viable strategy. Phillips wrote of the use of gangs for only certain jobs, such as clearing land of timber, in South Carolina areas mostly committed to the task system. He more generally wrote, "The great mass of the common negroes . . . were regarded as suitable only for the gangs." Certain crops, such as rice, were seen as ideal for tasking and others, like cotton, for gang labor. Seasonality likewise mattered, with stripping of tobacco, for example, especially apt to be tasked. "I do not believe in tasking negroes all the time," one planter wrote, but rather "in cases of a push, when the crop is suffering." There was no necessary link of gangs to pushing production harshly and tasks to paternalism. Tasks such as hoeing could be projected for the day in defined spaces, so that overseers could see how slaves were doing relative to one another. Others, such as plowing, might be too risky to be tasked in that the temptation to slight the work by performing it hastily, or to push animals and equipment too hard, would be great. Those supervising the driving of slaves had to acknowledge differences among workers, with the historical sociologist Charles Post identifying five distinct types of gang labor. The crude distinction that masters repeatedly made in making rosters of their slave property between optimally productive "full hands" and "half hands" suggests some attempt to balance individual and group productivity, and to place workers on gangs that included individuals who could work at the same speed.[33]

The harshly managed task of cotton-picking was also most susceptible to being measured in terms of individual productivity. Planters recorded picking results on forms provided in *Affleck's Southern Rural Almanac and Plantation and Garden Calendar* with an uneven zeal but to an extent at least comparable to monitoring of individuals found in British industry. At times the driving of gangs was used to set tasks. As the agricultural historian Lewis Gray writes of a Louisiana plantation:

The fastest worker took the lead. An overseer, whip in hand, followed the line of slaves on horseback. If any slave fell behind the leader he was whipped. In picking cotton, a new hand was "whipped up smartly and made to pick as fast as he can." Thereafter, the amount thus accomplished became his regular task.[34]

Thus while the formation of workers into a gang that, as many planter-managers boasted "could be driven," was explicitly cast in racial terms (and became part of the postbellum white managerial lore justifying chain gangs), race management on plantations always brooked complications as the possibilities of managing under a slave system were tested. Management-by-race sought not to simply degrade but also to extract labor, and it kept contradictory views of "negro character" at play to do so.

Personifying a System: Samuel Cartwright, Everyday Practice, and the Extremes of Race Management

University of Louisiana professor Dr. Samuel Cartwright, perhaps the most eminent professional produced by the Old South, is also a figure easily dismissed as a "medical extremist" given to fanciful views. Both his eminence and his extremism arose from the confidence born of mastering everyday practices of race management, making him a fit figure to sum up much of the discussion of slavery.[35] Cartwright was a leader in understanding and treating cholera and yellow fever. A physician at times to both Andrew Jackson and Jefferson Davis, he held, in Davis's words, "the first place" among doctors in the Old South. The doctor followed slavery west. Born in Virginia, and trained by the celebrated Philadelphia physician and race theorist Dr. Benjamin Rush, he followed slavery west, migrating to Alabama and Mississippi. He settled into an illustrious career in New Orleans before dying in the service of the Confederacy. His articles on medicine appeared in professional journals, but they also circulated widely, alongside his controversial theological and ethnological writings, in De Bow's Review, whose editor counted him in 1859 as "one of the most ingenious and far-famed writers of the Southwest." Honored well beyond the South, Cartwright attracted attention in Europe and his work won prizes at Harvard and elsewhere. If an extremist, he was extremely well regarded.[36]

When he lived, Cartwright's works concerning theology and race sparked far more controversy than the medical writings that strike post–civil rights era readers as so controversial. But as he went far out on limbs in reinterpreting the Bible, Cartwright received respectful attention even from his critics because he so incorporated the alleged wisdom of race managers to reinterpret the Old Testament past. His forays into Bible-based ethnology developed the minority proslavery racist position that Africans were an unperfected pre-Adamic creation. Indeed, the source of Eve's temptation was said to be a black worker, a badly managed "negro gardener" who had somehow become a slave to Adam. Although human, Africans were so inferior as to profit greatly by enslavement under superior Caucasians, according to Cartwright. He read plantation management back into many of the Bible's earliest pages, retranslating to make Ham not the father of Cush but instead a "head man," the "manager, or overseer of the nacash [Negro, in Cartwright's view] race." Thus the Bible, Cartwright wrote in 1860, making a characteristic claim that management of slaves enriched medical, theological, and practical knowledge of race, "tells us certain facts about negroes which none but the best informed planters and overseers know at the present day." His own approach modeled how to marry Bible-reading with watching Africans at work when he maintained that an observed posture of slaves at labor fulfilled the Bible prophecy that "Upon Thy Belly shalt Thou go." Africans needed white management, with a comparison to Indians clinching the point. The former group "requires government in every thing"; the latter "submits to government in nothing whatever." Cartwright fully premised his scholarship in theology and ethnology on the need managers of slaves had for racial knowledge and their capacity to acquire it. Those lacking such Bible-based practical knowledge, he maintained, "have great trouble in managing negroes." He continued, "If [the slaves'] ethnology were better understood, their value would be greatly increased."[37]

Such convictions regarding management and a separate creation of the races did not place Cartwright at the extreme edge of proslavery ideology. It is true that most master-class intellectuals expressing a view held to the idea of a common creation of all races, with God allegedly later cursing Africans. Such a formulation maximized the possibility of racial development and the positive role of paternalist plantation management. *De Bow's Review*, so admiring of Cartwright otherwise, therefore subjected his theological ideas to respectful but withering criticism. Nevertheless, an outspoken body of opinion went still further than Cartwright, not only positing separate creations but also flirting, as one scientist and clergyman warned, with "degrad[ing] their servants

below the level of those creatures to whom a revelation has been given."
Cartwright himself was so at pains to acknowledge "the black man's
humanity"—albeit somehow within a different species—that historian
James Guillory has suggested that the physician's ethnology sought to
"reconcile" theories of the unity and mankind with separate creation
arguments, taking a middle position, not an extreme one. Indeed, De
Bow's sustained critique of Cartwright, made from a "one-creation"
stance, spends much of its space elaborating their agreements, including
the former's assent to the critical proposition that "the Creator has
given the negro a nature suiting him to the servitude to which it is
revealed that he should properly be subjected." On all sides, exegesis
of the Bible merged with the needs of those who defended slavery and
managed slaves.[38]

Within medicine, Cartwright's continuing fame rests on his
seemingly ridiculous descriptions of work- and discipline-based slave
"diseases" that he helped to discover by reflecting on the process of managing "the negro." In elaborately labeling the slave's desire to run away
to freedom and his or her refusal to work except listlessly in bondage
as pathologies with elaborate Latinate names, Cartwright tailored his
science to proslavery ends in ways that seem prime examples of medical
extremism. However, so much did his medical opinions grow out of
everyday practices and dilemmas of slave management, and so much
did they express the supposed wisdom of race managers on plantations that even his most fanciful theories excited little skepticism from
planters when he wrote.[39]

Indisputably, Cartwright consistently put the interests of his region
and class far above any dispassionate practice of scientific investigation;
nonetheless, among Old South managers and professionals he was
not an isolated extremist but an expounder and extender of established managerial wisdom. The Cartwright passages most excerpted
for their seeming extremism and implausibility were first elaborated
in a thoroughly respectable, jointly produced report commissioned in
1849 by the Louisiana State Medical Convention, which asked him to
head a group studying "diseases and peculiarities of the negro."[40] His
wisdom, Cartwright asserted especially when challenged as to lack of
scientific evidence, rested on the "every-day experience of the Southern
people" with slaves representing "half the value of Southern property."

His activism on behalf of a specifically Southern medical education leaned heavily on the same valorization of the Southern elite's racial knowledge. "Our planters do not go to the North . . . to learn the art of making sugar, cotton, rice, and tobacco," he reported but he complained that they do send sons there for medical education. The result, he added, was a necessity on returning from northern medical schools "to study Medicine over again, in the school of experience . . ., particularly among negroes."[41]

In two distinct ways, Cartwright's science was the wisdom of a master and manager. He first chided northern scientists for being blind to matters so clear to planters and overseers who were in daily contact with slaves. He claimed that free blacks in the North almost universally displayed more acute symptoms of the diseases he discovered, but that their master-less status made both diagnosis and cure impossible outside the South. He then confined surpassing Southern knowledge of Africans to the slaveholding class, underlining the conclusion of much advice literature on slave management by insisting that the master's racial knowledge excelled that of overseers.[42]

When specific diseases came under discussion, the same dynamics applied. After a terrible yellow fever epidemic in New Orleans in 1853 fell more heavily on white workers than on slaves, Cartwright drew lessons based as much on race management as public health. He insisted that the pattern of deaths proved again that "nature scorns to see the aristocracy of the white skin . . . reduced to drudgery work under a Southern sun," and that she "has issued her fiat, that here at least, whether of Celtic or Teutonic origin, they shall not be hewers of wood or drawers of water . . . under the pain of three-fourths of their number being cut off." The immigrant population courted its own death by flouting nature. Doing hard construction work in summer and clearing the "filthy mud" from gutters exposed them to the "miasmatic vapors" that led to their illness. The slave, given "his enormous liver and the peculiar construction of the skin" perfectly fit such labor. The structural solution for the problem, Cartwright held, was to end "the process of making negroes out of the master race of men."[43]

When Cartwright turned to the disease of "dirt-eating," he inherited a heavily racialized discourse but managed to descend further down that road by applying managerial nostrums. The disease already carried the name *Cachexia Africana*, as observers in the Caribbean had regarded its only victims as Africans. The received wisdom made the cause a profound longing for home among the imported and a superstition that eating dirt would ensure return to Africa on dying. Cartwright elaborated an alternative that was biblical in origin. The disease grew out of the African's alleged biological affinity to the mule and fulfilled the Bible's prophecy "And dust shalt thou eat all the days of thy life."[44]

In pressing for "cures" in situations where theology, biology, and superstition were all presumed to be at play, Cartwright and others reflected real conflicts on the plantations and the need to use all methods at hand to manage. One of Cartwright's colleagues urged making more powerful African-style "countercharms" to combat dirt-eating. In discussing cholera, Cartwright similarly described a war for hearts and minds on the plantation, mixing the use of "wild African dance" and the lash:

> The ashy-coloured, dry skin conjurers, or prophets, who had alarmed their fellow-servants with the prophecies that the cholera was to kill them all, and who had gained, by various tricks and artifices, much influence over their superstitious minds, were by my orders, at twilight, called up, stripped, and greased with fat bacon. . . . After being greased, the grease was well slapped in with broad leather straps, marking time with the tam tam, a wild African dance that was going on in the centre of the camp among all those, who had the physical strength to participate in it. This procedure drove the cholera out of the heads of all who had been conjured.

Proof of the miracle came the "next morning [when] all who had been able to join in the dance . . . were ordered into the cane-field to work," their health restored.[45]

The vivid descriptions of two particular diseases helped establish Cartwright not as an extremist but as a powerful leader within the mainstream of managerially inspired racial medicine. The supposed pathologies were named *drapetomania*, or "absconding from service" to seek freedom, and *dysaesthesia Aethiopica*, an illness whose "diagnostic" was an inefficient, seemingly "half-asleep" performance on the job and destruction of the master's property. *De Bow's Review* parceled out in installments the report on "diseases and peculiarities of the negro" that Cartwright's committee completed for the Louisiana State Medical Convention, after the study had first appeared in the *New Orleans Medical and Surgical Journal*. Since the *Review* circulated far more widely and ran the report with Cartwright named as the author, the diseases became associated with his scientific reputation.[46]

Cartwright and his associates spoke the language of managers of black labor as they pathologized resistance, transforming it into disease. The prescriptions were simple: "preventively . . . whipping the devil" out of potential *drapetomaniacs*, and avoiding any possibility of "negro liberty" to ward off *dysaesthesia*. The contradictory combination of emphases on the status of the conditions as individual maladies and as parts of a complex of inherited "racial" inferiorities spoke to a pattern running through race management. The enterprise hinged on both a firm sense of biologically determined white supremacy and on the malleability that made managing of improvements among the inferior possible. Long-standing managerial concerns, such as the fear that slaves were "addicted to sleep," or listless by day because they made the night into the "nigger day-time," could be addressed "scientifically" in Cartwright's view by treating an individual in light of knowledge of the race. His committee's report argued that Africans literally possessed an inherited racial "instinct," housed in the feet and knees, to genuflect before whites. Without knowledgeable management the loss of this instinct produced contagious disease and disaster. Also conveniently "innate" were a "love to act as body servant," or "lacquey," and a tendency to "glory in a close, hot atmosphere." Fortuitous too was the supposed fact that, like mules, Africans could not be harmed by overwork. "The white men of America," according to Cartwright, had "never yet been able to make a negro overwork himself." Cartwright further posited an "ethnological peculiarity" ensuring that "any deserved punishment, inflicted with a switch, cowhide or whip, puts them into a good humor." At the same time, overseers' power to punish was seen as something to be curbed by imparting the knowledge that slave "rascality" was diseased rather than willful. Moreover, the slave had a "right . . . to be punished with a switch or a whip, and not with [a] stick or the fist." Cartwright made management the palliative for "negro peculiarities." Control rested on violence, wielding the "broad leather strap," but with a restraint that would preserve the slaves' "instinctive and most mysterious love for their masters."[47]

Cartwright's most famous work is widely cited as foundational to scientific racism, but his related role in the history of management in the United States is just as striking. Indeed, even the treatment that he prescribed for the slow-working "hebetude" accompanying *dysaesthesia Aethiopica* was a race manager's medicine. Cartwright urged making slaves work harder, thereby sending more oxygen to their brains to mitigate their disability. Though he alleged that the brain of "the negro" was a ninth smaller than that of whites, the main problem lay in the respiratory system. Oxygenating the brain through hard work would alleviate the "defective atmospherization of blood in the lungs" of the slave and increase productivity of the plantation. White management could compel the African to speed up, to "inhale vital air," and to be transformed from the "*bipedum nequissimus* or arrant rascal" into a "good negro that can handle hoe or plow." Thus transformed and driven, the slave could work effectively, accomplishing "about a third less than what the white man voluntarily imposes on himself"—with Africans not rebelling as whites "naturally" would. Such a "science" of work captured much of the sense, nonsense, and circularity of race managements to come.[48]

Race Management after Slavery

The total failure of the slave system has made it difficult to appreciate the powerful appeals made even beyond the South by a confident proslavery white managerial ideology that embedded the control over black labor within discourses on the fostering of reproduction and the husbanding of land recently held by Indians.[49] The paternalism of masters, however much its close association to the trade in bodies and breeding of babies left it open to abolitionist attack, was modern, market-driven, and heartfelt enough to convince planters and northern allies that slavery was not so different and deadly a system after all and that it paid off in comfort and splendor. Belief in white settler colonialism's role in maximizing the profits drawn from land appealed to values shared with the North and gave the defense of slavery purpose and plausibility for a time. Indeed, these advantages of the slave South arguably worked too well. Rates of reproduction by slaves were so great that the slave system appeared capable of improving much of the free (that is, Indian) land in the West. Such a prospect ultimately held little appeal for northern farmers and industrialists coveting that same region. Taking advantage of such contradictions, slaves gained freedom but freedpeople and their descendants did not escape from the race management ideas that so defined the modern United States.

The self-emancipation of slaves between 1863 and 1865 both changed everything and all too little. Edmund Ruffin, who had pioneered Southern proslavery management journals, took his own life after it was clear that the Confederacy would be defeated. Cartwright's wartime efforts to combat contagious diseases on the behalf of Southern victory left him dying of one such disease. Others proved exceedingly resilient and adaptable. Noah Cloud, whose *American Cotton Planter* had been willing to encourage aggressive pursuit of European immigration to the South as early as the 1850s, became Alabama's first commissioner of immigration as a Republican, joining with forces formerly despised as antislavery. Indeed, some in the Republican-backed Freedmen's Bureau themselves plumped for greater immigration from Europe to the South as part of the cure for the "educated idleness" of ex-slaves.[50] Editor J. D. B. De Bow recalled that it had scarcely been possible to imagine "free white immigration [as] practicable, or even desirable" before the war, and that masters had only begun during slavery's last years to think of Asia or Africa as places to gather "coolies, apprentices, or [laborers] under some other name" to repair a region "greatly retarded by a deficiency of labor." After the war, he could imagine European immigrants as a key ingredient in the mix of Southern development.[51]

The white Southern practice of claiming racial knowledge in order to manage, while emerging in slavery, thus outlived the end of that system. New conditions of freedom made postbellum Southern employers profess even higher regard for their own managerial skills. Fitzhugh predicted that the "great negro nursery" of the postwar Freedmen's Bureau—"the largest zoological gardens ever seen"—would fail disastrously for lack of racial knowledge on the bureau's part and lack of full humanity on the part of freedpeople. Such extravagances flourished as the material interest in valuing black bodies diminished.

Counter-discourses that acknowledged black capability and value waned. Fitzhugh imagined after emancipation that in the entire slavery period "not a single negro, in the whole South, was ever found capable of managing a farm." Predictions of a coming decimation of the black population wasted no time in drawing connections with American Indians. One account held that freed slaves and even free blacks from the North were settling near oyster banks to live on nature's bounty, allegedly replicating patterns of precontact Indian settlement and lethargy.[52]

By Reconstruction pro-"coolie" planters saw importation of Chinese labor as a way to break "Sambo" from the sense that he was "master of the southern situation." One newspaper editorialized that most planters sought Chinese labor because they believed it to be "more easily managed" and to "do better work, although much slower." The writer praised racial competition as much as the virtues of any race, promising that the entry of one hundred thousand Chinese workers would "make the negro a much more reliable laborer." Former slave trader and slave master, the murderous Confederate General Nathan Bedford Forrest became an entrepreneur in new arenas and a railway manager after the war, as well as the leader of terrorist Ku Klux Klan. He alternated between proclaiming African labor the world's best, and therefore seeking new importations of African workers, and encouraging schemes to import Chinese labor, in both cases to compete with existing local labor supplies, including a growing sector of convict labor.[53]

Labor management shaped white terror against freedpeople. In the early 1870s, federal action against Klan violence in the Piedmont discovered a pattern of railway contractors, some of whom had worked for the Confederacy as construction engineers, doubling as Klan terrorists. The Klan sought political power, but also disciplined black labor, acting at times as an employers' association, prefiguring later open shop, anti-union efforts in the South. The notorious convict lease system featured race-specific targeting of black workers, typically managed in gangs and under the lash according to theories inherited from race-management practices developed during slavery. At one mine worked by convict labor, the leather strap for whipping those not keeping pace was called the "negro regulator." It was not the convict but "the negro" who was seen by state officials as unable to "get along" without the whip. During

Reconstruction, ex-slaves sometimes succeeded in calling white land-owners and employers "boss" in order to banish the term "master," redolent of slavery as it was. However, with the reassertion of white elite power in the later nineteenth century came the insistence that all blacks call all whites "boss," a striking example of the staying power, and ability to re-create itself, of whiteness-as-management.[54]

In some New South industries, race management persisted and ramified. In a revealing 1901 article in the Cleveland-based iron and steel journal *The Foundry*, an observer revisited Southern stove factories that he had observed sixteen years earlier. The visitor had found on his first visit that the slavery-era practice of using African American craft workers produced a postwar work force of molders centrally including skilled, and prized, black workers. In one factory a manager rhapsodized regarding the unique racial fitness of "the negro" for molding, which he saw as requiring the worker to be "an artist" rather than "a mechanic." In this romanticized view, the same knack that made the African "pick up music" made his craft work as a molder intuitive, delicate, and deft. On the return to the same plant at the turn of the century, the observer found a different manager reflecting the heritage of a harder strain in slave management, as well as the ripening logic of Jim Crow. This manager found black molders to be thieving (a "race trait"), "unsteady," destructive of equipment, and unable to judge "the proper heat at which to pour." His ideal factory would "not have [had] a nigger about the place at any price." Characteristically, he produced numbers to make the case: the black molder was paid only 4 percent less but supposedly produced 10 percent to 15 percent less. To the manager's chagrin, African American molders persisted in the foundry. As he explained, "This is an open shop, and some of our people think it is good policy to keep enough negroes to show that we could fill up with them" if unionization threatened. Indeed, from day to day even the manager advocating a color bar saw the logic of playing races against each other. He concluded, perfectly capturing one strand of logic within race management, "If a white man gets 'cocky,' it does seem good to ask how he would like to see a nigger get his job."[55]

PART II

FACING WEST

3

Frontiers of Control

Infrastructure, Western Expansion, and Race Management

AS POWERFUL AS DIRECT INHERITANCES from slavery were in managing New South industries, U.S. innovations in race management played out on much larger stages after the Civil War. Such innovations unfolded in processes intimately linked to settler colonial expansion in the American West and to the growth of empire. In his sections on labor in the 1857 novel *The Confidence Man* author Herman Melville brought South and West—slavery and expansion—together in stark and profound ways. The novel captures the dynamics and implications of race management in ways that also presage what was to come. Everything in the it prepares us to think of the story, and the nation, as moving on a North/South axis, defined by the differences of free labor from slavery, until the moment that Melville calls such distinctions into question. Before the Mississippi River boat on which the story is set crosses the confluence with the Ohio River, the water divides "free" and "slave" states. Below the Ohio, passengers enter—as the nation seemed about to do itself in 1857 when the Supreme Court delivered the proslavery and white supremacist *Dred Scott* decision—a place where all territory is slave territory.

At the novel's very center, Melville's characters debate not only abolition and bondage but also labor more generally. A contractor of unfree labor parading as a sentimental reformer—critics have generally taken him to be the shifty title character in disguise—offers to provide a "good boy" to a "misanthrope" who is pessimistic regarding whether any young worker would be able to satisfy his need for steady and honest help and, it is hinted, his desires for considerably more. The labor contractor carries a brass plate advertising his business, the wickedly named Philosophical Intelligence Office. Since "intelligence office" at the time meant employment agency, the man with the brass plate supports a market in free labor leavened by a feel-good worldview, as he arrays himself against racial slavery. The misanthrope remains unconvinced, denouncing abolition as "the fellow-feeling of slave for slave." In answer to the self-interested reformer's pieties regarding the essential goodness of all boys, the misanthrope underlines that buying "free" labor was itself racialized, reciting a litany of the young workers who already have failed him. He had tried, in "fifteen years' experience; five and thirty boys; American, Irish, English, German, African, Mulatto; not to speak of that China boy sent me by one who well knew my perplexities, from California; and that Lascar boy from Bombay. Thug! I found him sucking the embryo life from my spring eggs. All rascals, sir, every soul of them; Caucasian or Mongol."[1]

As much as Melville casts such racial choices within the landscape of free and slave territory, he undermines such distinctions simultaneously. The misanthrope is a Missourian, and mostly identified as only that. He disavows slavery and abolition alike, castigating "slave states" and "slave pens" that he believes hold sway from the Northeast to Georgia. Other characters identify him not as a master but as a rural product of the "back-woods," terming him a "'coon," as country white people were still called in this period. From this perspective the Mississippi marked not only a North/South trajectory but also an East/West divide. As soon as the Missourian exits, a "stranger" takes his place, entering "with the bluff *abord* of the west," the shift from English to the italicized French placing the ship between the area of the British-ceded Old Northwest and that of the Louisiana Purchase from France. The stranger goes on to rehearse the "metaphysics of Indian-hating," drawing on atrocity stories from the history of Illinois and predicting recurrences farther west.[2] When Melville wrote of "China boys" and South Asian workers, the debate over uses of Asian labor was lively in the South, but the actual importation of such labor was proceeding dramatically in the Far

West.³ Within a decade, the political economy of the latter region and the nation would be transformed by the pitting of Irish and Chinese workers against each other in building the Transcontinental Railroad.

The Edge of Management

Frederick Jackson Turner's famous historical writings on the frontier West hold that history was made at the margins, with processes developed on edges defining the nation.⁴ His insight applies with special force where the history of management is concerned. The U.S. West, the Pacific world, and the American-controlled enclave abroad were leading edges in reshaping the labor process around race. In large measure the cohabitation of race management and management science matured in U.S. managerial discourse in the West before the industrial East and Midwest. Settlers in the West most suddenly and brutally displaced indigenous people. They relied on racialized labor to permit the completion of huge and dangerous infrastructural projects and to extract wealth through mining. Managerial knowledge from the West then spread beyond U.S. borders, engineering infrastructural projects and mines abroad. Such managerial jobs became associated with experts trained in the U.S. West, who could claim knowledge of race management as well as of technical matters.

In western fiction and film, a single racial division predominates, with Indians and white settlers facing off in military activities, not production. When railroads, which played multinational and multiracial labor forces off against each other, do find their ways into classic Westerns, they are represented as a source of graft and conflict among presumably racially homogenous "whites." When mining enters the picture, it is often in the person of the white prospector victimized in the hills or in town. Settlements appear in the forms of the white family farm or ranch, where managing other people's labor seems peripheral to the story. Drovers drive cattle; gunslingers sling; and the white characters, the occasional Chinese cook or beautiful Mexican woman notwithstanding, occupy center stage.⁵

A general challenge to the idea of the "frontier" as the locus of white pioneering, leavened by skirmishes with Indians, deserves to briefly frame matters. Over the long run of western history varied racial groups

were critical in providing different forms of coerced labor. The pre–
Civil War West saw thousands of American Indian children kidnapped
by settler families in California, Basque and Chinese miners imported,
and indigenous workers transported from Russian Alaska and from
Hawaii.[6] Prior to the war, Jefferson Davis argued for the desirability of
using African American slave labor to develop California, putting solid
logic into the service of that retrograde political stance. "Till canals
are cut, ditches and dams made, no person can reclaim the soil from
Nature," the future leader of the Confederacy held. He added that
"an individual pioneer cannot settle . . . with his family" and see the
land "reduced to cultivation" without the "associated labor" of coerced
workers necessary to build infrastructure. Davis erred in his prediction
of the use of slave labor, but ultimate mastery of the desert through irrigation involved the mobilization of divided and desperate workers who
were American Indian, Japanese, Chinese, Asian Indian, Filipino/a,
Mexican, African American, Armenian, and Italian.[7]

By discussing the role of race management in railroad building and
mining this chapter challenges the view that the post–Civil War West
was marginal to the national and international economy and that its
development was the product of the individualism of whites. It argues
that managerial patterns learned in both realms were vital to U.S.
national development. Varied forms of race management set important
patterns. Railroad construction at times followed the example of slavery
in seeking to find a single race best suited to the job and most willing
to accept its dangers. Later railway construction management recruited
a handful of races and nationalities to ensure labor supply and foster
competition. In mines, dozens of different groups came to vie for the
safest positions and best pay beneath the earth and for spots in camps
that companies set up for white men.

Racing Railroads: Choosing a Most Profitable Race

The 1869 completion of the Transcontinental Railroad, connecting
Council Bluffs, Iowa, to the south shore of San Francisco Bay, was
a miracle of construction and management. In six years, the Union
Pacific (UP), moving west, and the Central Pacific (CP), moving east,
lay almost eighteen hundred miles of track, building requisite bridges

and tunnels, conquering rock, mountain, and desert, and moving through Indian Territory. The CP forces started later, had the harder geological and engineering problems to confront, and constructed only about three miles of track for every five put down by the UP workers. The lines competed in a way that engaged the popular imagination around the drama of a race. They gained government subsidies parceled out by the mile. Cash payments, adjusted for difficulty of terrain, and land grants both followed a per-mile formula, with an incredible 6,400 acres of trackside land being the subsidy for each mile. The construction was a high-stakes competition between capitalist enterprises hoping to grow richer as they proceeded. Because the CP so dramatically chose one "race," the Chinese, to provide the grueling labor used to build its sections of the railroad, it is a revealing case. It, along with the later and partially analogous Great Northern (GN) line, therefore commands attention as a precedent-setter, staking out one extreme of race management strategy. Postbellum race management far more often, like the UP, employed a variety of races and nationalities, often pitting them against each other. To choose a group—the Chinese in building the CP and the Japanese in the case of the GN—as the best work force risked losing the advantages of competition, but benefited from using labor subject to significant amounts of coercion.[8]

Structuring the difference between the CP and UP were the dramas of race and sectionalism in the United States. Southerners in Congress blocked antebellum legislation on transcontinental railroad construction by insisting on a Southern route, so that approval of construction had to await Southern secession from the Union. The land grants to corporations eradicated Indian claims to land along the tracks, and the construction of the UP route especially involved eliminating Indian resistance, sometimes by forming alliances with friendly tribes and using Indian labor in construction. Attempts to curb journalistic coverage of Indian resistance were unevenly successful, and the Indian problem became a labor problem, as railway construction workers left jobs in areas considered to be unpacified. The defense of railroad construction thus contributed to accelerated aggression in Indian policy. It was in this context that California investor, Civil War hero, and subsequently commanding general of the U.S. Army William Tecumseh Sherman wrote, "The more we can kill this year the less will have to be killed the next. . . . They all have to be killed or be maintained as a species of paupers." Sherman repeatedly expressed a desire to "befriend" the "Great Pacific Railroad" and encouraged President Ulysses Grant to do the same, as "far as the law allows." The interest in the railroad's fortune was also self-interest for military men. Grant, who speedily outlawed Indian "trespassing" on railroad land, and Sherman realized that the railroad promised to shuttle troops in defense of white settlement onto Indian lands speedily, making defense of the West far more practicable. Indeed, Sherman thought the railroad would be the solution to the Indian problem.[9]

For a time the dislocations of war and emancipation seemed to suggest possible railroad labor forces. In the wartime beginnings of transcontinental railroad construction, as labor shortages limited progress, massive use of Confederate prisoners of war became one contemplated solution. After the war ended, there were high hopes that emancipated slaves might become a significant part of the railroad construction force. Charles Crocker, the most powerful figure shaping CP labor recruitment, avowed himself to have been an abolitionist "agitator" aiding escaped slaves through the Underground Railroad. Collis Huntington, another of the "Big Four" at the center of CP enterprises, directed that "his principal charities were extended to Negroes."[10] When Abraham Lincoln called eventual UP engineer Grenville Dodge to Washington to discuss the projected railroad, Dodge at first thought he was the subject of disciplinary action for having so precociously armed black people under his command in the Civil War, running far ahead of changes in military and political policy. Henry Varnum Poor, a leading U.S. railway editor and investment analyst, penned an 1865 *American Railroad Journal* article urging the building of the transcontinental railroad by thousands of African Americans, in uniform and under military discipline. Entitling his piece "The Negro and His Uses," Poor regarded his suggestion as patriotic, businesslike, and humanitarian.[11]

Such schemes amounted to little, even if the impulse to connect race and railroad labor recruitment continued. Although black workers significantly labored on certain stretches of the UP, their central roles in the railroad-building process were as "Buffalo Soldiers," U.S. Army troops defending the tracks from Indians during and after the construction. They also served as a reserve labor force to be used to threaten largely

Irish workers when the latter organized. After unproductive earlier inquiries about the possibility of recruiting freed slaves under military discipline, the CP's only significant brushes with African American labor centered on a hasty request in 1867 to mobilize ten thousand blacks as replacement workers to be brought in to crush a strike by Chinese workers. Also rejected after consideration by CP management was an early plan for "importing, under contract, thousands of peons from Sonora and other Mexican states." In the Mexican case, a supposed "constitutional inertia of the breed . . . well-known to California employers" counted as the reason for scotching the plan. Charles Crocker and his lieutenant James Strobridge reportedly found Mexicans "too slow and indolent to work." Therefore, they were "discussed and discarded," though Mexican Americans soon became mainstays in track labor in the Southwest.[12]

Even with the labor force thus delimited it turned out that there could be no separation between the race to lay track and the racial management of those laying it. In her historical novel *China Men*, Maxine Hong Kingston captures this reality especially well. "The demons" who managed the CP, Hong Kingston wrote from the perspective of Chinese workers building the line, "invented games for working faster. . . . Day shifts raced against night shifts, China Men against Welshmen, China Men against Irishmen, China Men against Indians." As the races and nationalities raced, the CP and UP "won the land on either side of the tracks."[13] As work began the racing crews were mostly separated by many hundreds of miles but as a climax was reached they came together. The decisions to racially structure a labor force seemed in the telling of the capitalists and managers who made them to be commonsensical. In their relentless judging of racial and national groups in terms of efficiency, cost, manliness, and willingness to face danger, those decisions magnify and typify what capital got out of race management and put into it. While including depressing wages and forestalling labor organization, those benefits also included more subtle advantages in getting dangerous labor performed day after day.

In the case of the turn to the Chinese labor by the CP, the fullest version of an official account lies in the testimony of the "Big Four" member in "charge of construction," Charles Crocker, in his 1876 testimony to a joint congressional committee on Chinese immigration.

Under very friendly questioning from an attorney who often represented importers of Chinese workers, Crocker repeatedly emphasized that for eighteen months the CP had made every effort to hire "white labor," offering high wages and advertising widely.[14] On a job that ultimately would require upward of fifteen thousand men, Crocker claimed it had proven impossible over that long period to assemble more than eight hundred white workers, with up to a quarter of them leaving each payday. "All of our people," but especially "Mr. [James] Strobridge and myself," were "prejudiced against Chinese labor" and determined "not to employ them," Crocker recalled. Strobridge, as construction superintendent under Crocker, thought the size, diet, race, and alleged effeminacy of the Chinese disqualified them from building railroads. Some accounts had Strobridge at first flatly refusing: "I will not boss Chinese." But the behavior of the white workers "compelled" the CP managers to experiment with the Chinese, a position they were "driven to."[15]

The result was a series of trials of groups, each consisting of fifty Chinese workers. The first group of fifty so succeeded in "vindicating its race" in doing light work that more groups were tested in heavier tasks. At first thought to be "nearly equal" in productivity, they came to be seen far more glowingly. Gradually they "worked themselves into our favor," according to Crocker, so much so that he added, "if I had a big job of work . . . I should take Chinese labor to it, because of its greater reliability and steadiness, and their aptitude and capacity for hard work." A racial or national proclivity for "teamwork" among the Chinese counted as a major virtue. Characteristically, the clinching evidence came in the form of a race. In digging the difficult Summit Tunnel through granite, the CP secured a group of "very good Cornish miners and put them in the tunnel so as to hurry it." A gang of these miners and a gang of Chinese laborers worked at the same task on different sides of the project. "We measured every Sunday," Crocker reported "and the Chinamen without fail always outmeasured the Cornish miners" on this stretch of "bone-hard" work. The Chinese workers were "skilled in using the hammer and the drill . . ., very intelligent, and they live up to their contracts." When the Cornishmen quit, Chinese "had possession of the whole work," Crocker remembered.[16]

Aware of anti-Chinese public opinion, CP management thus told the story that it had reluctantly, but pragmatically, hired steady but only slightly cheaper Chinese workers. They did so because a "certain class of white laborers" refused "to elevate themselves" through railroad labor, and instead chose to "work just long enough to get something to buy liquor with."[17] In Crocker's telling, entry of the Chinese benefited white labor. It freed them from "shoveling dirt" and allowed them to be "teamsters, mechanics, foremen . . . in an elevated grade of labor, receiving wages far above" those who shoveled, much as slavery had been said to elevate poor white Southerners. If skilled, white workers might also, it was promised, be able to hire a Chinese servant. However, CP management's concern for white skilled workers had sharp limits. Later in life Crocker testified that entry of Chinese workers into the skilled work of masonry came in the midst of struggle to break a strike by Irish workers. Nonetheless, the emphasis on the Chinese worker producing the rise of the white foreman made Crocker's narrative especially interesting. At least in a literal reading, it would seem that white labor, tried and found inferior to the Chinese, became management.[18]

In defending the turn to Chinese labor as the practical result of the necessity to quickly build a railroad, men like Crocker and Leland Stanford had to leave out a great deal and indeed barely suggested the enormous advantages accruing to the CP. Crocker insisted that he "preferred white laborers to Chinese" until he "could not obtain white labor." However, this dramatic story of response to a failed 1865 recruitment of whites clashes with CP payroll records showing employment of a full gang of Chinese workers in early 1864. Stanford, a Big Four stalwart, was already on record by early October 1865 as declaring to President Andrew Johnson that without the "quiet, peaceable, patient, industrious and economical Chinese . . . it would be impossible to complete" the CP's work.[19]

The problem was not an absolute lack of white, mostly Irish, unskilled workers but that they preferred agriculture and mining to dangerous and dictatorially bossed railroad work. Moreover, they occupied a labor-market position from which to make choices. Some certainly qualified as "slightly over-age forty-niners," who defected at first rumor of gold discoveries, but less poetic labor-market considerations also made labor for the CP less attractive than other options. As Stanford once wrote, in contrast to the pathologizing of white unskilled workers by Crocker, such workers avoided the CP because they could find "more profitable and congenial employment" elsewhere.[20]

Issues of dignity, control, and safety made those with alternatives likely to leave. Both Crocker and Strobridge carried, and indeed cultivated, reputations for a threatening style of management. The former prided himself on acting "like a mad bull" in interactions with workers and the latter managed with an ax handle, his "persuader," in hand.[21] The blows and curses fell more heavily on Chinese workers because Irishmen had a far greater chance of avoiding abuse by leaving. With labor highly concentrated at certain points, railroad construction was intensely bossed. Lewis Clement, the CP's assistant chief engineer, specifically identified "the discipline of railroad work" as what the "independent" and "high-priced" white workers found unacceptable.[22] The Irish and other white workers quickly left CP railway construction camps upon ascertaining working, living, and safety conditions in them.[23]

Nor did management countenance reform. In testimony before the Pacific Railway Commission, Crocker himself recalled that proto-unionism, not Irish drinking, motivated the turn to Chinese labor. Confronted in the spring of 1865 by the threat of a negotiating committee demanding a raise, Crocker remembered in this version, "I told Mr. Strobridge to . . . get some Chinamen and put them to work." Strobridge's hesitation gave time for the Irish to reconsider and, Crocker continued, "The Irishmen begged us not to have any Chinamen and resumed work."[24] In the case of the later strike of Irish masons, the employment of Chinese workers reportedly had the same effect. Only after the first strike threat, on this telling, did the concerted experiments with Chinese labor begin. That they supposedly would not organize became a selling point justifying use of the Chinese, at least until they did dramatically strike in 1867.[25]

Reportedly superior in work, the Chinese laborers received far less pay, though some management writing muddied this issue. White laborers were said, with some oversimplification, to receive thirty-five dollars a month plus board and the Chinese thirty dollars monthly without board. This racial wage differential, five dollars extra a month for white workers in the same classification, was sometimes presented as less than consequential, but there are strong reasons to question such a judgment. An 1870 account in a magazine of "eclectic engineering" concluded a racial comparison of wages with "the white men . . . paid about the same, but with their board thrown in." In fact, white wages were a sixth again as much as Chinese, and board constituted a very considerable expense, so the total outlay for white unskilled workers was half again as much as for Chinese labor and by some reckonings double. Moreover, as Crocker briefly hinted in his comparison to the Cornish miners, management got Chinese skilled labor (in masonry, blasting, and laying track, for example) for a dollar a day plus what Crocker recalled as "as little more." White labor in those tasks would have cost two to three times as much.[26]

Indeed, the quaintness of rehearsed stories from management suggests a close knowledge of Chinese workers' skills but also a tendency to make such abilities into racial and national traits to be cultivated by white management rather than individual, marketable, modern knowledge. One continuing sticking point in Strobridge's balking at using Chinese labor came when he protested that no such worker could do the skilled work of a mason. Crocker asked him, "Did they not build the Chinese wall, the biggest piece of masonry in the world?" Soon Chinese workers did the masonry work and among the prominent features on engineering maps of the Summit Tunnel were the "Chinese Walls." When their blasting skills were called into question, references to traditional Chinese gunpowder use clinched the point. In fact, these Chinese workers had skills derived from extensive experience in blasting and mining both outside the United States and in California, not from a misty racial unconscious transmitted over centuries.[27] One story had Chinese miners solving a major construction problem that stumped CP engineers by calling on prior experience and being lowered in wicker baskets into tight crevices in hard rock to plant charges.[28]

The biggest advantage to CP management in turning to a majority Chinese construction labor force was that those workers were considered expendable and vulnerable, having often been forced into service jobs until opportunities for railway work opened. The decision to take on Chinese labor drew upon a long, public, and transnational debate over the importation of "coolie" contract labor to replace or supplement slaves and ex-slaves in plantation agriculture. Some accounts credit CP attorney E. B. Crocker's positive relationship to a Chinese servant as leading to his advocating for the use of Chinese railway labor before his brother Charles did so.[29] Chinese labor in California had often devolved into service labor in laundries, restaurants, and households because entry to other jobs was blocked. White workers not wanting to work alongside the Chinese tried hard to connect the latter to slavery and servility, calling the Chinese "niggers" and "Crocker's pets." Management sought just such a servile workforce.[30]

Company expectations and white labor's fears of the servility of Chinese workers proved wrong, though tragically management's knowledge of Chinese vulnerability did not. The massive weeklong 1867 strike by Chinese CP workers showed them to be anything but compliant. Indeed, press accounts of the conflict identify opposition to beatings, insistence on the right to quit, higher wages, and shorter hours among the strikers' demands. Some gains preceded the work stoppage, and these seem to have continued after the men were forced back to work. Day-to-day attacks by Irish workers drew responses in kind from the Chinese, so much so that the UP's Grenville Dodge reported the use of blasting materials by each side against the other—a cautionary tale for race managers and a barometer of Chinese self-assertion.[31]

If not in the position of a slave-like "coolie," imported in bondage, Chinese railroad workers did suffer from coercion at the hands of labor recruiters and the state. The railroad wanted to profit from increased recruiting efforts in China and did benefit from the extent to which workers were kept in debt to companies that had facilitated their passage. However, it took substantial time for import networks to satisfy the CP's needs for labor. Although Big Four leaders dreamed of attracting one hundred thousand or even a half million speedy arrivals "to bring the price of labor down," nothing like those numbers could be delivered. The initial and ongoing Chinese labor force on the CP line consisted mainly of Chinese men long resident in the United States, migrating from China before transcontinental railroad building began, often to be miners. Sixty-five percent of the key early Chinese labor force building the railroad through Nevada fit this description. Thrown out of the best opportunities in the mining industry and out of a host of other job possibilities by legislation, violence, and discrimination, these men could ill afford to lose a CP job. Often in debt to Chinese and American merchants and saddled with family responsibilities to succeed and save, Chinese workers had to think carefully before leaving or risking jobs, even in the face of managerial brutality and manifest dangers at work.[32]

Another factor that conditioned the vulnerability and expendability of Chinese workers was their lack of the protections of citizenship. Without the rights to vote, to testify against whites, and to serve on juries, Chinese Californians often relied on merchants to broker their relations to white structures of power.[33] In short, the vulnerability that made Chinese workers subject to coercion was made in the United States. As noncitizens and as a racially despised population the Chinese could claim little in the way of sympathy or relief if thrown out of work. The expectation was that they would move on after doing their work, often in the 1870s and '80s to central roles in other railroad construction projects. After the celebrations of the driving of the last spike joining CP and UP in 1869, the Chinese often disappeared from the historical record.[34] A crew of "Crocker's Chinks" of the CP laid an incredible ten miles of track in one day to beat the Irish of the UP in a famous race to see who could produce more late in the construction process, but the victory was later memorialized by recording the names of eight Irish rail handlers on the CP crew, leaving the mass of Chinese workers anonymous.[35] The ability to produce and then disappear was part of what made Chinese workers desirable. As Crocker put it before congressional investigators, "I consider that as [long as] they are wanted for labor they will come, and when there are too many . . . they will go away."[36]

The expendability of the Chinese presented itself most starkly in deaths on the job. The CP crews, composed overwhelmingly of Chinese workers, faced smallpox, snowslides, landslides, falls, collapsed structures and tunnels, and blasting accidents. Management offered premium pay, in very low amounts, for especially dangerous tasks like blasting with nitroglycerin and working in cold water, jobs that fell especially to Chinese workers.[37] The death toll in CP construction probably reached over thirteen hundred, with five dead for every three miles of track on one estimate. Another study suggests that one Chinese worker in ten died. The evidence is very fragmentary, in part because the CP did not keep records on the deaths, and many of the fatalities were discussed in a single newspaper source. However, Chinese labor clearly performed, and white labor often refused, extremely perilous work on the CP.[38]

Understanding that Chinese workers might be preferable because they were vulnerable and expendable helps define the limits of the support Crocker and Stanford sometimes expressed for such workers, while also favoring a continuation of their lack of rights. Managerial multiracialism, and even preference for nonwhite workers on some jobs, was anything but antiracist. CP leaders rehearsed how they overcame "prejudice"—Stanford ran for governor of California early in the Civil War by opposing the Chinese as "that degraded race" but was singing the praises of Chinese workers in 1865.[39] They did not overcome an urge to discriminate against the Chinese and still less did they develop an ethic requiring respect for the labor rights of the Chinese. To break the 1867 strike, they undertook the massive recruitment of black strikebreakers, and threatened cutting off food, taking away tents, and leaving strikers stranded without transportation from the camps. The threat of using freedpeople as strikebreakers, E. B. Crocker wrote to Huntington, "would tend to keep the Chinese quiet as the Chinese have kept the Irishmen quiet." The idea of importing Japanese strikebreakers also quickly emerged.[40]

Imposing wage differentials by race, and barring the Chinese from good jobs in the railroad running trades, suggested that CP managers could simultaneously admire the Chinese worker and discriminate against him. Crocker proudly told investigators that he had paid "bigger wages" to white men he reported to be less productive than Chinese workers. He testified that the whole Chinese gang was paid a sum, delivered to a designated head man, and relayed to the men. While this practice was not out of the ordinary in late nineteenth-century labor arrangements, CP management offered a particularly revealing rationale for their practice. They declared that individual wage payments could not be made because Chinese workers had such incomprehensible names and so looked alike, as to open possibilities of the same worker drawing double pay. "Chinaman" thus supplanted the actual name of Chinese workers in some cases. This pattern also applied where the CP used American Indian labor. For all the praising of Chinese abilities, Strobridge insisted that Chinese workers were merely "reliable," while whites qualified as "mechanical." The former counted as "good laborers" but not "expert." As a *San Francisco Chronicle* reporter described it in 1868, "The scientific part of the job is superintended by white men [and] the rough work is done by the Chinese." Those whites superintending were called "herders" or "Riding Bosses."[41]

Regarding civil rights, Crocker was careful to insist that he did not advocate citizenship or voting for the Chinese. He regarded their presence as sufficiently troubling to urge a ceiling on Chinese population: "One laboring Chinaman for ten white persons." More than that would be "thick" and "unpleasant." Crocker argued that any Chinese aspiration to political power would be "very undesirable," but he added that such aspirations were happily absent in any case. Such lack of support for Chinese civil rights might have partly reflected a calculation that anti-Chinese opinion ought not be inflamed, but it also reflected the self-interest of management. For the Chinese to continue as the overwhelmingly favored (but fiercely exploited) preference in a largely one-track system of race management their continued vulnerability and expendability were required.[42]

Mixing as Necessity: The Great Northern Railway

A boom in Far West railway construction followed the 1869 completion of the first transcontinental route and it seemed for a time that Chinese labor might continue to dominate Far West railway building. Other transcontinental routes, and countless trunk lines, followed. Although there were dislocations, Chinese workers were thrown into building new projects and maintaining existing lines. The CP had served as a "school for Chinese labor" and had helped to develop supply networks for importing workers. In 1869 Chinese workers turned to constructing the critically important line to the Comstock Lode mining region. The Northern Pacific (NP) soon hired half of its twenty-five thousand workers, building eastward from Oregon to Montana, from among the Chinese. The Southern Pacific (SP), developed by the CP's Big Four and with Strobridge managing in an even more dictatorial fashion, likewise used Chinese workers centrally in building lines, the proportion nearing 90 percent for a brief time among three thousand SP workers in Texas construction in the early 1880s. However, violent anti-Chinese opposition from nativist forces continually threatened to disrupt production.[43]

The key factor restructuring the labor market in western railway building was that the very vulnerability that made the Chinese desirable too often made their availability unpredictable. By the

1870s, local pogroms anticipated the 1882 success of the passage of the Chinese Exclusion Act. The Chinese would only temporarily be the preferred labor force, never again as overwhelmingly so as on the CP. The trend toward building networks able to recruit other races and nationalities aimed to ensure ongoing labor supply and competition among workers.[44]

The best-documented and most interesting example of these dynamics lies in the Pacific Northwest and particularly in the western portions of James J. Hill's Great Northern Railway line. In the nineteenth century Pacific Northwest, the fur trade and then lumbering, mining, fishing, canning, and milling required increased labor forces. The Fort Blakely sawmill in Washington state employed Mexican, white native-born American, African American, Chinese, Chilean, English, Irish, Italian, Filipino, Japanese, Scandinavian, Hawaiian, and Austrian workers as early as the 1870s, some as "free" labor and some as contract labor. Chinese immigrants were so prominent as a source of unskilled labor in the Northwest region after the Civil War that early Japanese labor contractors themselves often furnished employers with Chinese workers. Even after the 1882 exclusion and riots targeting them in Seattle, Tacoma, and Portland in 1885, the Chinese shaped the unskilled labor market. Subterfuges remained possible, and workers could be brought in from Canada, where restrictions on the Chinese took the form of taxes, not exclusion. However, by the beginning of the twentieth century, major Chinese contractors gave up and moved operations out of the Pacific Northwest.[45]

Having long used the Chinese Quong Tuck Company as its labor contractor, the GN tried Greek and Italian immigrant workers in the 1890s but reported dissatisfaction with them. Even after the Chinese experience, the GN remained attracted to the idea of a single "race" answering its needs. In 1898, as Japanese entrepreneurs Charles Takahashi and Ototaka Yamaoka founded the Oriental Trading Company (OTC), the GN was negotiating for a very limited experiment to "try Japanese" section hands. As in the case of the CP, it took a short time between the plans for initial experiments and a general turn to a new Japanese labor force both as section hands and in gang labor.[46] By 1899, Hill had settled on a close relationship with OTC and by the following year the question was not whether to continue to use the

Japanese but how to extend their range of work on the GN. Both the perceived Japanese unwillingness to work in cold and snow, and the fear of violent opposition from white tunnel builders and coal chute workers entered calculations about how to "carefully extend the use of Japs" to new sites. However, such decisions took place in the context of certainty that the Japanese were the "best laborers that we can obtain," and management for a time insisted that "we do not need any Italian laborers."[47] Indeed, in 1900 the general superintendent of the GN so preferred the Japanese as to abjure all "Italians or other outside labor." By 1903, the hope was to obtain as many as five thousand workers from OTC, gradually extending "Jap laborers further East."[48]

James J. Hill is widely quoted as saying, "Give me Swedes, snuff, and whiskey and I'll build a railroad right through hell!" If that was his first preference for common labor on the railways, he abandoned it dramatically. The choice to make a near-exclusive turn to Japanese labor was both inspired and ill-fated. Hill's commitment to "rock-bottom" wages made the workers OTC provided especially appealing. Their wages could be a fifth or more below those of "Greeks, Italians or white labor" despite the Japanese being thought "more reliable" and altogether preferable. One account had Greeks and Italians doing half the work of Japanese workers, for twenty cents per day higher wages, but equal pay for superior Japanese workers was regarded as an exotic position when briefly raised in 1905. When particularly favorable labor market situations raised the possibility of obtaining cheap white labor, as after a raft of 1903 sawmill closings, the GN sought to capitalize, suggesting that the commitment to Japanese labor could be challenged by the same market forces structuring the preference.[49]

However, the commitment to the Japanese at GN also drew upon complex political and economic rationales transcending supply and demand. Hill himself feared limits to the U.S. domestic market and tariff-driven shrinkage of the British one. Beginning in the 1880s, he had therefore moved to build a strong Asian trade. Such trade could further ensure that GN's lumber-hauling trains from the Northwest would transport Midwest and Great Plains grain on the return trips west, an appealing proposition for Hill, who thought "the empty car was a thief." Hoping to convert Indian, Chinese, and Japanese diets from rice to wheat flour, GN first used Quong Tuck Company and then

OTC officials to forge trading networks and appeal to the Chinese and Japanese governments for favorable policies. Japan's own imperial ambitions at times made officials susceptible to schemes that encouraged labor migration, giving young Japanese men experience in jobs in a developing extractive economy like that of the Northwest.[50]

The problems with so focusing on Japanese labor nonetheless soon equaled the advantages. OTC relied on "book-men" who both assembled gangs and doubled, sometimes problematically, as foremen. From workers through "book-men" to the OTC, the common interest lay in having more wages, and therefore less turnover and more steady contractors' fees circulating in the system. GN management received continual requests for raises. Although Hill gloried in 1900 that the "clean, faithful and respectful" Japanese workers presented not the "slightest danger . . . of cutting a figure in labor circles," such pressure from OTC proved insistent. The supposed "racial" traits and habits that made Japanese workers desirable could even be recycled as justifications for raises. Thus an alleged love of gang labor morphed into an argument for premium pay for more isolating jobs.[51]

The established Japanese dislike for dangerous and unpleasant work in snow soon included refusals to do such work. This caused GN to threaten taking away the company-provided tents at Kalispell, Montana, leaving workers there exposed to the freezing cold if they did not agree to labor in wintry conditions. Workers resisted poor conditions by quitting, taking off at various times for the higher seasonal wages of fishing, picking, or lumber hauling or to take other railway and industrial jobs. GN leaders persistently complained that OTC did not provide the promised number of workers, causing substantial economic losses. When relations frayed most seriously, the company even suspected that Takahashi's manipulations lay behind lawsuits filed in Japan by "alien widows" of deceased GN workers. For their part, the contractors complained that the engineering department and other forces within GN gave common labor that should have gone to the Japanese to white workers.[52]

The OTC necessarily sought to please Hill by retaining workers but risked being discredited in the eyes of Japanese laborers if other contractors secured greater wages, as sometimes happened with the Northern Pacific, for example. To keep workers the GN held out

10 percent of pay to be redeemed as a "bonus" at season's end. As Takahashi allowed, "We schemed this bonus system merely for the purpose of holding men till the end of the working season. We called it 'bonus' and not 'hold back' simply to avoid the bad sound." However, historian Kornel Chang shows that huge numbers of men, a majority in certain instances, still opted to forgo bonuses to take fishing and other jobs, one factor in causing GN to persistently entertain the idea of doing its own recruitment of Japanese labor or shifting to another firm. While GN advocated for Japanese immigration, its management also had reasons to regret that "many opportunities present themselves to Jap laborers." Market forces did not solve GN's problems retaining Japanese workers. Even in acute labor shortages, the idea that the Japanese should be cheap labor could not be breached. In one such instance in 1907, management balked at paying $1.65 a day for Japanese laborers and then authorized $2.00 as the daily wage for Italians. To do otherwise threatened to have the "whole Japanese labor question thoroughly disorganized."[53]

No cures for such chronic problems seemed at hand outside of a large increase in the supply of imported Japanese labor. Increasingly the OTC and the GN faced doubly downward pressure on the supply of such workers. The growth of an anti-Japanese movement threatened supply, and Japan responded by imposing limitations on emigration as early as 1900 to avoid diplomatic conflicts. Moreover, if Japan's imperial ambitions made it more willing for a time to send labor, its victorious prosecution of the 1905 Russo-Japanese War encouraged keeping Japanese youth at hand, first for military purposes and then, as a world power, needing to protect its subjects from being slighted abroad. After 1908 U.S.-imposed exclusions made the shortage of Japanese labor an enduring one. While OTC and other contractors sought mass importations of Japanese labor from Hawaii, enticed Japanese workers from Canada, and sought to influence Japanese government policies in maneuvers exposed in the *New York Times*, these avenues were inadequate. At best, OTC had provided about half of the five thousand workers GN requested from them. Increasingly that level could not be reached so the need to resort to Italians and others deepened.[54]

By 1911, GN had converted overwhelmingly to European immigrant labor, sometimes Bulgarians and Austrians and sometimes Greeks and

Italians, although with no diminution of complaints about the workers and contractors involved and with continuing "racial" opposition to the new workers from weak maintenance-of-way unions representing native-born whites. Under these circumstances, OTC continued to do some recruiting for GN, which along with other railroads in the region sought a multiracial unskilled labor force. Plans for using black, Mexican, and Puerto Rican labor on the GN began to be broached by World War I.[55]

Mixing as Management: The "Miner's Frontier"

The extractive industries of the West, especially mining, departed monumentally from the railroads' conceptualizations of race management as finding the best race, or the best handful of races and nationalities, of available workers for construction and track-labor jobs. In doing so, extractive industries, especially western mining, developed sophisticated strategies for managing race against race. Turner's insistence that history was made at the margins nowhere applied better than to what he called the "miner's frontier," especially in the coal and metal mines of the West.[56] Unlike management in railway construction and track labor, many such mines sought to retain a large workforce over a long period of time. Requiring various skills, and able to provide newly built company towns, western mines desired, attracted, and played against each other the workers of the world.

Such enterprises precociously faced opportunities and problems defining modern industrial management. They attempted to glory at once in the differences among peoples whom they had assembled and in their own abilities to make those differences productive. In sparsely populated states, these mines brought in sufficient numbers of workers to create political possibilities for the election of both pro-labor candidates promising shorter working hours, and pro-white native-born candidates urging exclusions of Asian workers and limitations on the numbers of southern and eastern European noncitizens in workplaces. The ideal became creating a "white citizen-worker" or a "citizen-miner"—English-speaking, well-scrubbed, unlikely to brawl, immune to strikes, indifferent to labor politics, and sufficiently assimilated to reassure nativists. Indeed, the "questionably white" position of new immigrants from southern and eastern Europe positioned them perfectly as both urgently needing guidance from the company and the reformers it hired and as presenting a fair possibility of racial development. Grand schemes to Americanize and homogenize a wildly diverse workforce thus coexisted with the crudest efforts to keep alive a sense of differences among races, all competing for the precarious favor of management in western mines.[57]

Such mines could perversely typify Turner's further insistence that the frontier, albeit disappearing, was "the line of most rapid and effective Americanization" of immigrants, and a terribly hard place characterized by "captains of industry" brutally "applying squatter doctrines to the evolution of American industrial society." One of the first major studies of U.S. mining, written by the Johns Hopkins–trained historian Charles Howard Shinn in 1884, beat Turner to the punch in making the frontier central to national history, focusing on the mining camp, diversity, and white supremacy as creative forces within American democracy. Shinn identified the mining camp as "the original contribution of the American pioneer to the art of self-government." Its creative energy, for Shinn, stemmed from the reality that "the heterogeneous population of the mining-region included a strange medley of races from the islands and shores of the Pacific, from the provinces of Mexico, and the countries of Southern Asia." Difficulties with "such foreigners" were "inevitable, and only served to weld Americans into a closer union."[58]

In 1902, a management periodical described "the racial features of the workmen" at a particular complex of workplaces as "more varied than in any other industry of our polyglot people." Among the seventeen thousand workers there were "32 different nationalities or races, including, besides all the English-speaking races, Austrians, Bohemians, Danes, Dutch, French, Germans, Hungarians, Indians, Italians, Japanese, Mexicans, Norwegians, Poles, Russians, Swedes and many more." The twenty-seven languages spoken did not begin to exhaust countless dialects. "Here, then," the reader learned, "was a great field for sociology, in its most primitive and essential phases."[59]

This vast managerial and social science laboratory did not arise from the spectacular meatpacking plants of Chicago, the burgeoning steel industry of Pittsburgh, or the strife-prone northeastern textile plants. The site was in Colorado, a state with scarcely half a million people in

1900, but remarkably urban and, like many mining frontiers, highly cosmopolitan. Indeed, the publication came from Colorado Fuel and Iron (CFI), the giant John D. Rockefeller–controlled coal mine and steel mill complex built in and around Pueblo. Just after the turn of the century, CFI became probably the first U.S. industrial enterprise to open a Sociological Department. Fifteen years later, Henry Ford's similar efforts, seen as an early hallmark of Fordism as a system, took the same name and apparently modeled practices on those of CFI.[60]

CFI experts chose *Camp and Plant* as the title for their magazine, combining images of factories and frontier outposts, as they tackled problems that put them on the cutting edge of new forms of welfare capitalism and race management. When the eminent sociologist E. A. Ross described the process of "foreignizing" workplaces that was unfolding nationally in 1914, CFI figured centrally in the discussion. At one CFI mine in 1902, for example, the less than three hundred workers included sixty Italians, forty-five African Americans, thirty-two Japanese, and twenty-three Mexicans, with but forty-seven white native-born citizens employed.[61] Such mixing seemed the essence of managerial wisdom, with *Engineering* writing in 1901 that any mine manager would be "aware of the advantages of working 'mixed crews' mingling nationalities as a sort of insurance against labor combinations." To produce enough "citizen-miners" out of such a managerial strategy seemed to require what was at the time called the "necessary science" of sociology, increasingly undertaken by female staffers at CFI. Through kindergartens, hygiene programs, night schools, and publications, the experts set out to produce American workers from the immigrant employees.[62]

Despite these efforts labor conflicts rocked CFI. The mass coal strike among southern Colorado coal miners in 1903 amounted to an immigrant rebellion. The bloody April 1914 Ludlow Massacre, in which the National Guard and company colluded in intransigence and brutality, left twenty-one dead as a result of gunplay, execution of a strike leader, and a terrible fire in a tent colony of evicted strikers. Policing and use of the National Guard against strikers who were said to be "savage" relied on weapons, techniques, and cruelties used by the United States in a variety of Indian wars. The first strike wave led to a firm commitment to the Sociological Department, and the second to the shelving of sociology in favor of company unionism as a strategy of control and publicity.[63]

As the journalist John Reed and the novelist Upton Sinclair argued at the time, the company attempted to accent racial division even as it also funded Americanization. Reed reached Trinidad, Colorado, ten days after the massacre and found that the experience of living through eviction and death, terrible as it was, gave miners what segregated towns and sped-up mine labor had denied them: "time to know one another." The experience of "living together" eroded "the petty race prejudices and misunderstandings that had been fostered between them by the coal companies."[64]

Sinclair's ambitious 1917 novel *King Coal* was so based on events at CFI that he appended an afterword on his sources, drawing especially on congressional investigations of the massacre at Ludlow. Sinclair organized the first long section of the book around the "domain" of King Coal and the second around the "serfs" of that eponymous monarch. Hal, the central figure in the book, a young college student trained in sociology and experiencing life as a worker, at first thinks that the strategy of managing by race overmatches any attempts by workers to retain humanity, let alone to organize. Alec Stone, the "nigger driver" mine boss, is said to control men like a stage manager who shouts orders to actors by the names of their characters. But the characters are assigned roles of race or nationality in what is literally race management: "You, Polack, get that rock into the car! Hey, Jap, bring those tools over here! Shut your mouth now, Dago, and get to work, or I'll kick the breeches off you. . . . Load those timbers, Hunkie, or I'll carve you to bits." The pit boss tells instructional "nigger" stories to a captive immigrant audience and every horrific division seems to work for capital. Among the diverse men in the saloon, "race-feelings seemed to be stronger than . . . class-feelings."[65]

Indeed, Hal finds the domain of coal and capital extending via race into the hearts of the working population. "The Americans and English and Scotch looked down upon the Welsh and Irish," who in turn looked down on "the Dagoes and Frenchies"; they, in turn disdained "Polacks and Hunkies," who despised "Greeks, Bulgarians, and 'Monty-negroes [Montenegrins]." After another spate of eastern European distinctions came "Greasers, niggers, and, last and lowest, Japs." However, when

Sinclair turned to life, joy, mutual support, and organization among the
"serfs," Hal began to question the "haughty race consciousness of the
Anglo-Saxon" as immigrants crossed lines, including language barriers,
meant to divide them.[66]

Employers nevertheless believed, sometimes at their own peril, that
they could depend on race and nationality injecting ongoing divisions inimical to labor organization. Management brought in new, or
newly numerous, groups of workers explicitly to undermine assertions
of strength by existing organized or organizing workers. Sometimes,
the animus toward these new workers could be defused with time and
new experiences. Missouri lead miners, for example, were said to have
migrated with little knowledge of the labor process in western mines.
The lack of fit between what they were said to have known and how
employers valued them was mocked in the phrase, "I'm from Missouri,
you'll have to show me [how to mine in new settings]." Over time
Missourians became less identified with threats to labor unity and the
"Show-Me" jab returned home to become the proud motto of the state.
Italians, W. E. B. Du Bois once noted, were mobbed to force them into
unions and African Americans were mobbed to keep them out.[67] At
times western miners proved exceedingly able to realize that, as one of
their leaders put it, "the scab of today is the striker of tomorrow," and
experience taught them that "Americans," whether from nearby farms,
from Missouri and upper Michigan metal mines, or from coal mines
in the east often proved more eager strikebreakers than transnational
migrants. Nonetheless, in the case of southern and eastern European
and Mexican strikebreaking migrants, acceptance as something other
than people racially coded to be scabs took time.[68]

The presence of racially despised and suspected immigrants alongside
native-born white citizen-miners also served mine management's interests where safety was concerned. The perils of western mines made hard-
rock mining the most dangerous U.S. industrial occupation during
this period. In Colorado between 1909 and 1913, coal miners also died
in accidents at astronomical rates, three and a half times the national
average, at a time when the United States was the deadliest coal-mining
nation. Before 1900 liability issues presented themselves only slightly in
such cases, as "contributory negligence" and "assumed risk" doctrines
often absolved the companies when disasters occurred. However, stark

safety risks potentially produced great fellow-feeling among those working below the earth, leading to organization and militancy. As law and patterns of litigation changed during the Progressive Era, maimed victims of accidents and survivors of men killed in disasters did begin to more successfully sue for damages as well.[69]

A set of powerful stories about race and nationality provided a counternarrative to those holding mining corporations responsible for accidents and encouraging organizing for change among the imperiled. When the dangers of mining fell on those considered nonwhite, or European but inferior, the costs of disaster could be reckoned as less. If "American" workers died in accidents, they were typically named but other victims might be counted as "a Mexican" or as a group of Greeks or Slavs. Overwhelmingly noncitizens (or in the case of many U.S.-born Mexicans nonvoting citizens) racially marginalized miners commanded little strength to demand reforms as voters or to decide on liability for accidents as jury members. The new immigrant death and permanent disability rate in U.S. industry in the early twentieth century may have been double than for the native-born worker, and one western employer reckoned non-English-speaking workers nearly two and a half times as likely to suffer "mishaps" that were often fatal. Absolution of the employer from responsibility for injuries was a common response, sometimes followed by employer-initiated English-language classes. Inquiries into how and why European immigrants and Mexican American workers were being slotted into the most dangerous jobs and places within mines seem not to have entered the science of management.[70]

Blame for accidents thus fell on immigrant victims more heavily than on mining corporations. State mine inspectors and mine management reinforced each other's contentions that the "careless" immigrant worker left accidents in his wake, though employers could only go so far without calling the open immigration policies they supported into question. When workers responded to pay schemes based on production of ore by slighting construction of timbering supports needed for safety, or by blasting aggressively, race and inexperience could be blamed in preference to indicting a system inviting disaster. Since the term "English-speaking race" stood in for native-born European workers of western European descent, the invocation of miscommunication as a cause of tragedies lent itself to "racial" as well as cultural explanations.

Thus the *Engineering and Mining Journal* blamed "non-English-speaking common labor, represented by emigrants from southern Europe" as culprits in mine accidents in 1902. At times the charge could be both specific to a nationality and expansive enough to cover more, as in an 1888 report from a Colorado mine inspector identifying "Italian and other inexperienced miners" as the cause of deaths in the mines. The Winter Quarters Mine disaster of 1900 in Utah saw the mine superintendent successfully blame Finnish workers as reckless, deflecting charges that the mine's ventilation allowed dangerous levels of dust to accumulate.[71]

CFI mine superintendent David Griffiths exemplified the symbiotic relation of the state and corporation in racializing tragedy. In an earlier career as a mine inspector, he had argued against company liability in a major mine disaster and had praised mine owners for concern with safety. In 1912, as a CFI manager, he offered perhaps the most spectacular double displacement of blame away from mining capital for continuing safety problems: "The consumer demands our product, and in our necessity we must hire everything that comes along, be it Jap or Greek. . . . There must necessarily be more accidents and casualties."[72]

In blaming Finns, "Japs," Greeks, and other victims for accidents, management potentially undermined the sense of unity derived from facing common dangers in the mine. Similarly, safety could never be a fully unifying issue for workers in and around most Southwest mines, as Mexicans were generally barred from underground work that provided the best-paying jobs, but also the ones most dramatically identified with danger and masculinity. Instead, the most dangerous above-ground jobs, often in the smelter, went to Mexicans. A similar pattern of exclusion from jobs presenting one danger and placement in another job presenting equally dire threats occurred among African American smelter workers in the Anaconda complex in Montana. In the mines themselves, unionists were capable of great sophistication in resisting attempts to collapse safety into a "race" issue. At their best they blamed management and not immigrants for the "holocausts" that regularly occurred, and emphasized as a safety issue not the employment of immigrants but the blacklisting of veteran union men who raised issues about unsafe conditions. Employer negligence leading to the deaths of immigrant workers, including many Finns, in the terrible fire at the ominously named Speculator Mine in Montana in 1917 energized renewed wartime militancy among mostly Irish "settled workers."[73] However, unions too often paired immigrant exclusion with prevention of accidents, pressing, for example, for barring Japanese workers or for laws requiring 80 percent of workers at any mine to be English-speaking on the grounds of safety. Despite some inspiring campaigns by mining unions, and embrace of the principle "An injury to one is an injury to all" by not only the Industrial Workers of the World but also at times by the United Mine Workers and the Western Federation of Miners, the production of difference typically served the production of metals, coal, profits, and death on the job.[74]

The employer's aim could never solely be to produce only something as abstract as difference or even simply to offer a self-serving explanation for accidents. The goal had also to include getting workers to return to workplaces unsafe even for the most privileged miners without successfully demanding a full share of the wealth produced in them. Keeping a core of expert workers in a place like Butte was seen as central to the survival of the community and the safety of the mines. Mine management, both as it related to extracting daily production and to keeping a lid on possible insurgencies by labor, rested on maintaining and deepening a series of stark but shifting dichotomies. Each pairing—white versus Mexican (or versus "peon," as it was sometimes put); settled versus transient; American versus foreign; native versus immigrant; English-speaking versus non-English-speaking—had its moments of particular utility and none lacked racial inflection. The literal construction of the mine compound as a "white man's camp" was the foundational managerial decision, with entry to company housing and other amenities prescribed in a way that deepened older distinctions between Mexican or Chinese areas and white settlement dating from the era of the prospector and small mines. Complicating these pairings was incredible diversity among workers. Anaconda Company's giant complex in the Butte area gathered workers with what one federal official called "kaleidoscopic . . . racial characteristics." They came from thirty-eight countries in 1918, including, at a time when managerial comparisons of the world's miners were rife, Persians, Egyptians, Bolivians, Syrians, Armenians, Turks, and Afghanis. Sixty-one percent of Colorado's miners were reportedly of nonwestern European origins, and twenty-five languages were spoken by workers in 1912.[75]

Changes in the racial composition of the labor force could occur very rapidly both in response to changing labor markets and because employers tried to avoid hiring groups seen as able to organize militantly and effectively. Between 1916 and 1918, Anaconda's workers went from being 9 percent new immigrant to five times that. Mexican immigrants and New Mexicans, seen as "less turbulent by nature than the European," received preference in employment in some Southwest mines. However, the reputation of a race for either quiescence or militancy could turn on a dime. Employers cherished the presence and proximity of jobless and low-paid Mexican workers, even though they were often skilled and experienced miners, as a threat to restive white workers. But Mexicans were variously figured as shiftless and excellent workers, as ready to be exploited and as ready to engage in both formal strikes and in short assertions of workers' power on the job known as *strikitos*.[76] Their transience to Mexico seasonally presented real problems for employers, but it was also a result of management's practice of putting Mexicans onto "extra gangs" whose labor was casualized. Italians often served as strikebreakers, but when titanic struggles involving Italian immigrant unionists unfolded in and around Coeur d'Alene in the 1890s, one large mine transformed rapidly from having crews over 50 percent Italian to employing a workforce over 80 percent native-born. By 1899, that area's Bunker Hill and Sullivan Company mine, which had less than a quarter native-born Americans working four years earlier, boasted a workforce 75 percent native-born with only "2 or 3 Italians."[77]

Race management of labor militancy and of production favored employers in everyday practice as well as at dramatic moments. It was possible, as one western-based coal mining labor organizer complained, to construct gangs by placing "an Italian with a Greek . . . and so on down the line" so that "no two of them shall get together and discuss their grievances." As early as 1883, mine bosses in the West turned to such mixed crews to break up national affinities said to lead to loafing. The cowboy, writer, and Pinkerton private police agent Charlie Siringo regarded the "mixing of nationalities" by mine owners as designed to both weaken unions and to destroy small solidarities on the job.[78] When unions did make headway, or threaten to do so, the press sometimes branded their agitation as threatening "race war" rather than expressing class conflict. Even in areas with a working class overwhelmingly European in its origin, a pro-management press constructed the drama as between "aliens" and the "white element." An epic, multiethnic labor struggle could be reduced to the title "Greek Strike," as was famously the case in the walkout of Grays Harbor, Washington, lumbermen in 1912.[79]

In that strike and many others settlements seen as favoring native-born workers, or one nationality over another, created lingering suspicions among workers. At a dramatic meeting during a 1901 miners' strike in Utah, Finnish workers promised to never join another strike if the Irish-led union returned to work without a contract. Their point was underlined when a band present broke into a rendition of "I'll Not Go Out with Reilly Anymore." Veteran groups of skilled Cornish and Irish miners persistently divided, often eying union decisions, and even the existence of a union, as possibly advantaging their national rivals.[80] When unions successfully organized, and especially when they seemed ready to organize new immigrants and Mexicans into their ranks, the repression they faced also drew its fierceness from a nativist edge, most famously in singling out of Mexicans and Slavic new immigrants in the notorious Bisbee deportations of 1917, but also in the "Irish Scare" around the wartime militancy of Butte's workers.[81]

No state exceeded Arizona as a site where mine management so institutionalized a stark, bifurcated racial division and elaborated myriad further variations. In the state's giant copper mining and smelting operations, the "white camp" versus "Mexican camp" loomed as a major spatial and social divide. Jobs in the very best categories at the Copper Queen Mine in 1917 went almost nine-tenths of the time to British or native-born U.S. miners, while the worst ones went overwhelmingly to Mexicans. Nearly three-quarters of surface workers were Mexican and almost 80 percent of Mexicans worked above ground. At the exceptional Clifton-Morenci mine complex, where Mexicans could work below ground, they were paid far less than whites for similar work until union demands interrupted that differential in 1916. In Arizona mines, Anglo workers generally made about double the wages of Mexicans, according to a 1910 federal report; other sources suggest still greater disparities. Even when differentials reflected skill categories, such designations were constructed in ways making skill inseparable from race and nationality. Thus Mexicans could scarcely benefit from being among the most highly experienced western miners in the late nineteenth century. Designations of skill likewise followed racial categories in the lumber industry in the West, sometimes leading to highly dangerous and intricate work being done by workers of color at low rates.[82]

The seemingly simple white/Mexican split in Arizona mines was enormously complicated by other "races" and other segmentations in the workforce. A foundational feature of copper mining in Arizona and most of the West was the exclusion of the Chinese from mine labor, a color bar not much resisted by management. Bisbee was an anti-Chinese "sundown town" where the Chinese were barred after dark. The resulting anti-Chinese practice solidified in particular a sense among white workers that management had some regard for their manhood as white miners. Concentrated in the lower reaches of the "miner" and "mine laborer" categories, Mexicans were paid considerably more than the American Indian workers grouped as "general laborers." Mexicans could rightly regard themselves as not without advantages over, for example, the miners forced to stay at "Ajo Indian Village," with no provision of housing, or the excluded Chinese.[83]

With the twentieth-century increase in southern and eastern European immigration to Arizona's mines, the question of whether such new immigrants belonged in the white man's camp sharpened, especially in the case of Italians. On the whole, new-immigrant wage rates hovered between Mexican and what might be called "unquestionably white" pay scales, moving at times dramatically toward the lower wages paid Mexicans. Close to Mexicans in religion, language, sporting passions, wages, and at times left politics, Italians often made ties, even family ties, in the Mexican camp. Slavs joined Mexicans in being removed as radicals in the Bisbee deportations, and at times "Irish Mexican greasers" seemed a threat to order in the camps.[84] At Bisbee, Finns, Serbians, and Montenegrins joined Mexicans and Italians in filling the ranks of the working poor. When coerced Americanization became both military and labor policy in World War I and the strike waves after it, management switched in some instances to an "American camp," signaling inclusion of loyal immigrants even as radical immigrants were being removed. While creating the possibility for broad labor alliances, though seldom including Mexicans or Indians, and consistently excluding the Chinese, the separations enforced by management also left almost everyone involved with something to lose, something to defend, and much to fear. Such coercions and incentives would shape how U.S. mining engineers managed labor around the world and would inform the celebrated creation of scientific management in industries in the Northeast and Midwest.[85]

4

Crossing Borders

Racial Knowledge and the Transnational Triumphs of U.S. Management

HERMAN MELVILLE'S SHORT STORY "The 'Gees" offered an enigmatic and rollicking satire of how white managers of maritime work claimed racial knowledge of the Afro-Portuguese from the island Fogo. Melville located the production of the U.S. racial knowledge within an Atlantic system of trade, folklore, and, above all, management. The broader target of Melville's merciless satire was U.S. ethnological writing on race, particularly that of Dr. Samuel Cartwright. Melville's account undermined all claims of racial knowledge to scientific rigor, perfectly capturing its offhandedness, circularity, and selfishness without losing sight of its import. Ethnology regularly collapsed in Melville's sketch into a ridiculous managerial how-to manual, advising captains on methods to capture the "beam of evil" in the eyes of experienced 'Gee sailors attempting to pose as more desirable, innocent, and tractable "green 'Gees." The most important judgments regarding 'Gees hinged on which ones to hire. Such decisions were best left to " 'Gee jockeys," men "well-versed in 'Gees"—that is, management experts—who then were exposed as knowing nothing either.[1]

South, West, and the wider world met jarringly and repeatedly, in fiction and real life. Melville set his even more bitter satire of white managerial racial hubris masquerading as racial knowledge in the Pacific in *Benito Cereno*—a novella in which a sea captain spouts pretenses to know "the negro" even as he is oblivious to the occurrence of a slave revolt.[2] However easily ridiculed, such hubris underwrote claims to be able to manage the world's races. Well before the 1898 push to formal overseas empire, a striking number of former slave-owning or slave-trading Southerners from the United States found work and wealth by claiming expertise in the capture and management of Pacific Islanders being brought as coerced labor into Fiji and Queensland, Australia. Indeed, in the 1870s the Ku Klux Klan became briefly powerful in Fiji as it waned in the U.S. South.[3]

Southern knowledge of cotton culture and expertise regarding the management of workers producing cotton, having failed to thrive in antebellum experiments to export them to plantations in India, were transferred more enduringly by the German empire to Togo after the war. Leavened by the ideas of white and African American associates of Booker T. Washington, such exported knowledge of management, coercion, and industrial education contributed to an African regime of sharecropping held out as a model of "free farming." The experiment quickly devolved into incidents of "brutal Texas racism" and floggings, especially under the management of Texas A&M graduate G. H. Pape. Southern management techniques and lessons from anti-Indian wars were also applied to nominally "free labor" in British Honduras in the postbellum years. After trebling sugar production in the colony in five years, most of the transplanted planters failed, often indicting as inadequate the available labor supply and the levels of state-sponsored coercion available to keep imported Guatemalan and Spanish Honduran workers from fleeing. Local labor, mainly African, seemed still more mercurial, unwilling to trade a life based on plentiful coconuts, rice, and other foodstuffs for wage labor.[4]

Southern managerial experience was also key to the most detailed fictional depiction of the U.S.-based transnational engineer, a neglected figure who was central to the logic and practice of race management between the Civil War and World War I. George Cary Eggleston's *Love Is the Sum of It All: A Plantation Romance* (1907) portrayed the dashing and calculating Warren Rhett who fled a declining postemancipation Virginia plantation to become an "expert engineer" in Peru, Mexico, and Africa. His experience in Arizona and New Mexico made his successes abroad possible. In every case he obsessed over the alleged inefficiency and inferiority of those from whom he extracted production—races of men who lacked "any interest in life except to shirk work and eat and drink in idleness." He emphasized the need for firm command not only to exact efficiency but also to avoid being murdered by those being bossed. Rhett wrote the maudlin song from which the book derives its title while building a mine railway in Peru "utterly without human companionship." But he soon added that this terrible solitude occurred as he was surrounded by two thousand "Chinese coolies, Mexican peons and convicts" working under him—"the dregs . . . of humanity [and] refuse of civilization and semi-civilization." Rhett found such transnational workers so lacking in conscience and the human ability to laugh, that he briefly pined for "the plantation darkey [singing] absurd ditties." Fear alone made the workers in Peru manageable, and it was the experiences of settler colonialism, of knowing natives, and of bossing slaves that enabled the production of such fear.[5]

When Rhett returned to Virginia after his father's death he found he could not produce fear in the black labor force on the family's failing plantation. Attributing inefficiency and open resistance to his "experiment with negro labor" to both the race of the workers and to their living memory of emancipation, he made elaborate plans to convert the enterprise to a truck farm, bringing in an Italian gardener as manager and contracting under the padrone system for Italian farmworkers, while keeping on only a few faithful "negroes." The plantation thus redeemed, he could marry and honeymoon in Africa, superintending a building project and managing colonial "native" labor there.[6]

Race was ultimately central to both industrial management at home and to imperial capitalist expansion. After the 1848 Treaty of Guadalupe Hildalgo added much of Mexico to the United States, one U.S. editor summed up the triumph of the white managerial ethos: "The nation that makes no outward progress . . . that wastes its treasures wantonly—that cherishes not its resources—such a nation will burn out [and] become the prey of the more adventurous enemy."[7] The argument that the "English-speaking race" embodied wise management continued to add its part to empire building. In 1896, U.S. steel manufacturer Andrew Carnegie, commenting on British actions in Venezuela, would acknowledge the "dubious" ways that indigenous land had been seized, but nonetheless conclude that "upon the whole the management of the land acquired by our race has been for the higher interests of humanity." Indeed, for Carnegie "civilization" made "the acquisition of the land necessary." It was "well that the Maori should fade away, and give way to the intelligent, industrious citizen, a member of our race."[8] Carnegie's assertion reflected the American prejudices that had attended the Mexican-American War and prefigured the United States' "overseas" expansion into Panama, the Philippines, and elsewhere. The "problem" of how to get the land without coming into contact with overwhelming numbers of allegedly inferior people was a constant source of anxiety for these modern architects of racial management though, in building infrastructure within expansionist projects, the labor of just such peoples was often desired.[9]

Panama: Infrastructure, Imperialism, and the Intimacies of Race Management

Managers and ideas moved back and forth between domestic and foreign workplaces. Building a large, difficult infrastructural project like the Transcontinental Railroad through territory occupied by those seen as racially inferior had precedent in the Panama Railroad Company's completion of a trans-isthmus line between 1850 and 1855. In turn, railroad building in the Far West gave engineering, colonizing, and managerial expertise to those who created the Panama Canal half a century later. Although the great triumphs of transnational engineering by U.S. experts would largely take place in the world's mines, the two Panama ventures suggest that both the origins and crowning glory of transnational engineering by those from the United States featured state sponsorship, infrastructural goals, and at times military force. Race management guided the Panama projects.

Energized by the California Gold Rush, the earlier Panama railway project saw U.S. capital, with government subsidies, carve out control over an enclave within the independent republic of Nueva Granada, even though managers expressed impatience with its "nigger Government." Eschewing annexation, the railway investors respected the abolition of slavery in Nueva Granada in 1852 and therefore could not play slave labor against free. Local workers—African, Indian, and mixed race—had enough access to free and cheap food and to better-paying, nearer-to-home jobs in water and mule-based transport that they "were largely uninterested in the dangerous wage labor offered by the company."[10]

The result was that the project faced chronic labor shortages, especially as deaths decimated the workforce. Race quickly entered managerial judgments. An urgent concern with susceptibility to disease made labor from the region seem preferable even if sufficient numbers of workers could not be easily found. If the breathlessly laudatory contemporary history of the railroad is to be credited, labor in the region was often seen as African with "lusty half-naked negroes descended from the African slaves of the old Spanish dominion" forming "a large proportion of the littoral population of the Isthmus." In any case, local labor remained insufficient in quantity to complete the work, and recruiting trips to Cartagena found workers there also largely unwilling to commit to six-month contracts on jobs known to be perilous. Moreover, in a twenty-two day stint management could insist on "20 and two-thirds to twenty-one and one third" days of labor and still complain about the absence of a willingness to work among those employed.[11]

As the need for labor grew, the bosses turned to West Indian workers—Afro-Jamaicans appeared especially hardy in the face of disease—but fretted about the islanders' strength and work ethic, while parroting the view of slaveholders that African workers "require driving or tasking." Irish American workers were likewise tried but went on strike when management attempted to give them direct orders. "Desertion," as quitting was called, came to be criminalized but labor was still a problem at the end of 1853, when a report to the company president broke the workforce into the following categories: "white men 649, Jamaican & coolies 160 [and] natives 1301." At that point, the owners turned to British sources of Chinese indentured labor, importing over a thousand workers, half of whom would die from disease or suicide within a few months. A company history blamed the deaths on "previous habits" and a supposed "melancholic, suicidal tendency" among the Chinese. Ultimately, according to the first major history of the railway, laborers came "from almost every quarter of the globe. Irish were imported from Ireland, Coolies from Hindustan, Chinamen from China, English, French, Germans, and Austrians." When individuals became hurt or ill, or when whole groups like the Chinese were given up on, they were transported out so that the company was "relieved of their care." Amidst such misery, the railway was completed in five years.[12]

Much given to emphasizing the virtues of having a racial mixture within the workforce, the Panama Canal's chief engineers paid their laborers on two tracks, the far less favored one in silver and the more valued in gold. Crosscut by skill and citizenship, the system was increasingly shaped by racial hierarchy after 1905.[13] The exceptions around the edges tended to apply to dark Spanish-speaking Panamanians and sometimes to skilled West Indians who still managed to receive wages in gold. So clear was the racial logic of the pay system's general application to black immigrants that when a West Indian woman visited a dentist in the Canal Zone she was said to have noted the use of gold and silver in fillings and asked, "Oh, Doctah, does I *have* to have silver fillings?" Attempts to make the gold/silver wage distinction track race or nationality more exactly did not fully work, with efforts to remove all black workers from the "gold" list in 1906 being undermined by a desire of managers to retain skilled West Indian workers. When Theodore Roosevelt moved in 1908 to reserve gold wages for U.S. citizens and a few Panamanians, management created further exceptions to policy by placing some white Europeans on the gold payrolls and by confining the few African American workers overwhelmingly to the silver rolls, even though they were U.S. citizens. If anything, such failures to elaborate a firm racial system only made race and nationality more enduring and contentious nodes of managerial power.[14]

Harry A. Franck's journalistic account of his work as a "Zone policeman" during construction revealed encounters with an astonishing variety of workers and residents. Franck's police work was punctuated by the task of census taking, with the enumeration focusing on nationality and race. After a challenging effort to cross language barriers in enumerating people for six weeks, he produced a break-down for the area he surveyed: of 4,677 residents, over half were

Jamaican with large contingents from the United States (the source of many skilled workers and managers), Greece, Spain and Portugal, as well as "Martinique negroes." As many as seventy-two nations and dependencies furnished residents, with Jamaicans and Barbadians especially successfully recruited.[15]

Two rules prevailed. "White" U.S. men, with a few mostly early exceptions, were not to dig. That is, they did not belong in the most dangerous, dirty jobs on a project in which as many as one West Indian unskilled worker in ten died in accidents or from disease and many more were disabled. Indeed, Franck had hoped to write as a worker actually digging the canal but was disabused of that notion when he "arrived and learned of the awful gulf that separates the sacred white American from the rest of the Canal Zone world." Franck noted the occasional "sunburned blond men" amidst Basques, "English niggers," and "French niggers" on shovel gangs. Since, as he wrote, even on the isthmus the U.S. "caste system . . . forbids white Americans from engaging in common labor side by side with negroes," the blonds were "invariably Teutons or Scandinavians."[16] The second rule enforced the conspicuous absence of the "states nigger" from the labor force. Foremen, sometimes white Southerners and very often "military men," wanted no such "corrupting" influence, though sometimes the employment of "our Southern negroes" was also said to be "impracticable" because it would disrupt "our Southern industries." By 1912, only sixty-nine black U.S. workers labored on the Canal, at wages just above half those of white U.S. workers. In contrast to the railway construction of a half century earlier, a Jim Crow social order was transplanted to canal building, with the siting of lodgings supposedly ensuring that even the best "breezes" were reserved for places accommodating whites. Although only a third of the U.S.-citizen workforce was Southern, the Canal Zone reflected U.S. patterns of segregation. Leading management and engineering experts were familiar with Jim Crow practices. The chief engineer with the longest tenure, George Washington Goethals, was a New Yorker, but fresh from building the Muscle Shoals Canal in Alabama and Tennessee, and the long-standing division engineer for the Pacific Division was a Virginian, via the Spanish-American War.[17]

The engineering genius laying the early foundations for the canal in Panama was John Frank Stevens, whose experience was overwhelmingly gained in the American West, mostly at work for the Great Northern railway empire. A New Englander by birth, Stevens achieved notoriety as both an engineer and as one of the last white explorers of the Pacific Northwest. Accompanied in 1889 by a Kalispel Indian, he "discovered" the Marias Pass, although Indians had long known of it. In constructing an early management and engineering team in Panama, Stevens drew from his associates in the Northwest and especially from within James J. Hill's enterprise.[18] Stevens reported himself "a little in favor of the Chinaman . . . as a laborer" based upon his contact with Chinese people in the U.S. West and particularly hoped for contingents of Cantonese laborers. He found them preferable to the West Indians who were so "indolent, childlike, and unintelligent" that it was almost "impossible to think of building" the Panama Canal with Caribbean labor. However, his early campaign for securing permission to recruit the Chinese as coerced labor ran afoul of protests by labor and of U.S. commitments to Chinese exclusion. Chinese officials, Stevens further acknowledged, "were not altogether favorable" to sending workers to an area where so many had died during earlier railway building. Attempts to ensure that Chinese workers came as "free" labor faltered since many would surely have "deserted" if able to do so. Stevens soon lost enthusiasm for trying to bring in Chinese workers.[19] Given these problems, Guatemalan Indians and "hindoos" seemed promising, but only for a time, and local Panamanian and Colombian labor was deemed too unwilling to work and obey to be extensively employed.[20]

Thus management "regretfully" returned to black Caribbean laborers as the main builders of the canal, replicating patterns from work on the Guatemala Railroad in the 1890s. Those whom Stevens once derided as the "sorriest excuse" for workers he had ever encountered soon came to be portrayed as capable of improving and of acquiring skills. The genius of management, and particularly of diet specialists, got the bulk of the credit for their development, despite the fact that segregated messes for West Indians served, according to Canal Zone native Lancelot Lewis, "three times as many people for one-fourth the cost of feeding the gold employees." Southern Europeans supplemented the West Indians, with special preference for the Spanish as "white men, tractable, and capable of development and assimilation." White managerial opinion held that "the Spaniard" was the premier type of worker imported in railway or canal building. "Stocky," "muscle-bound," "cheery," and "law-abiding," the Spanish came to Panama expressly "to shovel dirt." Indeed, Spaniards, who made up two-thirds of the about twelve thousand European contract laborers imported from 1906 to 1908, at first seemed to increase West Indian workers' productivity, as did the presence of Italians. As Lewis put it, management acted not only to increase the labor supply, or even to secure better workers, but also to destroy the "attitude of indispensability" black workers allegedly held. Stevens wrote to a member of the Isthmian Canal Commission that West Indian "usefulness . . . correspondingly increased" once their "complacency [was] badly disturbed" by competition. Such optimism soon dimmed. Management suspected that southern European immigrants learned to loaf from the "lazy negroes who, where laborers must be had, are a bit better than no labor—though not much." Charged also with spreading labor radicalism, southern Europeans provided less labor after 1908.[21]

On one hand, Stevens's casting "around the globe for an alternative source of labor," but then finding that "every potential worker was either too lazy or too assertive for his tastes" stood as standard fare among employers, always wanting more. But as the example of southern Europeans spurring on West Indians suggests, the sullen multiracialism of Stevens marked out a managerial strategy, not merely a series of complaints. As a thoroughly racist contemporary account on the "silver men" of the Panama Canal observed, division and competition were sought, even in recruiting West Indians: "No large proportion of men is to be brought from any one place, for [management] tries to profit by the rivalry that exists between the different islands."[22]

Foremen prized racial competition, often requesting both a Spanish gang and a West Indian one "to keep them both on their metal by rivalry between the two," but problems persisted. Stevens saw the West Indians as "childlike" and as so accomplished in their resistance to management demands that they were capable of halving production via their "unceasing, and continuous effort to do as little work as possible." Segregated gangs supposedly kept Spanish workers from so quickly learning such stratagems and enabled Europeans to set a benchmark from which to measure Caribbean workers. Locating southern Europeans in production best shows how management reinforced the idea of race by fostering distinctions and heightening tensions on the job. The Spanish, by virtue of their overwhelmingly unskilled work and lack of U.S. citizenship, took home pay in silver. Given long-standing and powerful connections between the rhetorical appeals of the gold standard and those of white supremacy, for a U.S. contractor to adopt such a mode of payment positioned southern Europeans as "semiwhite," at best. Such labeling was very much felt by the workers involved.[23] However, the pay scale for "silver" workers immediately reintroduced white supremacy, factoring in race and nationality, so that an unskilled European made twice the wage of an unskilled West Indian and an amount equal to or greater than the wage of a skilled West Indian. The wages of semiwhiteness were justified at times by the belief that Europeans outworked West Indians by a ratio of 3 to 1, but by later reckonings supposed that productivity was roughly equal across racial lines, with West Indians more often absent. The very militant Spanish workers, influenced by anarchism, often enough found themselves tragically involved in protests defending their racial positions, however indistinct, or lamenting consignment to the silver rolls as a racial slight, much as did Panamanians and white West Indians.[24]

Canal management's commitment to what would now be called a multiracial labor force did not assuage racial animosities or even alleviate management problems. Foremen seldom spoke Spanish, which exacerbated frictions with Spanish and local workers. Lower management adopted the general American practice by which "all black peoples are designated 'Niggers,' " as Lewis writes.[25] Whatever habits they arrived with, Spaniards learned to slow down work to beat the heat and prolong their period of employment. They provided militant challenges to management prerogatives regarding race and class. And yet, Stevens's telling conclusion, in a 1915 book he coauthored with William Sibert, was that racial competition as a management strategy was nonetheless a "marked success." While it was true that "Spaniards did not hold up to the standard first developed," their presence "did exactly what was expected in changing . . . the negroes," who soon "exhibited the aspect of men who were afraid of losing their jobs." In later recollections, Stevens wrote that the move to Spanish labor "succeeded beyond my hopes" because it disabused "the blacks" of the notion that they had "the whiphand in common labor."[26]

Gender, Empire, and Home: Household Race Management and Its Discontents

Infrastructural and imperial projects requiring large and multinational workforces encouraged a view of "whiteness-as-management" that reached far beyond those paid by companies to act as bosses. Domestic workers of color serving in the homes of white employees and catering to travelers were likewise judged and managed. Two accounts by travelers from the period of the building of the Panama Railroad illustrate this process, particularly around gendered white American judgments of service labor across color lines. Medicine brought both these observers to the isthmus. Mary Jane Megquier arrived in 1849 and stayed for weeks, heading with her physician husband to California, and Robert Tomes, a Scottish-trained ship surgeon, scholar, and writer, arrived in Panama in early 1855 and published a travelogue within six months. The differences in perspective between Megquier and Tomes were great, but they shared an easy resort to claiming knowledge, and indeed bodies, of other races.

Tomes waxed eloquently about diversity in the isthmus, eagerly ranking workers and the service that they provided. "Distant parts of the world supplied the laborers," he wrote. "From Ireland came crowds of her laborious peasantry. The Negroes, stimulated to unusual energy by the prospect of reward, thronged in from Jamaica. The surplus populations of India and China contributed their share." The "mixed races of the province of Carthagena, the Indian, Spaniard, and African completed this representation of all nations, in which the Caucasian, Mongolian, and African, the Anglo-American, European, Negro, American-Indian, and Asiatic, with all their diverse temperaments" took their places. But multiplicity had to be judged as well as celebrated. While speeding past them on a train he could divine productivity in a "rapid glance," observed that "sturdy Jamaica Negroes in throngs were plying the pick and the spade, in company with the turbaned, lithe-limbed Coolies, who were lending an indolent hand, and an occasional Chinese, who might be seen loitering lazily by the roadside."[27]

Above all, Tomes appraised the bodies he looked at and the quality of service labor and pleasure that they delivered to him. One "negro waiter" wept when Tomes returned from a trip: "My arrival brought tears of joy into the eyes of Negroe Thomas who brushed my shoes over and over."

Tomes assessed native and Jamaican women as vendors of fruit and drink and as sexual objects in particularly overwrought passages. Native women were "full-formed, ripened in the shade," and their "modest flutter" accompanied a rising to serve when Tomes surprised them in repose. They were "dark women in Panama hats and loose draperies." African women were "slouching Negresses in flaunting calicoes" with "expansive black bosoms," and a "clamorous eagerness." Ultimately, the discussion turned to mixed-race women. Tomes described the local population as a "mongrel race—in which the Indian, Negro, and white blood is indiscriminately mixed." He mocked claims of even the elite to "pure Castilian blood," holding that a "shrewd Mississippi dealer in the Negro variety of mankind" would know better. Even so, mixture had advantages, producing "some fine specimens of physical vigor, and the laborers show great strength and powers of endurance." The women in general seemed "far from handsome, and, being ill-educated, have no social attractions, but are lifeless and uninteresting." However, in the right combination, an appeal came to life: "The prettiest females are those in whom the Indian and European blood intermingle, producing that beautiful mixture of the *blonde* and the *brune*—where the former gives richness and the latter ripeness of beauty."[28]

Tomes, who had worked on translating Hermann Burmeister's *The Comparative Anatomy and Psychology of the African Negro* from German, combined casual observations and race theory. He memorably captured the omnipresence of pestilence and death in the area of construction, producing figures showing how hard death fell on the Chinese. Tomes ranked hardiness of races according to the proportions of deaths during construction. In his last days in Panama, he visited a fellow doctor in a death house in which worker-patients of various races lay dying or barely hanging on to life. His thoughts turned to ethnology in a way that would have interested both his fellow scientists and managers of labor when he wrote, "An anatomical collector would have watered his mouth over the gaunt show of grinning skulls and dangling skeletons of all races."[29]

The letters of Megquier, said to be the first woman from the United States to cross the isthmus, reflect pressure to embody domesticity while in Panama. Megquier, like Tomes, remarked on the absence of commodity production in Panama as an index of its backwardness. But while he focused on the inability of the region to furnish supplies like wood for construction of infrastructure, she zeroed in on household items. She especially lamented the absence of "any good bread, milk, no butter, cheese, pies nor cake." The lack of dairy products indicted a native population "too indolent" to milk cows and generally squandering their access to what she judged "the finest soil in the world." Local markets served her poorly and she found local service slow. It took six native women to cook two meals daily for her party of about ten.[30] When Megquier and her husband got to their California destination, servants likewise disappointed. She promised to write more "when I get a negro to do my work" but a subsequent letter complained, "I have a black man here who pretends to be a cook but he don't [sic] know as much as a jackass." An Irish woman pleased but departed and the "Chinese boy" was at first industrious, if sickly, but then his "particularly unruly" attempts to raise his pay occasioned "domestic trials" for Megquier, who eagerly noted the arrival of "a cargo of Chile women."[31]

Amidst such trials, Megquier likely looked back to a missed opportunity in Panama. On a walk there, she saw a mother whose "beautiful child" extended a hand to Megquier, who had recently written home to her teenaged daughter of a desire to acquire in Panama "a girl about your size to help me" with housekeeping. Megquier asked the mother to give her the child. The mother agreed but asked for a hundred dollars in return. "I should have taken her," Megquier wrote, but for lack of ready cash. The failure to strike a bargain occasioned disappointment and amateur ethnology. Regretting the loss of "the only thing I have seen in Panama that I wanted," Megquier remembered the child as impossible not to love—the shining representative of an amiable, inferior people who were at once "simple" and "inoffensive" and "very little above the brutes." The girl would hopefully retain the "very pleasant disposition" of the local population, some of whom were "quite good looking but most of them . . . intolerably ugly."[32]

On a far grander scale, management during the canal-building period replicated concerns of Megquier and Tomes. Canal managers assumed the need for household labor to clothe and feed male workers, and accepted the inevitability of sexual contact by male workers, although campaigns for monogamy and a morality criminalizing sex work were also present. Especially among gold standard workers, the policy implication was that the transportation of wives, or fiancées, to the Isthmus received material encouragement in the form of much preferable married housing, YMCA clubhouses, and quality schools for children. For West Indian workers, the standard differed considerably. While being connected to an employed canal worker facilitated the migration of Caribbean women, processes encouraging West Indian family formation were far more haphazard, serving larger numbers of people, and receiving fewer resources. Construction was scarcely under way before the importation, under Stevens's orders, of several hundred women from Martinique brought the charge that traffic in prostitution was greasing the wheels of production. Management replied that it sought wives for West Indian workers. In two-thirds of the cases, the newcomers lived as wives of construction employees, even if officials accepted some level of prostitution. Although scant evidence of sex work among the Martinican migrants emerged, a leering U.S. Senate investigation kept the issue in the news, and for a time the women were subjected to a 9:30 curfew.[33]

The entire affair unfolded as a dissection of morality among West Indians but of course the presumed "need" for sex workers in the isthmus was to service white workers as well. Acceptance of "*quasi* wives," as one early account had termed women of color in temporary and/or informal relationships providing sex and service labor to whites building the railroad in Panama, was clear. Similarly, inquiries into unmarried cohabitation involving white workers were desultory and individualized until late in canal construction. One canal commissioner, in tepidly condemning white male workers engaged in cohabitation with women of other races, allowed that they were perhaps not "any worse" than workers traveling off-site to visit prostitutes and that "single men on the Isthmus are in a somewhat peculiar position as regards sexual intercourse." For racialized sex workers, official toleration was far more scant as the domestic arrangements among black workers seemed to authorities to indict the morals of a race, not to flow from conditions of production and social reproduction common to labor camps in infrastructural and extractive projects.[34]

Stevens's second justification for allowing the entry of the women from Martinique—"the desperate need for more domestic servants and washerwomen"—reflected not just a desire to attract and retain black workers but also a desire to serve white families in the Canal Zone. Some recruitment of "elderly" West Indian female labor, between ages thirty and fifty, specifically targeted the need for service labor, into which West Indian and Panamanian women were overwhelmingly slotted. The wife in a white Canal Zone household soon stood as a manager of household labor, bossing those whose knowledge of tropical housekeeping must often have exceeded her own. Within families in which the husband managed West Indians in construction, the wife managed shifting combinations of Panamanian and Caribbean labor in the household, fighting what one combatant called the "Battle of the Maids and Houseboys." Currents of closeness and exasperation—of racism, rage, and reliance—resulted.[35]

The particular situation regarding race, gender, and service labor in Panama not only spoke to a wider imperial world of mines, army bases, and infrastructure building but also interacted with patterns of service labor in the United States. Practices from the American West in particular found their ways into imperial possessions and vice versa. Stateside sex work, for example, consistently reflected the ways that race shaped vulnerability to legal prosecution and to violence while structuring marginalization within labor markets. Managers of sex workers often sought a variety of races and nationalities among their employees to exploit all vulnerabilities and to cater to demands of clients. The deflection of moral censure toward women of color that led to the scrutiny of Martinican workers in Panama had applied with special force to Chinese women in the 1870s in the West. Indeed, even after the 1875 Page Act subjected Chinese women to racial and gender exclusion, 1876 hearings on Chinese immigration fretted over the effect of Chinese prostitution "on white boys" more than a dozen times. Testimony also suggested that the Chinese presence was turning young white males into jobless "hoodlums." Allegations of sex work also served to discursively connect Chinese workers with "slavery." Intolerance for anything but bourgeois marriage for imported workers of color was strong, even when legislation limited women available for such marriages.[36] On the other hand, in opening frontiers and areas of backcountry trade, the acceptance of interracial concubinage and "*quasi* wife" relationships with Indians for white men was great, setting the stage for similar toleration in Panama. Purchase of sex was likewise tolerated in ways that somehow did not undermine the images of the available brown female and the "irresistible American" white man.[37]

White women in the United States, and then in imperial possessions, shaped the racial choices made in hiring household labor. "Help Wanted" ads often preferred that the applicant be (or not be) of a certain race or nationality. Job competition domestically between black and Irish servants in the nineteenth century was common, and more broadly the choices were remarkably varied. Possible servants included Indians, Mexicans, Japanese, Swedes, and Filipinas, with different choices made at different times. Such choices involved fascinating crosscurrents, and often enough working-class "white" women, themselves in highly exploitative jobs, also managed the domestic labor of women of color. One Irish immigrant chose to manage African American "help," judging the generality of black maids to be prone to theft, but her own servant, "a cathelick," as a good worker. During the high tide of the anti-Chinese agitation in California, the middle-class woman's decision regarding which race to hire and manage became the subject of political appeals by advocates of white unity and Chinese exclusion. Conversely, when an attorney in 1876 in California attempted to defend the ability of labor contractors to import Chinese labor, he understood that the appeal had to be made to the interests of white female employers of household labor. The Chinese male servant should be seen, F. A. Bee argued before the California legislature, not as a cause for sexual alarm but as "a direct divine blessing" to white women. Providing "the balance of power between Bridget," as the Irish servant was stereotyped, and her mistress, the Chinese "protect[ed] the . . . housewife from imposition" by the servant. White middle-class women at times acted on such appeals, defending Chinese workers against exclusionist movements, or at least choosing to retain their own Chinese servants.[38]

The point that white American women participated in race management at home and abroad is both important and subject to overstatement. Those employing servants of color often claimed special racial knowledge in the communities where they lived. The forms such management took could be insulting and ugly. In the Philippines, Anna Northend Benjamin advised that it was "impossible to be too firm" with native domestic labor, that whipping was an apt form of interracial communication, "speaking to [the native] in terms which he can understand." Nonetheless, to imagine white women as solely responsible for managing hired labor, with the household a wholly separate female sphere, claims too much. Race management directed toward household production and race management directed to commodity production outside the household could never be wholly separable. Probably more white women in households than white men in industry managed racialized workers in the nineteenth- and early twentieth-century United States, since the low wages of domestic workers made it possible for whites of relatively modest means to have at least part-time "help," especially in low-wage areas such as the American South or Panama. But white men also were extensively served by workers of color, in barbering, shoe-shining, livery, laundering, and sex work, for example.[39] Managers, male workers, and wives thus all brought to Panama an expectation that workers of color might serve them.

Nor can it be said that in the management of household workers the wife held sole authority and full capacity to shape labor relations. When she was in California, for example, Megquier beat her "China boy" for real or imagined transgressions, exercising what would seem the most straightforward authority. However, as she wrote to her daughter, she administered the whipping using "a rawhide your father bought for the purpose." The husband seemingly took over managing that conflict at some point, dismissing the Chinese worker and replacing him with a small French boy.[40] More broadly, the decisions regarding household management could lead men and women to differing conclusions, as when white wives in California reportedly preferred Chinese male servants, but men worried over such a presence in the household, opting more for Irish women.[41]

Transnational U.S. Engineers as Race Managers

The early twentieth-century American engineer was a man of the world. Indeed, the celebrated "Test Course" for the training of engineers at General Electric (GE) boasted that its graduates had "scattered over the . . . globe, doing their share in the fascinating work of electrifying China, harnessing the waterfalls in India . . . substituting electricity for steam or hand labor in the mines of Alaska and South Africa, building railways in Australia and refrigerating plants in the Philippine Islands." GE's overwhelmingly American-born and northern European–descended engineers paid considerable attention to managing new immigrant workers, especially Slavs. Indeed, immigration gave GE the possibility to depress wages and experiment with managerial techniques.[42] Such inquiries into race and management at home would find their ways from Detroit to Port Elizabeth, the "Detroit of South Africa" as it was called, via Ford's and General Motors' expansion there. Thus civil, electrical, and industrial engineering all regularly applied U.S. views of race to the world and to some extent vice versa.

Nonetheless, the greatest U.S. export in the quarter century after 1890 was the mining engineer and, with him, U.S. capital goods and U.S. race-management ideas. Technically well-trained, such engineers replaced European experts in Asian, Mexican, South American, Australian, and African mines in significant measure because they so successfully proclaimed a knowledge gained at the intersection of race and management. Such engineers often gained experience in mines in the western United States, where varying decisions regarding which "races"—the term then marked differences of European nationality as well as broad "color" divisions—could live in the "white man's camp" were central to management. Indeed, biographies of mining engineers sometimes took the form of western adventure stories told across a transnational landscape.[43]

In Columbia University's ambitious 1950s oral history project collecting the reminiscences of mining engineers with far-flung careers, Ira Joralemon was one interviewee who learned race (and gender) management in the Southwest and took it into wider worlds. In Arizona's Ajo mine, he recalled, "a lot of Papago [Tohono O'odham] Indians" did the dangerous and hard work of sinking the pit. Swedes from Minnesota, typed as "jackpine savages" when they mined in proximity to Indians in that state, soon joined the ranks of the Ajo mine's drill men. The Swedes, according to Joralemon's observations, were so tough that the "squaw men" around Ajo, who lived with their Indian families out in the desert, called the new drillers "the savages."[44]

Increasingly trained at elite schools rather than through hands-on, shop-based experiences, men like Joralemon claimed an ability to know and to boss "native" and racially divided labor worldwide. The transnational mine engineer emerged as a white man-of-the-world, with the *Engineering Magazine* mixing emphasis on the isolation and the cosmopolitanism of the transplanted expert/hero and trumpeting in particular U.S. prospects as global engineers of the "Anglo-American industrial ascendancy." In a 1913 account of the "mines of Mexico," the "thousands" of American and European engineers in the country were said to hold a nation of "mixed tribes and races, mostly aborigines," fragilely together. South African mines saw the most spectacular influx of U.S. management. There, fully half of new gold mines had U.S. managers by 1895, with William Honnold the most powerful of the "Yankee engineers" among them. Finding that "some employers are unqualified or temperamentally unfit to manage crude labor," Honnold argued in 1908 that "to recall American experience" with the "efficiency of negroes" could clarify much in South African mines. But he urged resisting proposals to bring actual African American miners to South African mines with the judgment that "American niggers . . . would be the very worst thing that could be introduced." U.S. western mines also produced Hennen Jennings, who helped South Africans consider what racial lessons could be learned from mining in Venezuela, where he had also worked.[45]

Indeed, the Yankee engineer was so ubiquitous and mobile that he increasingly could propose transnational comparisons based on expert knowledge purporting to characterize races and nationalities according to productivity and habits. Nowhere was such comparative experience more dramatically deployed than in Korea's extensive gold mines. From the origins of their presence in the 1890s, the dominant U.S. interests exploiting the mines relied mainly on native labor, though they also massively imported Chinese and a few Japanese as well as "Occidentals." One of the early partners in the enterprise, British-born Henry Collbran, had long constructed mine railways in Colorado. J. Sloat Fassett, whose investments made him one of the "fathers of mining in the Far East," had married into the Crocker family, so prominent in completing transcontinental rail lines in the United States. Herbert Hoover visited the Korean mines, whose principal investors from the Coors, Hearst, and Mills families would become his close political associates in conservative causes. The many experiences of those involved enabled a confident judgment that the fifty thousand Korean miners they trained were the best in Asia, and among the lowest paid in the world. After 1910, Japan added to the transnational mix in Korea, as a colonial occupier that continued to give mining concessions to U.S. investors. Interlocking directorships united those running the four major companies, whose investors also controlled enterprises in Peru, the Philippines, and Nevada, and whose managers drew on practices used in Mexico to run Korean mines.[46]

Although the term "Yankee engineer" stuck, it obscured both the role of western mines and contributions from Southern engineers, though studies show that relatively few turn-of-the-century engineers from Southern engineering schools went abroad. The central figure in the cult of the U.S. "Yankee engineer," Herbert Hoover, was an Iowan who was educated at Stanford, the western university most directly beholden to railway expansion. He was first hired as an engineer in California, working for Louis Janin, a Louisiana-born mining engineer active in the Far West and Mexico, and contracting for the Japanese government. Effectively publicized as the "highest-salaried man of his age in the world" for his work as a transnational engineer, Hoover brought the ideas of an efficiency expert to Africa, China, and isolated areas of Australia. He might as easily have deserved the simpler title of "race manager."[47]

In Australia, Hoover thought that the "saucy independence" and "loafing proclivities" of local white miners required a counterweight. He ranked groups of indigenous Australians eagerly but called all of them "niggers" and judged even physically and mentally "superior" ones to have "too little intelligence to work very much." Since Hoover incredibly professed to believe that "infanticide is universal" among indigenous Australians, he could hardly have viewed them as an ongoing and major source of labor in any case. He therefore pitted the "races" against each other by importing crews of Italian immigrants and keeping them "in reserve" in order to "hold the property" against the possibility of a general strike. In the context of an Australian Labor Party–backed inquiry into the use of Italian labor, Hoover's associate explained the logic behind the choice. Italians, he reckoned, were more "servile," "peaceable," and productive. Hoover himself put the advantage in productivity of Italian labor at a ratio of 26 to 15 on one work gang, but the real benefit lay in the racial competition itself. Management would be "in a hopeless mess if they had all aliens or all British." It was "mixed labor" that provided the real payoffs. Hoover largely sat out the controversy but he reacted strongly to the charge by Labor supporters that he was a "slave-driver."[48]

An eager consumer and producer of reports judging the relative efficiency of African, Chinese, and white miners on the Rand in South Africa, Hoover was accustomed to calculating productivity by weighing "colored shifts" and "colored wages" against the white. His own most extensive calculations on race and management involved Chinese workers. Hoover, who once extravagantly wrote that he had strongly supported restriction of "Asiatic immigration" to the United States from the moment that he could "think and talk," did not let borders keep him from making much of his early career as an engineer in North China. He frequently commented on race and productivity there, at times spinning that data rosily to attract investment in China and at others gloomily to explain why more dramatic gains in efficiency had not been made under his watch. In an early prominent appearance before an international congress of engineers in London in 1902, for example, he wrote of the "mulishness" of Chinese miners and of their "capacity for thieving [which] permits the abstraction of nails, screws, nuts, and even coal." However, he cheerily concluded, money could be saved on timbers supporting mines because the resulting tragedies only had to be compensated at thirty dollars per death, given what he perversely saw as "the disregard for human life" among the Chinese.[49]

Hoover's mixed impressions and calculations regarding the Chinese worker could always claim knowledge, if seldom consistency. Chinese "thieving" was epidemic, but at other junctures was judged as no worse than the global norm. Hoover could credit charges that supposed Chinese cultural baggage regarding mining fatally interfered with operations and then turn on a dime to offer the more plausible view that to dwell on "superstition" among the Chinese was a "great mistake." He once held that the "Chinese mine as fast as anyone if they believe that there is anything in it for them. The main reason for the riots against our mines and miners was the Chinese dislike of seeing foreigners make capital out of their soil."[50]

The ratios of race and productivity that Hoover fabricated, particularly before audiences at international conferences, varied wildly. In 1900, he supposed that Chinese in mining produced a fifth of what white workers did, since for the former group "to work, in the sense of Western miners, is an unheard-of exaction." Two years later, the Chinese worker had "no equal" in the world for crude labor, though an accompanying chart counted him only a quarter as productive as the "American" in such work, for a twelfth of the pay. Soon the newly calculated ratio was 1 to 8, with Chinese miners paid a sixth as much and therefore more expensive than whites, although Hoover's mathematical mistake led him to the opposite conclusion and then to a disquisition on hidden costs of "superintendence" and "eternal vigilance against fraud" to explain why costs could be high in Chinese mines.[51]

When he published *Principles of Mining* in 1909, Hoover produced a chart on South African mines, amalgamating data on African and Chinese workers there, but also incorporating data on Chinese miners in China. Ratios abounded. He concluded that in simple tasks like shoveling "one white man equals from two to three of the colored races." In more highly skilled work, "the average ratio is . . . one to seven, or . . . even eleven." Hoover's memoirs explained the productivity differences as racial, though all of his writings offer the possibility that enduring cultural habits mattered as much as biology in making race. "Our inventions and machinery came out of our racial instincts and qualities," he held. "Our people learn easily how to make them work efficiently." The Chinese, "a less mechanical-minded people than the European-descended races . . . require many times more men to operate our intricate machines."[52]

Groping toward an ersatz uniting of the interests of capital and white labor around race, Hoover departed substantially from the editorial view of the influential *Engineering and Mining Journal*, which maintained that "mine operators find it economical to make the best of whatever native labor may be available," training it up to "American or European" standards, rather than deal with sickly and entitled imported white miners. An article in the *Engineering Magazine* on "the uprising of Dutchmen and half-breeds" in 1900 echoed this view in concluding with the observation, attributed to the explorer David Livingstone, that "for any white man merely to live in Africa is a great achievement. . . . We must not expect from him very much in the way of moral, or intellectual, or physical energy." Indeed, Hoover rhetorically preferred white labor more consistently than his older brother, Theodore Jesse Hoover, Stanford's first dean of the School of Engineering and author of the influential *The Economics of Mining (Non-Ferrous Metals)*. Theodore Hoover warned that "labor costs are almost always greater in districts depending heavily on native labor" because "irresponsibility, incapacity to use explosives and machinery, lack of judgment and initiative, and need for constant supervision are such marked traits of most of the races furnishing large bodies of cheap labor." On the other hand, he wrote of Chinese miners in Burma matching American standards at about a seventh of the cost, with similar success stories among Turks mining in Asia Minor and "Kaffir boys" in South Africa.[53]

In practice Herbert Hoover likewise proved able to act in pursuit of mixed labor forces even while praising the superiority of whites. Between 1895 and 1898 alone, seventy-five thousand white United Kingdom residents had migrated to South Africa, overwhelmingly to take mining jobs, but their turnover proved astronomical as the migrants moved through what historian Kornel Chang calls "imperial circuits of labor" fortified with a strong sense of their own worth. Tom Matthews, as general secretary of the Miners' Union, one of the prime adversaries of the plans of Hoover and others to employ Chinese miners in South Africa, perfectly illustrated such imperial circuits. Matthews was a Cornishman who had cut his teeth in labor organizing in the U.S. West and who trumpeted "White Australia" policies of Chinese exclusion as productive of civilized labor relations. In South Africa Hoover never argued that nonwhite labor must be barred from unskilled work, only that wages, opportunities, expectations, and conditions of competition be adjusted by knowledgeable race managers whose ability to calculate advantages of racial choices aggrandized their roles. He claimed to know just what work could be profitably done by "savages of low average mentality," the "Kaffirs." Hoover teamed up with Honnold so effectively that historian John Higginson has termed the pair "formidable enemies of South Africa's black and white workers." For all of his doubts as to their efficiency, Hoover played an active role in recruiting over sixty thousand indentured Chinese to labor in South African mines, after the costs and efficiency of possible

Cypriot, Hungarian, and Italian workers had also been assayed. At a time when African miners withdrew their labor from jobs in which wages had been decreased and danger of accidents was rising, and when organized skilled white miners commanded great social power in the industry, the Chinese seemed to offer great opportunities to play races against each other, though they soon resisted management impressively. The particular task of sinking ever-deeper mines rested on new technologies for recovery of less rich ore, bringing more dangerous conditions and attempts to hide management's role in producing them. Chinese and African miners were made to perilously drill into hanging walls in shafts insufficiently supported by timbering. Chinese miners were regularly blamed for the resulting cave-ins. Out of such carnage, Hoover's reputation grew. As late as 1921, well on the road to a political career, Hoover still entertained an offer of joining in a partnership with the Guggenheim mining interests in South Africa.[54]

Empire: Race Management, Occupation, and Infrastructure in the Philippines

As the cross-Panama adventures in infrastructure underline, U.S. state-supported race management took various forms, from subsidy to colonization. The more typical, and less understood, forms of U.S. expansion into private enclaves, or simply around the activities of transnational engineers and managers, similarly defy easy categorization in their relation to state-sponsored empire. Hoover, for example, would seem the epitome of the supranational free agent, working often with British capital to build enclaves controlled by mining corporations, sometimes with the support of the nations in which he operated. However, during China's Boxer Rebellion, he was evacuated by U.S. Marines, dramatically recalling hearing the strains of the marine bugles playing "There'll Be a Hot Time in the Old Town Tonight," and knowing that he and his wife would be safe. Hoover, raised as a Quaker, later guided the marines and drew the conclusion based on his China experiences that "diplomacy with an Asiatic is of no use. If you are going to do business with him you must begin your talk with a gun in your hand."[55]

When employing nonwhite labor, Hoover from time to time indulged in paternal visions of generalized racial uplift appealing to elites in the hosting nations. He balanced racial competition with what was called "race development" in the early twentieth century. Such alternating currents within race management helped to give rise to a thoroughly modern U.S. imperialism. That the flagship journal of modern U.S. empire, *Foreign Affairs*, evolved from the tellingly titled *Journal of Race Development* suggests that few architects of U.S. empire did their work outside a racial framework. Perhaps the firm that most famously practiced race management in part via race development was Ford Motor Company in its ill-fated rubber-growing and "man-making" ventures at the Fordlandia plantations in Brazil, a venture succeeding in little else but convincing a modernizing Brazilian state that Ford valorized the mixed-race workers of Brazil and could develop those workers further. Ford's South Africa enterprises, on the other hand, promised that a progressive Jim Crow factory regime could develop the chronically impoverished and therefore racially suspect members of the dominant race, contributing to solving the "poor white" problem.[56]

It was in the fin de siècle U.S. occupation of the Philippines that moments of force and moments of development perhaps most clearly unfolded and that U.S. state-sponsored race management reached deepest into the racial categorization of local people. U.S. participation in expelling Spanish colonialism in the war of 1898 gave way to a series of overlapping applications of the idea of whiteness-as-management during the brutal, bloody periods of U.S. occupation and rule that followed. In fighting the Spanish, and then Filipinos who had believed that independence from Spain could mean independence, the United States made managing military and civil affairs into a matter of race. Justifying a "race war" on Filipinos as a continuation of wars of conquest against indigenous peoples at home coexisted with claims to be preventing race wars among fractious natives in the islands. Soaring rhetoric of race development coexisted with pioneering use of "re-concentration" camps and what would now be called water-boarding. Laments as to the "utter unfitness," racially based, for self-government of Filipinos yielded at strategic moments to rosily optimistic environmentalist pronouncements regarding the extraordinary capacity of the natives for "imitation" and of colonizers for accruing ameliorative racial knowledge. This was especially the case when racial and racist arguments from anti-imperialists holding that the United States should abjure connection with the benighted inhabitants of the Philippines needed combating. Such necessarily contradictory claims ensured that the new colony would be perhaps the most-studied area of the world where race, society, and health were concerned. More than military and political domination was being managed. Colonizers' claims to be able to "calibrate capacity" of various groups of Filipinos focused on assessing their capacity to labor. The occupation was hardly under way when the governor-general of the Philippines, William Howard Taft, urged systematic study of Filipino "indolence." He argued that "one must know them and study their traits"—that "before satisfactory labor can be obtained [the colonized] must be under the control of a master who understands him."[57] Empire needed to claim racial knowledge for both its implementation and its justification.

Those with various tasks in the conquest of the Philippines saw the intersection of race and management with different inflections and imagined the racial landscape of the islands very differently. However, none escaped the assumption that whiteness conferred a right to manage natives or missed the ongoing importance of labor to the colonial project. The influential Indiana senator Albert Beveridge described U.S. imperial success as proof of the general rise of "English speaking and Teutonic peoples" as the "master organizers of the world." For the initial occupiers, especially military men charged with managing counterinsurgency, the racial distinctions were starkly drawn and in need of little elaboration. The defeat of the Spanish was seen as marking U.S. racial superiority, especially in terms of masculine vigor, so that a stalled Spanish colonial project could be perfected by the Americans. With regard to the Filipino anti-American insurgents, the brutal Major General Arthur MacArthur attributed the "almost complete unity of action of the entire native population" to "ethnological homogeneity." The architects of occupation insisted on a settler-versus-savage dichotomy but also supplemented it. Theodore Roosevelt, hero in another theater of the Spanish-American-Cuban-Philippines Wars, reduced the resistance to "the Tagal insurrection," bizarrely claiming it to have been conducted by a "syndicate of Chinese half-breeds." Negotiating independence, he held, would be "like granting self-government to an Apache reservation." The occupation was justified by the same "reasoning which justifies our having made war against Sitting Bull." On the ground, U.S. troops racialized, feminized, dehumanized, and infantilized their opponents as "goo-goos" and, to the alarm of restive African American occupying troops who formerly patrolled the U.S. West, as "niggers." Troops frequently described combat as hunting. José de Olivares's photos and sketches of occupation, which sold hundreds of thousands of copies at the century's turn, critiqued soldiers' usage of the word "nigger" only because the "mirthful" African so excelled over the "treacherous and bloodthirsty hybrid Malays."[58]

Such crude race-making had its uses in rationalizing an incredibly deadly campaign, but its logic frayed around the edges, leaving room for other, equally race-based logics acknowledging differences of the occupation of the Philippines from race management in the U.S. West. Settler colonialism in the Philippines could not unambiguously be a U.S. goal because scientific and managerial opinion held that whites could not thrive in the climate there. Both the ability to labor and to coolly manage labor were put at risk in a land in which whites functioned as if they were "underwater." In one of the first publications of the islands under U.S. occupation, Frederic Sawyer wrote that the new territory would never be a country for the "poor white man." He reasoned that "a white man cannot labour there without great danger to his health. He cannot compete with the native or Chinese mechanic." For Sawyer, racial superiority became disability in the heat of the Philippines. He concluded, "For my part, I would never employ a white man there as a labourer or mechanic if I could help it, more especially an Englishman or an American." Whites, according to a 1903 Bureau of Insular Affairs report, forfeited "flesh, vitality, and energy" away from a "bracing climate."[59]

Thus unable to imagine white settlers displacing native people, the architects of the occupation of the Philippines faced a broad problem of modern colonialism: how to make the differences between colonized and colonizer sufficiently great to justify white rule without making the costs of contact with the conquered and of living in unfavorable climates so high as to call the whole enterprise into question. Science and race management helped ensure that the "white man's burden" would not be seen as too heavy to endure. With arguably the most significant anti-imperialist movement in U.S. history questioning the occupation, the need to show progress and justify a continued U.S. role took on special force in the Philippine case. Civil authorities there came to emphasize not homogeneity and fixed inferiority among the islanders but instead multiplicity and flux. Racial knowledge and capacity for research were central to managing crises and transitions, so much so that colonial education expert and *Journal of Race Development* contributing editor David P. Barrows could argue that men like himself should dictate Philippine policy because they "knew Filipinos as no other body of white people will ever know them."[60]

A zoologist already studying animal life in the Philippines before the war with Spain, Dean C. Worcester, proved the pivotal colonial bureaucrat through the first fifteen years of U.S. control in large measure because he successfully claimed to know how to manage race. Worcester argued that there was no formidable, unified Filipino people but rather a "jumble of savage tribes." Making the prospects for military victory over rebels seem more sanguine, such a formulation also highlighted Worcester's own role as the lone "ethnologist" writing sections of critical policy reports. Studying "natives" much as he did the birds he had come to the islands to chart, Worcester influentially posited three broad racial categories: Negrito, Indonesian, and Malayan. He then elaborated eighty further tribes—more when he recounted—to be discussed, studied, and judged separately. "The Negritos," Worcester wrote, "belong to a distinct race. They are woolly-headed, nearly black, and of almost dwarfish stature. . . . Intellectually they stand close to the bottom of the human series, being about on a par with the South African bushmen." Moros, on the other hand, exemplified "the highest stage of civilization to which Malays have ever attained unaided."[61]

Even the "civilized" and Christianized majority of Filipinos seemed to be tribes, not national or ethnic groups, to Worcester. "Individual" differences, which Worcester posited as important among the Christianized Tagalogs, Ilocanos, Cagayans, and Visayans, turned out to be racial as well. "Very few of the present political leaders are of anything approaching pure Malayan blood," Worcester believed. "If one follows their ancestry back a very little way he finds indubitable evidence of the admixture of Spanish, other European or Chinese blood." Fearing that "the *mestizo* element is in control," Worcester actively promoted hostility between them and the "great dark mass of the people." Widely despised by Filipinos who picked up on what his biographer has called his "disdain" for many of them, and charged with being complicit in upsurges of "race prejudice" by a visiting U.S. government investigator in 1905, Worcester also professed romanticized affection for some groups within the "dark mass." Such paternalist love especially applied in his case to the Igorots.[62]

Assembling and retailing racial knowledge came to be seen as central to managing the colonial enterprise. Such occupation leaders as Worcester, Barrows, Albert Jenks, W. Cameron Forbes, and the anthro-pologist/lieutenant-governor Daniel Folkmar studied racial types as they ruled the colonized. The racialized medical literature from the islands was said to have carried "a greater scientific value than that of all the other countries combined."[63] Perhaps the most ambitious early colonial project, a census conducted between 1903 and 1905, enumerated a population, but not a nation, into existence through an ambitious and obsessive process, attending to the color ("*blanco, moreno,* or *amarillo*"), tribal, and citizenship status divisions. The central distinction of "wild" versus "civilized" highlighted religion, with the Christianized majority forming the latter group. However, acting on such calibration was by no means simple. The "civilized" had formed the basis of leadership for antioccupation struggles, and there was some hope that the allegedly imitative, trusting, and loyal "wild" natives would become supporters of the occupation. Barrows, Worcester, and other experts thus claimed to protect the "non-Christian tribes" against depredations and even slavery practiced by local elites, who were considered racially superior and even civilized but burdened by decadent Spanish and Catholic influences. The Bureau of Non-Christian Tribes was charged with the production of "ethnology" of a sort hoped to "lead to due respect, kindness and sympathy."[64]

Within the United States, the Philippines had to be made to seem manageable. The transnational high point of attempts to portray the islands as what Major General MacArthur called a "tuitionary annex" of U.S. civilization and a font of racial knowledge came at the 1904 World's Fair in St. Louis. The fair celebrated the centennial of the Loui-siana Purchase, but further westward movement to the Philippines generated its signal attraction. Six "villages" of colonized Filipinos, assembled by Worcester and visited by Taft and Roosevelt, captured fairgoers' imaginations. Multiplicity and hierarchy of conquered races were put firmly in the service of defeating anti-imperialist arguments, with considerable simplification seen as necessary to educate efficiently. At the fair the "anthrometry" section elaborately measured the "relative physical values" of the races assembled and tested their eyesight, psychology, and judgment pseudoscientifically, confirming white superiority in a collection of experiments in which the future expert on labor management at home, Hugo Münsterberg, participated. Through these connections, and on-the-ground managerial practices in the islands, the Philippines have as strong a claim as university- and factory-based American initiatives as the incubator of social engineering.[65]

The St. Louis exhibit simplified the racial dramas imagined to be occurring by adopting a primary focus on three hierarchically arranged types, although the twelve hundred colonized people on display allegedly represented over forty tribes. On one extreme, what experts organizing the exhibition saw as the hopeful-for-empire story of the Negritos was surpassingly hard-hearted. Anthropologists told fairgoers to see them quickly because the "savage but timid" group was destined to die out. Such a projected outcome removed the anti-imperialist, but racist, objection that conquest created long-term relations with those seen as very inferior people. Worcester thus portrayed Negritos as akin to "anthropoid apes . . . a link which is not missing but soon will be." One displayed Negrito himself came to be known simply as "Missing Link." So much was propaganda on this score believed by its purveyors that it was thought that many captive Negritos would die at the fair, and elite universities jockeyed for rights to their prospective remains. At the opposite extreme, the seven hundred mixed-race and Christianized members of the Philippine Scouts and Constabulary brought to St. Louis incarnated the possibility that a largely European layer of the population could help keep order in the islands and contribute to progress as junior partners of the occupiers. The displays suppressed the role of this layer in leading anti-U.S. struggles in favor of the view that the United States had easily overcome opposition from "wild" Filipinos, on show near the defeated Indian chief Geronimo at the fair.[66]

Critical amidst a welter of other groups, the representatives of the supposed middle layers who could be developed to make the

Philippines productive were the Igorots. Picturesque, at times seminude, and associated with head-hunting, they featured prominently in the imaginations and photographs of spectators and in the plans of the fair's powerful Anthropology Department to leave a sense that pliable if inferior groups could speedily progress under U.S. tutelage on matters ranging from sport to learning songs to industrial education. Jenks, the head of the War Department's Ethnological Survey in the Philippines, had concentrated on detailed observations of the Bontoc Igorots and reported that Igorot children constituted the "brightest and most intelligent" in a model school also enrolling Christians and Moros in the Philippines. Jenks perfectly exemplified the transcontinental and interdisciplinary flows that made those possessing racial knowledge able to take such confident leaps. He trained as an economist, and his graduate work detailed wild rice production by upper Great Lakes Indians, a study in "primitive economics." After his Philippines research, he was a founding leader in developing anthropology at the University of Minnesota, authoring a notorious tract on "racial purity" among the White Earth Ojibwe and producing seminal eugenics-influenced work on the problems of European immigration and labor.[67]

Predictably enough, the education of fairgoers undertaken by the anthropologists and policy makers risked being crowded out by sensational reports of nakedness among the "wild" tribes and of socializing with white women by the Scouts and Constabulary. So great was such negative publicity that Worcester backed off supporting future exhibitions. Nonetheless, the exhibits perfectly illustrated how the notion of a fixed order of white supremacy could coexist with ideas that race was partly environmental, and therefore malleable. Policy elites, from Roosevelt down, refused to choose between a hard racial hierarchy and possibilities of spectacular native progress, given changes in diet, wages, medicine, sanitation, and, above all, education under the tutelage of white experts. "Race," far from simply genetic, was seen consistently as in dialogue with cultural factors and with climate. "In the Moro," Worcester wrote, "native racial characteristics have been profoundly modified by religious beliefs." What on one level seemed biological, including white degeneration in the tropics, subsequently was portrayed as mutable. Such amelioration highlighted not only the capacities of natives but also and especially racial knowledge and managerial skill among the white U.S. colonial bureaucracy and employers of native labor.[68]

Even when colonial administrators quarreled, they agreed that the study and reform of the peoples of the Philippines hinged on managing them in production as well as in politics. When William Powell Wilson, a businessman, scientist, and museum director instrumental in the Philippine exhibition at the 1904 World's Fair, pronounced Filipinos in need of a "long apprenticeship," he balanced the language of colonial control and labor perfectly. Military men proved especially keen and hopeful students of Filipino labor and of its capacity to mature under U.S. managers. Major Edward L. Munson, a medical doctor, quickly analogized "military efficiency" with "industrial morale" so that military drill could be applied "with little or no modification to the industrial problems of civil life." When a report on labor was made in 1903, the fullest evidence came from Captain Archibald Butt, a quartermaster in the U.S. Army. Butt offered a sustained series of comparisons of Filipino and Chinese labor, preferring the former "as they are more amenable to discipline, more imitative in their methods, more enthusiastic in their work for the work itself, and more easily assimilated by American workmen." Emphasizing the importance of "picked" labor, "judicious handling," and "American foremen," Butt reported on experiments showing the usefulness of Filipinos for unskilled work and their ability to acquire a range of skills. Other managers backed Butt, finding the Filipino worker to be "quicker to pick up a thing, and at the same time takes more interest, consequently more pains with his work" than the Chinese.[69]

On the other hand, Manila's city engineer counted the "Chino" as producing 20 percent more than Filipinos, with less supervision. The latter group showed satisfactory "capacity" to do heavy work for "the standard of their size," but proved unwilling to "exert it as other races," unless motivated "under excitement or by stimulating them." A respondent from the firm building Manila's port emphasized that "to successfully employ Filipino labor is, to the American employer of labor, a new business, which has to be learned." Correspondingly, "the Filipinos have to be taught how to work," necessitating "intelligent high-grade American foremen and mechanics." The earliest accounts under occupation tended to emphasize how hard it was to secure steady supplies of native labor, especially in mining and lumbering. A 1903 report to the War Department reckoned that "labour is a great difficulty; wood-cutters are scarce, and they are a wild, unruly lot; only men inured to such a rough life can resist the malaria of the woods, and even they are occasionally down with fever. . . . Chinamen would not venture into the forests, and only the natives of each district are available, as they do not care to go far from their houses."[70] Filipinos acquired a negative reputation for hating hard manual labor, preferring other jobs even at lower wages. Even positive evaluations of work done by Filipinos included disclaimers and justifications for setting native wage levels far below that of other workers. In 1903, the road-construction engineer N. M. Holmes thus found "on some work—drilling, for example—the Filipino is entirely unable to handle the sledgehammer, but they do work on the hand drill, and in that drill about 2 feet a day to an American's 6 or 8."[71]

A brilliant series of reports on race and labor in the Philippines published in 1903 and 1904 by T. Thomas Fortune, longtime African American editor and leader of civil rights initiatives, bring urgently needed balance to the colonialist moralizing informing many negative judgments of Filipino labor. Fortune, sent by the Roosevelt administration as an investigator, regarded the Philippines as a hotbed of extreme white supremacist thought, with secondary leadership of the occupation dominated by Southern Democrats and their allies. He found Manila newspapers as given to "race-baiting" as those of Atlanta or Memphis. Fortune continually heard "the laziness of the Filipino . . . denounced" so much so that he offered in reply, "I have been in the Philippines two months and have not seen a white man working with their hands. . . . Why do you expect the Filipino to do what you will not and cannot do?" Fortune described a drama often replayed: "The white man . . . expects the native to labor as they labor in this country [the United States] and Europe, and because the native refuses to do so, as it would mean death to him, he is abused . . . as a worthless creature. The native laughs."[72]

The colonial bureaucracy combined sweeping denunciations of native "indolence" with high hopes for change. Thus Worcester wrote of the Filipino, "Indolent he surely is, but whether hopelessly so is another question." American women nurses, who predicted their own success but only in the very long run in training of Filipina nurses, were especially well positioned to see themselves as providing race development through fostering healthy habits among natives, working through the women whom they managed. Adding protein to a diet of polished rice, addressing hookworm, and, especially for Barrows, learning English, all promised racial development. As Butt had it, "When once a native becomes accustomed to eat meat once or twice a week and to provide the same for his family, from that time he can be looked upon as a high-class and steady laborer." After 1910, when schooling more decisively turned to an industrial education model pioneered in training black and Indian children in the United States, the results were likewise trumpeted as utterly transformative, changing even the alleged disdain for hard manual labor among the Christianized. While the colonial bureaucracy generally argued for the long-term prospects for improvement of all but the "lowest" tribes, it also judged tribe against tribe. Experts found Negritos could "neither reap nor sow"; the Ilocanos and the Igorots were "industrious"; and women of the latter group seemed the "most expert ore-sorters" in the world. Cagayans were reckoned "notoriously lazy" and Bicols as "energetic." The "wild tribes" from the highlands appeared especially promising as sources of labor for the military, with one proposal being to take on thousands of "highland" soldiers in the hopes of killing "two birds with one stone," civilizing "savages" and increasing security.[73]

The swirling currents of race development, political control, and production came together in constructing the Benguet Road, an incredible infrastructural project unfolding in the Philippines as the Panama Canal was being built. But while the canal linked two great oceans, the road attempted to provide reliable transport to what was then a tiny outpost at Baguio, far enough in the mountains to have pine trees and to remind some policy makers of New England in late spring or early summer. Planners billed the development of Baguio into a new city as having many possibilities. It was to be a colonial "hill station" providing a respite from enervation and a sanatorium for victims of dysentery, malaria, and tuberculosis. Baguio thus promised to support the racial adaptation of whites said to be threatened by the tropics and its diseases. One beneficiary found visits there to approximate inhaling champagne. Proponents also projected Baguio to be the colony's "summer capital," where decisions could be made away from sweltering heat. For Worcester it served as a potential fortress to be held in the face of renewed revolution in the lowlands. However, problems with the road continually washing away, opposition to it by Filipino political leaders, and changes in attitudes regarding tropical medicine left the city one perpetually poised to make leaps forward but never quite doing so. Although it led to Baguio's becoming a place of trade for Igorots and a destination for gold miners, the greatest achievement of the road was in many ways its own construction.[74]

Supporters of the Benguet Road regarded labor as a great problem of the project as well as one of its greatest opportunities. The construction was to provide an "education" for native workers. Building in "wild man's territory," and particularly in Igorot areas near gold deposits, offered the chance to test ideas regarding the possibility of imitative "savages" as ideal workers. Authorities sometimes believed that "wild men" were ideal for large projects. Even when construction was difficult, authorities lauded the "additional value of road construction as a means of improvement in the organization of native labor and in its increased effectiveness," especially with tools. For a time it seemed policies allowing indigenous labor to be drafted for work on the road would be speedily implemented, and in the early phases of surveying and construction, the remarkable ability of Igorot porters to carry heavy packets long distances impressed observers. A 1903 report underlined the conviction that "the Filipino, as conditions settle, can be made a good laborer; not so good as the American, not so good as the Chinaman, but one with whom it will be entirely possible to carry on great works of construction." Management reportedly profited from Igorot ideas about hydraulics and irrigation in laying out parts of the road, which historian Paul Kramer aptly describes as bringing all major "preoccupations" of the colonial bureaucracy together: transport, possible exports, and especially "control and productivity of Filipino bodies."[75]

As delay followed delay before the highly imperfect road opened in 1905, the "labor problem" loomed large. Solutions were no less racially based and racially divisive than those taken on the Panama Canal. Far from a simple uplifting project joining Filipino labor with white experts and "competent foremen acquainted with local conditions and native characteristics," the project attracted workers from forty-six nations. Workmen frequently stayed only a few months and then found other jobs or returned. From October 1903 until June 1904, the labor force never exceeded 3,793 workers in any month and the average stood at far less than 3,000, but medical records show over 20,000 workers hired in that period. Indigenous "wild" labor—all groups in this category were regularly lumped together as Igorots, differentiating them from lowland Christians, also lumped together though they were recruited and managed through the lens of tribal identity—proved especially reluctant to stay long or to follow construction far from home. Nonetheless, hope ran high and in 1903, one expert still held that "on road work the native does fully as much and as good work as the Japanese, is more easily managed, has better health, and costs about half as much."[76]

However, labor shortages and problems managing native labor caused increasing desperation by the end of construction. Proposals for a draft of natives to work on the road stalled in the face of Filipino opposition, though prisoners and coerced labor were important in road crews and American foremen sometimes doubled as jailers. A section of the report to the War Department in 1903 spoke of "2,500 Filipino laborers on the Benguet road," adding guardedly that "our engineer reports that, wages considered, they are doing good work," though only after "an unfortunate experience in obtaining labor for this road, due to a misunderstanding with the proposed laborers, and to the fact that the men were obtained from an undesirable class in Manila and the neighboring provinces." Workers being recruited from highlands in Luzon then seemed a potential solution. While some optimistic rhetoric on local workers continued in 1904, alongside blaming of foremen for limiting native production, near the end of the project it was said, "In the difficult and dangerous work it is found that the white men are the most efficient, the full-blooded negro next, while nearly a thousand Japanese are employed and are giving very good service." A Christianized and civilized group became the preferred Filipino laborers. Most of those had "had to be educated very gradually up to this sort of thing," but one group of Tagalogs were said to "have proved themselves to be very serviceable workers."[77]

The turn to foreign labor was sharp and significant, producing a highly segmented labor force on Benguet Road. As late as February 1904, well over 60 percent of the road's workers were Filipinos, a figure that fell to considerably below half by June. When construction hit its stride, Japanese composed 22.5 percent of the large imported labor force, doing skilled and unskilled jobs, and often undertaking hazardous "cliff work." The Japanese death rate approached 16 percent on a relatively short project. Despite official and private reassurances that imported Chinese labor was unnecessary, one worker in six was Chinese. Among the forty-plus other nationalities, Sikhs (a term management and states often stretched to include Hindu workers) were significant enough that managers fashioned a separate scale of rations for them. American laborers made four to six times or more the wages of native workers in the same job categories, and often double those of the Japanese and Chinese. The storied Igorot porters sometimes made only one-fifteenth of the daily rate of unskilled Americans.[78]

The rhetoric of uplift increasingly clashed with the reality of who got jobs and at what pay on the Benguet Road project. As construction proceeded, Archibald Butt wrote of his labor policies as army quartermaster, "The Filipinos were entitled to the labor of these islands as far as it was possible to give it. I have made every effort—at times it seemed almost at a sacrifice—to advance this cause. My efforts in this direction have more than repaid me for the experiment as I. . . . have seen the Filipino develop from what might be termed a shiftless laborer to a constant worker." In their later reflections on the Philippines, W. Cameron Forbes and Worcester wrote of wage increases of three-, four-, five- and even ten-fold as making U.S. influence different from that of the Spanish. For Forbes, such pay increases flowed from the "science of labor" that constituted the "greatest fundamental difference of American practice from that of other colonizing countries." For Worcester, wage boosts transformed Filipinos by "increasing their necessities."[79] Major General MacArthur had much earlier argued that replacement of the Spanish, who were "exploiters pure and simple," with munificent Americans employers would transform Filipinos. Taft echoed such points, although he also raised the fear that high wages would lead local workers to take more time off. The implication of such arguments was, like Barrows's hope that education for citizenship might compete with industrial education, that racial development might take precedence over racial competition and exploitation.[80] But such practices did not, even amidst perceived labor shortages, consistently apply in the signature early colonial project of Benguet Road construction. In less formal incarnations of U.S. empire and transnational race management, they were even less likely to prevail.

PART III

CHANGING THE WHOLE STORY

5

Continuity and Change

Scientific Management, Race Management, and the Persistence of the "Foreman's Empire"

THE SHOP FLOOR OF A FACTORY revolutionized by the scientific management methods developed by the patrician engineer Frederick Winslow Taylor and others in the later nineteenth and early twentieth centuries was a precise and exacting place. Taylorism, as such management was often called, required that workers learn the precise movements, and the timing of them, determined by management to be the best way to do a job. Arriving at the determinations often involved college-trained men scurrying about with stopwatches and slide rules. Taylorism fetishized respect for study and for system, as did the "Fordist" assembly line that engineered unheard of exactions in terms of sped-up labor in exchange for higher wages. Nothing was to be left to accident and little seemed to count except production.[1]

Race sat anomalously in such a system, but not because a choice had to be made between scientific claims and racial hierarchies. Claims of systematic observation of races, after all, were regularly put in the service of white supremacy and race management by anthropologists in the Philippines, physicians in the slave South, and American engineers in South Africa. Nonetheless, because modern managers set out to gather in their heads and their reports all of the knowledge necessary to run a factory, and because they refused to take the foreman's rule-of-thumb knowledge as the last word on organizing production, race management by foremen did present potential problems. Two logical courses of action were open to upper management and the outside consultants whom they hired. One response would have been to actually study race and productivity systematically, generating a body of racial knowledge rivaling the knowledge of the labor process that was being amassed. This would of course have produced no "pure science" of race, any more than Taylorism could purely study what was best in doing work without making foundational assumptions favorable to capital. Systematic study of race and the workplace would likewise have been far from necessarily antiracist, given management's goals, habits of thought, and long-standing practices. However, such studied racial knowledge would have acted as a counterweight to the impressionistic race lore acted on by foremen. The other possible sweeping response would have declared that race mattered little in production and that the data on time and motion they did collect could apply to the regulation of the movement of any worker.

Management experts in the early twentieth century pursued both of these positions sporadically but neither of them consistently and seriously. Experts continued to claim racial knowledge mattered, but never undertook the empirical studies of race and labor that matched studies of the productive process. Their efforts to write about the virtues and limitations of different races and nationalities as workers began and ended with simply assembling or excerpting the opinions of managers on the ground in workplaces, often foremen. Scientific management, along with its offshoots in industrial psychology and personnel management, therefore never put itself in a position from which to challenge fully the long-accumulated prerogatives regarding hiring, firing, and disciplining workers that were termed the "foreman's empire" at the time.[2]

This chapter thus concerns a dog that did not bark. The image comes from the most famous detective fiction of the time. As Taylorism was about to become highly influential and controversial in management thought, that other fantasy of total mastery of relevant knowledge, Sir Arthur Conan Doyle's Sherlock Holmes stories, achieved great popularity. In one famous case, Holmes unraveled a mystery by considering the implications of the fact that a dog had "not barked."[3] Connecting race management and scientific management requires a similar appreciation of the fact that what did not happen can powerfully illuminate what did. If only the respect for empirical data that energized investigations of the motion and skill of workers by managers, the acknowledgement of the importance of race in management literature, and a broad desire not to defer to the unsystematic knowledge of foremen had been at play, close investigation of race at work ought to have occurred. Indeed, such an undertaking was frequently called for. But it never happened. Scientific management seldom extended its empiricism to the study of race and work, and its feeble conclusions when it did so could not be heard over the barked orders and racial slights delivered by foremen. Management professionals were willing to leave the foremen's racial knowledge unchallenged, and this choice left foremen in control of other aspects of workplace rule as well.

That a deeply embedded connection of management to racial brutality and to hubris regarding racial knowledge had matured in slavery, settlement, and empire helps to explain why the writings of experts were equally unable to renounce race management or to deliver on studies of race. Late nineteenth- and early twentieth-century factory management in the most industrialized U.S. regions inherited much from older patterns of race management in other regions, This fact was not lost on those who lived through the period. As Frederick Winslow Taylor attempted to rationalize production at Midvale Steel in the late nineteenth century, that exemplar of modern scientific management heard white workers complain that he was a "nigger driver." Shortly thereafter, the rubber manufacturing executive Charles R. Flint held that "the American wage earner is raised to the dignity of an overseer, not over degraded humanity, but over a more reliable and effective slave—machinery." In one celebrated 1907 article, the expert opinion endorsing Italians over African Americans came from the almost unschooled but wildly influential scientific racist Alfred Holt Stone. Stone's main credential as a student of race was that he was a Mississippi planter, enough to vault him to be a division head studying "the Negro" at the Carnegie Institution.[4]

Connections of the frontier to the modern workplace occurred as insistently. When the eminent historian Frederick Jackson Turner went to deliver his early twentieth-century lectures on western expansion he walked through "the hall in Harvard's museum of social ethics . . . covered with an exhibit of the work in Pittsburgh steel mills, and of the congested tenements." The exhibit, according to Turner, captured the "long hours of work, the death rate [and] the gathering of the poor of all Southeastern Europe to make a civilization at that center of American industrial energy." Such a "social tragedy" inflected Turner's lectures on the Pennsylvania frontier with the knowledge that what had been the home of "painted savages in the primeval woods," had given way quickly to "huge furnaces [that] belch forth perpetual fires and Huns and Bulgars, Poles and Sicilians [who] live a brutal and degraded life." When Herbert Hoover sought to memorialize the Mexican War in a pageant, he placed the conflict in a context that resonated with the management of factories in the period. U.S. victory had allegedly settled the contest for leadership of the white race, with the descendants of the north of Europe besting those of the south.[5]

Nevertheless, the pattern in which managerial literature contained close study of the labor process, but loose, unexamined generalizations regarding race and productivity was not simply foreordained by history. Nor did the fact that racial invective by foremen survived within management even when the expert study of time-and-motion potentially clashed with it flow automatically from the past. Race management survived also because it seemed to work so well in the present, alongside scientific management, but largely as the task of those lowest in the managerial hierarchy. The tension between scientific management and race management was seen as a productive tension, best left unresolved, with both systems holding sway. Thus when John R. Commons proposed goading workers into racial competition as the sole "symptom of originality" in American management, he had in mind especially the meatpacking industry, one as systematized as any in the United States. In keeping both kinds of management at play, the desire for racial knowledge consistently gave way to the utility of what philosopher Charles Mills has called "white ignorance" regarding race, in this case packaging and validating the prejudices of managers, and leaving intact the existing racial practices of foremen. Indeed, Mills's characterization of such ignorance applies perfectly to the race-thinking described in this chapter: "Imagine an ignorance . . . that is active, dynamic, that refuses to go quietly—not at all confined to the illiterate and uneducated but propagated at the highest levels of the land, indeed presenting itself unblushingly as knowledge."[6]

In an influential essay, Marxist theorist Raymond Williams distinguished between "residual" forms of culture and power, hanging on by virtue of habit and tradition in changing settings, and "emergent" ones being created to address fresh realities. The temptation is to regard race management as a residual form, and it certainly was partly that. But it equally represented an emergent set of practices, adapting and growing in its applications even as scientific management emerged.[7] Race management, and the cultivation of "white ignorance" that it came to involve, represented a combination of residual and emergent forms, informed by backward looks but thoroughly modern withal.

Engineering, Scientific Management, and the Seeming Transcendence of Race

When he published "Phases of the Management Movement" in 1960, Wellesley's emeritus professor of economics and sociology Leland H. Jenks could plausibly regard himself as having lived through the entire history of modern management. It emerged, he held, as a movement with a distinctive and expanding print culture in the same year as his birth, 1895. Fifteen more years would pass before management was formally taught to any significant degree. Jenks, initially an expert on U.S. imperialism in Cuba, presented the "management movement" as largely progressive and without connection to racism. He did not, of course, deny that management itself had long existed, but its pre-1895 forms remained crude. For Jenks, the first stage featured ad hoc problem-solving within firms. In its second stage, planning and experimentation proceeded, but "without reference to what had been done by anyone else." Thus firms like Standard Oil, AAT&T, and DuPont developed impressive knowledge of their own internal processes before the "management movement" matured, but communication of such knowledge "beyond the individual firm was rare, accidental, or the result of individual transfer of employment."[8]

The presence of industry journals and of efficiency experts circulating through firms, often contracting as consultants, signaled for Jenks a "third stage," the first one deserving to be called a movement. As early as 1872, the *Railway Gazette*'s editor was urging that the "world advances by recording, studying, and comparing experience," but it was nearer the turn of the century that journals detailing management and technical problems achieved a critical mass. The journals profited from the "lack of a sharp line between careers in trade journalism and in industry" attracting practical-minded readers like Taylor, and helping to generate organizations like the American Society of Mechanical Engineers. What historian Arthur Cole later called "the spreading belief in the existence of good ways of carrying through business operations, and the belief that it is the duty of first-class business administrators to discover or learn and apply such ways" was thus seen as arriving only with the Progressive Era.[9]

Although the extensive management literature under slavery conducted itself within the broad "third-stage" model of modern management identified by Jenks, he and Cole rightly point out that managers of waged labor had reason to think of themselves as inventing something new and world-changing between 1895 and World War I. What Jenks regards as the center of innovation, the Works Management Movement, occupied the intersections of cost accounting and engineering in the context of tremendous innovations in machine tools. It unfolded in such journals as the *Engineering Magazine*, which interestingly evolved to become *Industrial Management* (with The World Is Its Field as its masthead motto). Participants nurtured a sense of "continuity" and even "literary self-consciousness." They balanced desires for respectability within professional organizations and "fair play" by capitalists, with a perceived need for "obtaining from employers an authority to manage." They invoked Darwinism more to trumpet progress and the virtues of cooperation, Jenks argued, than to give social hierarchies a biological imprimatur. The engineering impulse to modern management at first outran the parallel but quite separate rise of personnel management and the later, weaker impulses toward industrial psychology, which meant that an emphasis on "the human factor" developed tentatively, leaving engineering at the core of managerial reform. While more recent mainstream and Marxist histories of management inch its origins a few years earlier in time, they typically follow Jenks in concentrating mainly on the factory and in seeing an attempted unfolding of rationality, however contested at times by workers and foremen.[10] They share his emphasis on the influence of engineering as a major chord in managerial reform, and human engineering as a minor chord. Such an interpretation makes Taylor and the engineers of Henry Ford's assembly line central to the logic of the new management but also leaves room for Fordism's brief embrace of a Sociological Department to "improve" immigrant workers as well as for the rise of personnel departments.[11]

The seeming unimportance of race in Jenks's narrative of management reform squares with how the great figures involved in merging engineering and management, especially Hoover, Ford, and above all Taylor, made and described the changes they championed. In Hoover's case, race management had clearly been a hallmark of his career as a transnational engineer and mine manager. However, on the domestic front, his career parlaying the "engineer as progressive" image into commanding political positions as secretary of commerce and then president featured a striking unwillingness to think in racial terms where immigrant European workers were concerned. Within five years after the titanic, if unsuccessful, immigrant-led 1919–1920 steel strike, Hoover used pressure and persuasion to achieve what the unions could not, an eight-hour working day in steel. The Federated American Engineering Societies' massive 1922 report, *The Twelve-Hour Shift in Industry*, which Hoover arranged to be prepared as both secretary of commerce and president of the organization issuing it, served to sway industrialists by focusing on waste and labor markets. The word "immigrant" never appears in it, nor does "foreign worker." The three occasions where "foreign-born" is used all charge that immigrant workers were a roadblock to reform, seeking "the most money . . . regardless of how many hours they labor." Such a stance, forgetting that immigrants had formed the core of support for the strike for eight hours in steel, made the role of the outside expert all the more critical.[12]

Where Ford was concerned, the use of engineers to make auto plants showpieces of mechanically timed, subdivided, interchangeable assembly line labor outlasted the company's embrace of sociology. Such engineering remained compatible with a sense of developing races, and the human race, on and off the job. Indeed, engineering reforms tended to insist on the term "betterment" rather than "welfare" for corporate programs attempting to develop workers.[13] But in Ford's case, the company's Sociology Department experiments in racially developing immigrant workers proved even more ephemeral than the Colorado Fuel and Iron ones that had preceded them. Even the Fordist efforts at human engineering via sociology avowedly sought, regardless of Henry Ford's own anti-Semitic and fascist sympathies at times, to homogenize immigrant workers. Engineering, committed to technique over conflict, outpaced and outlasted human engineering.[14]

As a management consultant, though one with intimate ties to politicians and engineers, Taylor was more voluble in proselytizing the new management than either Ford or Hoover. The scion of a wealthy and prominent Philadelphia Quaker family, Taylor turned to industrial work and then to industrial management out of a combination of boredom and perhaps rebellion. He fell in love, by his own account, with working class life's color and camaraderie but in becoming a boss he faced a problem. Taylor knew from recent experience the techniques through which workers "soldiered"—that is, acted in concert to limit production. Accepting that his prime responsibility was to the factory owners, Taylor was grudgingly willing to accept the charge by workers that he was a "piecework hog," attempting to extract more production from workers who knew that piece rates often were simply cut after new standards of exertion and coercion were reached, but he wished for a new system. Thus the idea of managing groups of workers, so central to race management, was anathema to Taylor as he tried to reconcile the well-being of workers with the return of profits to capitalists. His solution stressed winning individual workers to the idea that they might become "high-priced men" in a new system offering incentives in exchange for working according to the directives of expert planners. Those experts observed work (and especially the existing practices of workers skilled in production) in order to specify the "one best way" for bodies and tools to move in doing a job, thereby eliminating the power skilled workers gained from their superior knowledge of production. At its most hopeful, Taylor's scientific management implied that the benefits in ease and wages that the system promised made it able to square the interests of labor and management. Taylor himself looked forward to factories run by "men of smaller caliber and attainments," although not necessarily lower-waged at the semiskilled level.[15]

Taylorism described a system potentially hostile to race management. As articulated in Taylor's prominent writings and congressional testimony after 1903, his system distrusted anything encouraging group practices, even taking meals together, among workers. Attacking the broad and arbitrary powers held by foremen, scientific management seemed to leave little room for the sort of racial invective that was so central to lower management's control over workers in labor novels from Upton Sinclair's *King Coal* to William Attaway's *Blood on the Forge*.[16] Separating execution from planning—a reform advanced by Taylor disciple Carl Barth's application of the slide rule to machine tool and other labor processes—converted work into a series of abstractions, perhaps reinforcing the idea that management was the province of white, Anglo-Saxon educated men, but seemingly not considering the race of those doing the work.[17]

And yet, despite such substantial tensions in theory between race management and scientific management, the two coexisted in practice. The modern practices of industrial capitalism and the atavisms of race proved so compatible that Commons, himself deeply interested in and appreciative of Taylor's work, was able to insist that race management was the U.S. managerial invention par excellence without questioning why scientific management did not eradicate management based on racial competition.[18]

Even the famous example that Taylor himself used to educate the public regarding his system's ability to create "high-priced men" suggests overlap between managerial science and race management. In the example, even as he insisted that the key to effective management was to remake individuals, Taylor chose "Schmidt" as the exemplar of a new regimen for labor. Schmidt was both archetype and stereotype. In charting the most efficient way to move an abandoned stock of pig iron suddenly made valuable by demand resulting from the Spanish-American-Cuban-Philippines War, Taylor required an almost fourfold increase in productivity and made Schmidt the human face, and pseudonym, for such an advance. The actual model worker's name was the less stereotypically German "Noll." The switch reflected a penchant for ethnic typing that elsewhere had Taylor discoursing on the "Patrick" type for Irish American workers, even as he elaborated the metaphors of "racehorses and dray horses, songbirds and sparrows" in describing factory labor. In the famous pig iron story, Taylor adjusted rhetoric and practice, and probably largely invented the details. He did so with the alleged "racial" attributes of workers, and his audience's (as well as his own) belief in those attributes in mind. After first experimenting with "large, powerful Hungarians" to effect the speedup, Taylor turned to a "racial" image of doggedness rather than brute force. The name Schmidt emphasized that the worker's agreement to submit to the new system and his ability to move the iron flowed in part from his membership in the German "race." Taylor wrote of Schmidt as embodying the strength, persistence, and love of savings thought to be peculiarly concentrated in the Pennsylvania Dutch, as Germans in the area were called. In the long process of cajoling and threatening workers until some of a newly recruited group conformed to the unheard-of standard of moving forty-seven long tons of pig iron per day, Taylor's deputies continued to think racially, blaming pressure brought to bear by Hungarians for resistance. Taylor thus identified Schmidt's productivity, if also his stolidity, with one of the "old immigrant" groups from northwest Europe. He met Schmidt at a time when "new immigrants" from southern and eastern Europe were coming to outnumber the old. If Taylor did allow that brutish capacity for heavy and heavily bossed unskilled labor might reach into the old stock immigrants, and might not be found in too organized and assertive Hungarians, he elsewhere left little doubt that the new immigrant groups generally were the workers "of smaller caliber" fit for driven and unskilled labor. Indeed, he gloried that when "American" laborers moved up to operate machines: "the dirt handling is done by Italians and Hungarians."[19]

George Preston, secretary general of the International Association of Machinists, tellingly mocked Taylor's contention that plenty of workers able to work up to Schmidt's standard were available. According to Preston, Taylor forgot to add "within a radius of three thousand miles." The assumed need for brutally exploited and racialized immigrant labor thus formed part of the logic on which scientific management was founded, at least where the mass of unskilled work was concerned. The former foundry manager C. T. Sears was acute in making this point, remarking on the logic of Taylorism's emergence largely in iron and steel, an industry "where man ha[d] been raced against man, gang against gang, mill against mill" as destructively as in any other. Often such "racing" pitted unskilled workers against each other based squarely on race and nationality.[20] The great student of Taylorism, Samuel Haber, found that Taylor believed that "negroes were of an inferior race." Even the limits of Taylorist successes could find "racial" explanations. There was, H. D. Minich wrote in *100%: The Practical Magazine of Efficient Management* in 1913, allegedly a "type of labor, usually Slavic, to which higher wages do not seem to appeal—which prefers the lowest wage scale to any form of greater effort," disarming the rational appeals of Taylorism.[21]

In other ways as well, Taylor incorporated race-thinking as he revolutionized management. In replying to the socialist novelist Upton Sinclair's critique of his celebrated "The Principles of Scientific Management" in 1911, Taylor cast matters globally in a way that suggested familiarity with Hoover's articles that featured fanciful racial ratios regarding productivity within transnational engineering: "The one element more than any other which differentiates civilized from uncivilized countries . . . is that the average man in one is five or six times as productive as [in] the other." More incredibly still, Taylor's use of race management apparently almost found its way into the classic work of African American sociology of the early twentieth century, W. E. B. Du Bois's *The Philadelphia Negro*. Du Bois mentions Midvale Steel, ground zero for the origination of Taylor's managerial techniques, as one rare Philadelphia industrial workplace in which African Americans found work in significant numbers at the turn of the century. Du Bois credited a manager "whom many dubbed a 'crank' " for the opportunities at Midvale. A reprint of Du Bois's classic study later identified that crank as Taylor in its introduction. Social historians Walter Licht and Jacqueline Jones added their own brief accounts, emphasizing that Taylor's hatred of ethnic solidarity and of on-the-job drinking at Midvale had led him to introduce African American workers into gangs across the plant. The strategy aimed to raise productivity by undermining unity within work gangs, especially those of "imported English workmen" whose drinking Taylor battled. Subsequent managers apparently resegregated Midvale, with black workers remaining but confined to certain departments.[22]

Taylor's racial logic in the Schmidt example and his use of African American workers at Midvale did not run through the whole of his writing. Most frequently his desire to uproot the arbitrary power of foremen and other petty bosses placed Taylor among those management experts whose formal system left the least room for day-to-day uses of stormy racial competition to extract production by playing races against each other. Taylor's disinterest in reforming workers off the job also meant that he scarcely engaged in the rhetoric of racial development of immigrants or of African American workers. He overwhelmingly marketed his management style as based on scientific expertise in manipulating processes not races.[23]

More broadly, the race-thinking that informed Taylor's presentation of his new system by introducing Schmidt, and his diffidence in pursuing the matter, did comport with larger patterns that saw race management survive, and even expand, in the early years of the era of scientific management. Taylor's example further showed that race management was so deeply entrenched that its "residual" power would have had to be systematically dismantled if management decided to commit to the idea that labor was abstract and raceless. Instead there developed a productive détente between the high-powered innovations of scientific managers at the upper reaches of management and the high-powered continuities of race management carried forward by foremen.

Staying Power: Strengths and Practicalities of Race Management

Managerial reform emerged within a larger set of racial and racist assumptions and was bound to reflect them. If those assumptions came under social-scientific questioning in the early twentieth century, especially from scholars of color and from Franz Boas and other anthropologists, the period was also a boom time for white, Anglo-Saxon supremacy. The nation accepted Jim Crow as a legal system of separation and oppression in the South and, with variations, in other regions. Color bars kept black workers from jobs in many factories and from the better jobs in those where they could work. Campaigns for immigration restriction matured. Newcomers from southern and eastern Europe were routinely seen as being either racially inferior to the earlier Anglo-Saxon and Celtic settlers in the United States or at best as "on trial" in terms of their abilities and their fitness for life in the United States. If a potentially antiracist science made its stronger appearance, so too did its opposite. "Objective," scientific histories of slavery and of Reconstruction gave respectability to massively popular racist cultural productions like the film *The Birth of a Nation* and the novel on which it was based, Thomas Dixon's *The Clansman*.[24]

Management reform literature featured the assumptions woven into the broader society and academia. Eugenics literature circulated widely with the World War I use of IQ tests for soldiers broken down to show difference by race and nationality, lending a seeming unassailable quantification to racist science and to anti-immigration campaigns. Connections between race and crime were powerfully imagined, drawn, and redrawn by experts and the broader population. Everyday racism shaped the framing and the language of expert opinion. For example, writing in *The Factory: The Magazine of Management* in 1914, Harry Franklin Porter puzzled over unaccounted-for differences in the acceptance of piece rates in a particular workplace and concluded that there had to have been a "nigger in the woodpile" somewhere, reproducing an old racist folk-saying. When introducing the technical matter of showing how management might make use of charts and tables, it was perfectly natural for another author to choose a graphic separating "foreign whites" from native-born ones.[25]

U.S. race management searched the world to validate its perspectives. Not only was this true in regard to colonized people but also in its consideration of the United States as a racially superior nation and Anglo-Saxons as uniquely fit for industry among Europeans. Perhaps the best example of the perils of assuming that engineers and managers thought in raceless terms where techniques and process were concerned came in an 1895 article from the *Engineering Magazine*. In it Albert Williams, Jr., tackled "Racial Traits in Machine Designing." While more nuanced than its title suggested—national characteristics of design practices hinged on "the habit of thought, the training, the experience, the natural bent" of the engineer, as well as labor markets— the leap from stereotype to product was swift and sure. Understanding

Scottish and English design depended on knowing those groups as "proverbially conservative, painstaking, and careful." The French "were quick, sensitive, innately artistic in all their perceptions . . . and somewhat given to an inordinate desire for originality." Austrians "turn[ed] out work resembling that of the North Germans, but showing less progress" so that their exports were rightly relegated to "semi-civilized lands." U.S. design, though it might according to Williams be expected to simply reflect its colonial origins or "racial admixture," somehow transcended such limits, producing "striking originality" and remarkable adaptations to the shortage and cost of skilled labor.[26]

The *Engineering Magazine* also featured Casper L. Redfield's commentary on the "Industrial Ascendancy of the Anglo-American Peoples." In a period in which the "English-speaking race" came to stand in for superiority among workers, Redfield, credited as an expert on heredity and degeneracy, tied language to inventive genius. Though fixed at other points on Anglo-Saxon brain size, the article's most arresting paragraph begins with: "Modern civilization depends on modern engineering," and concludes with: "Another illustration of the comprehensive knowledge of English-speaking people is found in the language itself. The number of words indicates the number of ideas, and the number of words in the English language is three or four times that of any other language."[27]

Management reformers of the early twentieth century entered workplaces that had been organized with race thoroughly in mind so that the practical advantages of continuing the system were fully on display. Commons wrote his line on race management as the "one symptom of originality" with his own recent studies of meatpacking very much in mind. As early as 1904, he had heard from an employment agent at Swift and Company that the "playing" of races against each other had been "systematized" in his factory, which rotated favored "racial" groups weekly. Commons worried that such "competition of races," especially when it included workers from the "non-industrial" Negro race and too many immigrants from the "backwards, shiftless and unintelligent races" of southern and eastern Europe and elsewhere, would lead to catastrophe for workers. At the same time he realized that competition served capital because it extracted productivity and exerted a downward pressure on wages.[28]

Indeed, as split-labor market theorists have observed, "potential" as well as "actual" competition benefited management. Such use of racial difference was not incidental to the exploitation of labor in meatpacking but central to it. Management manipulated racial differences to divide workers. The industry thought it "neither necessary nor prudent to conceal this policy of divide and rule." Meatpacking magnate Philip Armour urged that the industry work to "keep the races and nationalities apart after working hours and to foment suspicion, rivalry, and even enmity among such groups." Such seeming crudeness came in a thoroughly modernized industry, one pathbreaking in its engineering of the (dis)assembly line and soon to be at the cutting edge of post-Taylorist scientific-management pay-incentive schemes. Commons himself regarded these same packinghouses as also among the most "systematized" workplaces extant where the labor process was concerned. Even "the animal was laid off and surveyed like a map," he wrote, with the moving line producing innovations in engineering efficiency and speedups in pace of work.[29]

Iron and steel, closely studied by Taylor, similarly embraced both thoroughgoing rationalization of production and the continuation of unstudied race management. The industry's leader, Andrew Carnegie, received information from managers concluding that it was possible to know the optimal racial and national combinations of workers. That perfect mix impressionistically included Germans, Irish, and Swedes, groups which could and should be "judiciously mixed" with native-born rural white "Buckwheats" to make for the most "efficient and tractable" factory labor force. Machine shops, the other job sites most associated with Taylorism, and mines scarcely differed from steel and packing. Divisions based on skill overlapped with ethnic cleavages. One traveling British organizer of machinists and mechanics noted the "common practice" in U.S. shops for bosses "to quietly pit one nationality against the other in the workshop. Germans were ever ready to race the Irish, the Irish the Polander, Sweed [sic] or any other nationality."[30]

Such racing sometimes became literal. An article from 1914 in the journal *Factory* described the revolutionizing of production in a laboring job. A dozen and a half men loaded "dump cars" with clay to be transported by rail away from a dam construction site generating the clay. They loaded on average twenty cars daily. Three weeks later, the crew had been reduced by half but sixty, and some days eighty, cars of clay went out, making the productivity increases dwarf even Schmidt's. The key, as *Factory* put it, was "Management. The second manager knew how." Though recounted in the pages of a leading management-reform periodical, such transformative knowledge did not turn on slide rules and elaborate wage-incentive plans. A few technical improvements did occur, and workers came to receive maximum rates for their classifications as well as tips on shoveling. But "what welded the gang into an effective . . . working unit" was something else. The key to the transformation lay in the appointment of an effective "foreman of maintenance of way" who exploited "natural rivalry." The foreman split the gang of Italian Americans workers into two groups, Calabrians and Neapolitans, who raced to load materials. A green branch topped the car loaded by the winner. The scheme produced "cheering" and "cheerless" gangs, and the speedy removal of clay.[31]

Foremen in mines discriminated against Slavs and Italians by assigning them the worst places to dig coal.[32] Assignment to less productive sections of mines meant lower wages in an industry where miners were paid by weight of the product. Such assignments also raised questions of safety as the unfavorable placement in mines put workers in peril from gases, damp, and disaster. The most dangerous, unhealthy, debilitating jobs disproportionately went to new immigrant, black, and Mexican workers. In some times and places, the hot jobs around blast furnaces were typed as fit for Slavic workers and in others for Mexicans. Foundry work generally went to black and new immigrant labor. As one Hungarian cleric put in, after inspecting conditions in iron and steel in the Pittsburgh area: "Wherever the heat is most insupportable, the flames most scorching, the smoke and soot most choking, there we are certain to find compatriots bent and wasted with toil." The management and industry journal *Iron Age* linked new immigrants from eastern and southern Europe to not only the ability to withstand heat, but also to an "attraction" to "hot and heavy work"—in contrast to the northern European "aversion" to such conditions. Management expressed surprise, even alarm, when a native-born white worker applied for jobs considered "too damn dirty and too damn hot for a white man," though fine for Slavs.[33]

Management benefited practically by parceling out dangerous jobs along racial lines, though the patterns admitted exceptions. One study found nearly one blast furnace worker in six to be Irish—by then a nationality solidly considered white—as late as 1920. However, the notion that unsafe and unhealthy jobs fell only to the most racially marginalized mitigated the horror of epidemic accident rates, reaching as high as a quarter of recent immigrants who worked there killed or injured in the giant Chicago-area South Works mill from 1906 to 1910. Nonresident alien workers were in the main not protected, according to the courts, by Pennsylvania's workplace liability legislation. Frequent management and press references to the disposability of immigrant workers—"hunkies," as nativists called them—coexisted with the use of "hunked" as a verb to refer to becoming disabled at work.[34]

Studied Imprecision: Race Management and the Foremen's Role

It would have been difficult for management experts to systematically study race and productivity, not least because the former term meant so many different things in the early twentieth century. The results would almost certainly have reflected ideologically driven assumptions, beginning with the assumption that race in fact exists as a significant biological reality. Nor would any results have necessarily found easy application amidst the pressures of getting out production, a process in which the individual was more important than the stereotype.[35] Nonetheless, the absence of close investigation of race by modern management, and the willingness to countenance contradictory assessments of races by managers otherwise so committed to systematic investigation is significant, not least because it left the foreman's claims of productive racial knowledge so unassailable.

International Harvester's management expert H. A. Worman held that "each race has aptitude for certain kinds of work." His comments reflected an increasing, if offhand, rhetorical acknowledgement of the centrality of racial discriminations alongside the rise of scientific management. Indeed, the trend toward personnel management as a complement to Taylorism dramatically "extended the purview of scientific management from the factory itself to the surrounding community," a development that "flowed directly from the concern with recruiting from specific ethnic groups," according to labor historian David Montgomery. Racial difference also deepened the hubris of management. Historian of engineering David Noble observed that "precisely because they viewed the immigrants as 'aliens,' [managers] were able to manipulate them with considerable scientific detachment." But such an interest in race did not lead to an interest in precisely studying race. Montgomery has written that in the early twentieth century "all managers seem[ed] to agree" with Worman on the significance of race in job placement, adding however that they often disagreed utterly on "which 'race' was best for what."[36]

The "knowledge" that American race management produced in the era of scientific management was just as contradictory, and as just given to presenting matters in terms of fanciful ratios comparing groups, as it had been in running Southern cotton plantations, western railroads, and foreign mines. Upper-management literature sometimes specified which races should be slotted into what jobs. John Williams, who presided over the Philadelphia Association for the Discussion of Labor Problems, wrote during World War I that men grinding steel ought to be "Polish, Lithuanians or Americans." Williams also departed from accounts that made presumed similarities of gender override those of race when the management of early twentieth-century women's work was discussed, as it was only infrequently in management journals. Finishers, he said, were to be Italian or American girls with a preference for those who were "not flirty." Among men, heaters should be American or Polish, and forge workers either Americans or "American Poles" in his view. The 1911 U.S. Industrial Commission report on bituminous coal recounted preferences among managers for Slovaks and Poles, with Russians, Magyars, northern Italians, and Lithuanians in a second tier, and southern Italians and Croatians bringing up the rear in terms of "desirability." But any unskilled new immigrant worker, regardless of nationality, was vulnerable to being dismissed as "only a hunky." The psychologist Eliott Frost declared race and nationality the centerpieces of personnel management, elaborating his own 1920s views: "The Jew . . . is continually thinking of how much he is receiving for his labor. . . . The Italian's highly emotional nature lends itself readily to directions by the [union] organizers. . . . The German workman is of placid disposition, loves detail, [and] is particularly effective on precision work. The Pole and Croat usually do the dirty work in the plant." A want ad could read: "Syrians, Poles and Rumanians preferred."[37]

When rankings were hazarded, they reflected prejudices of managers, not sustained investigation of which groups produced most in which jobs. Even starkly different conclusions did not lead to study. The U.S. Immigration Commission report of 1911 posited virtual unanimity among employers around the judgment that southern Italians were "the most inefficient of races" and an *Iron Age* article from that same year placed the "races" in "about the following order: Slovaks, Poles, Magyars, Croatians, Italians," ranked according to "preferences of the employers." Pittsburgh Steel management meanwhile placed Italians in the most efficient third of all "racial" groups shortly thereafter. One steel manager might prefer "two Negroes" to "three Macedonians," while most ranked the "alien white races" above African Americans. Not only the basic question of who was white, but even that of who was black remained unanswered by managers otherwise fixated on race. "The 'black races' cannot do the work in three days that a white man can do in one," an Iron Range mine superintendent told a government investigator, using the former term to connote Montenegrins, Serbs, southern Italians, Greeks, and Croats.[38]

Even the rare, elaborately mounted examples of research on race and management sometimes rested on slight empirical evidence. In a long 1918 *Industrial Management* article "Negroes as a Source of Industrial Labor" the supervising engineer Dwight Thompson Farnam developed some new evidence beyond managerial common sense. Farnam moved perhaps more than any expert toward a scientific apparatus to investigate race and labor. He generated a plethora of graphs and insisted upon the possibility of gradual race development of inferior peoples with proper white managerial leadership. But such leadership ended up hinging on the instincts, and the nationality, of the foreman, a position Farnam had once held. The Irish, with their "cheeriness coupled with an occasional terrifying outburst of authority," typically "ma[d]e good negro bosses." One anecdote suggested an Irish foreman could extract as much production from "an engine room full of negroes" as from one "full of German square-heads." The "type of Scot or New Englander who has no patience with any except those thrifty souls who work unwatched from a strong sense of duty, has no business trying to handle [N]egroes."[39]

Farnam wisely kept his article's ill-described charts at some distance from his textual explanations of their contents. Four of the nine charts purport to quantify "negro" productivity under various types of foremen. Each type had a sample size of one; thus one foreman studied was Irish, lending the most slender possible support to Farnam's theses on nationality, race, and management. Other graphs and parts of the text suggested avenues for potential serious quantitative study of race and productivity, such as comparisons of African American, Italian, and "mixed-gang" productivity. However, despite its elaborate apparatus, the article ended valorizing the untutored opinions of foremen as keys to race management.[40]

The elaborate, striking, but atypical chart ranking three dozen immigrant "races" according to their fitness for three dozen job types and conditions, posted at Pittsburgh Central Tube in 1925, assembled a much more impressive number of opinions, but only opinions, systematizing a huge factory and the peoples in it in upward of a thousand multicolored squares.

The chart gathered managerial and professional folklore, summing up existing prejudices. Italians, according to the Pittsburgh chart, allegedly excelled with pick and shovel but could not handle serving as helpers for engineers. Armenians ranked "good" in none of the twenty-two job categories listed and rose to fair only once: wheelbarrow. "Americans, White" could do any job fairly well and excelled in most. Jews supposedly fit well into no industrial jobs. Portuguese workers rated as poor in seven of eight "atmospheric conditions" and joined Mexicans in lacking capacity to work on the night shift, or the day one. Greeks and West Indians rose beyond fair only in surviving heat and humidity according to the Pittsburgh chart.[41]

Purportedly scientific connections of race with productivity thus remained extremely crude. The weightiest research on productivity and race tended to be assembled by investigators writing in the government journal *Monthly Labor Review* and often focused on demonstrating the falsity of negative stereotypes regarding black workers. This data seems to have made scant impact on combatting such stereotypes, while the repetition of antiblack and xenophobic folklore took scholars to great academic heights. When the towering figure in American sociology, E. A. Ross, urged slotting the Slavic "race" into filthy and unhealthy

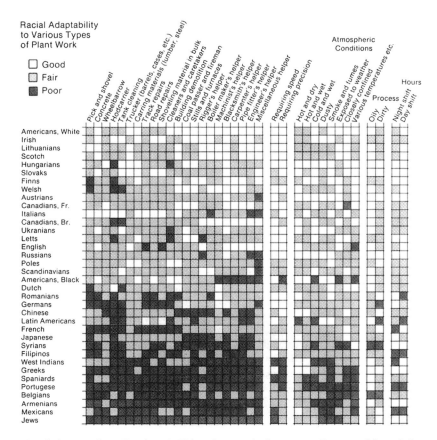

Untitled image from Pittsburgh Urban League Archive, 1925. Reprinted from John Bodnar, Roger Simon and Michael Weber, *Lives of Their Own: Blacks, Italians, and Poles in Pittsburgh, 1900–1960* (Urbana: University of Illinois Press, 1983), 240.

jobs because they were "immune" to dirt, he offered an opinion, not a study. The same was true of Commons's own assessments, such as "The Negro . . . works three days and loafs three [while the] Chinaman, Italian, or Jewish immigrant works six days and saves the wages of three." When the sociologist Jerome Davis researched his extraordinary 1922 study *The Russian Immigrant*, he had to drop plans for a questionnaire regarding Russian immigrant workers when one personnel department after another reported utter lack of basic statistical information on how many Russian immigrants they employed. They could not distinguish Russians from Jews, Poles, Finns, and others often listed as Russian in official sources. This lack of data coexisted with a high tide in pronouncing racial judgments on workers, and with a professed desire to limit hiring of Russians who were seen as potential Bolsheviks. In the absence of systematic data collection and study, those foremen carrying out on-the-ground race management remained free to proceed on their own assumptions.[42]

Some experts were aware of patterns of pronouncing much and investigating little where race and productivity were concerned. As early as 1913, Hugo Münsterberg's classic *Psychology and Industrial Efficiency* identified the discontinuity between precise studies of workers' motions and offhand assumptions regarding "race" and productivity. Münsterberg set out to assess how far scientific management had gone, and could go, and staked out a place for "scientific psychology" as congruent with the "revolutionary," but incomplete, innovations of Taylor. Race initially seemed to Münsterberg to present little difficulty to those bent on achieving such a breakthrough. "If a man applies for a position," he wrote, "he is considered [for] the totality of his qualities, and at first nobody cares whether the particular feature is inherited or acquired, whether it is an individual chance variation or . . . common . . . to all members of a certain nationality or race." Reliance on race in the search for the "best possible man" for the job would be checked because even if the "combination of mental traits" required occurred more often in specific races "psychical qualities may vary strongly in the midst of the group."[43]

In further developing his analysis, Münsterberg acknowledged that the search for the best man for the job did often depend on unexamined racial assumptions. That management at the plant level cared about race was not necessarily bad in his view, but that they cared so unsystematically and unscientifically was troubling. At one factory with "twenty different nationalities" the employment officers might declare the Italians best for one job, the Irish for another, and the Hungarians for a third. At the next factory, Münsterberg added, completely different conclusions would be reached. In one workplace, managerial lore judged the "hasty and careless" Italians and Greeks undesirable in risky jobs, which were to go to the Irish. In the next, it was the Irish who were too prone to court danger to do risky work. Münsterberg himself tended to credit the stereotype of carelessness as applying to Italians, Greeks, and Irishmen. But he abhorred the lack of system in studying race and accidents. "American industrial centers," he argued, offered "extremely favorable conditions for the comparative study of nationality," but the opportunity was not being seized. "Much more thorough statistical inquiries," especially into variations between nationalities in their responses to piece rates, were needed to ground "race psychological statements."[44]

Münsterberg's lament found echoes in the writings of the small number of experts attempting to study race, management, and labor together. Farnam noted in 1918 that "the racial tendencies of different classes of labor have so far been insufficiently studied in America." A year later Frost likewise thought that he was starting from scratch in developing an "analysis of racial psychology" appropriate to industrial education and management. One early 1920s management handbook saw the duties of the employment manager including "follow[ing] internal migrations of different races and nationalities . . . movements of negroes and Spanish-Americans," and hiring the "type of worker most desirable for [the] task: American or foreign, white or black." But management literature remained very close-mouthed and arbitrary in what judgments it did offer regarding just how to do so.[45]

Race mattered, but without provoking serious reflection, in postwar management theory. Ordway Tead, the coauthor of the first textbook in the new field of personnel management, introduced his *Instincts in Industry* (1920) with the remark that "differences in race, climate and civilization . . . may so modify human organisms as to cause radical differences in what is the substance of our . . . human nature." Tead also wrote of "employers who have a definite policy of hiring several different nationalities in one department of a factory in order that workers may be less able to communicate effectively and therefore less able to cause trouble." For Tead, that deliberate divisiveness focused, as in the Mr. Block cartoon, in part on keeping out unions. But he offered an investigation neither of how or whether such a strategy worked, nor of his contention that the southern and eastern European immigrants commonly exhibited an "instinct" to be submissive, albeit punctuated by the occasional "brave frenzy of self-assertion." In 1920, when the Social Science Research Council (SSRC) "mapped" the field of industrial relations, enumerating well over a hundred disciplines poised to contribute to the new field, it assigned to anthropologists the task of investigating "inherited racial characteristics" capable of "affecting work," offering the "alleged laziness of the negro" as an example. But the SSRC did not try to solve the problem of, to use Montgomery's phrasing, "which 'race' was best for what."[46]

In the 1920s and '30s, management experts Herman Feldman and T. J. Woofter, Jr. rued the fact that manufacturers, so scrupulously careful in choosing raw materials, "rely on hearsay and rumor as to the grades of labor hired." Everett C. Hughes and Helen M. Hughes observed that off-the-cuff opinions on racial difference so pervaded managerial choices and language, while hard data comparing racial performance remained so rare, that it was worth questioning whether "modern society is really guided by the impersonal concepts of the market and efficiency in choosing . . . its labor force." Taylor had written, "Under scientific management arbitrary power . . . ceases; and every single subject . . . becomes the question for scientific investigation." Where race was concerned, post–World War I experts increasingly joined Münsterberg in arguing that such a shift did not happen.[47]

Race, Nationality, and the Persistence of the "Foreman's Empire"

There were compelling reasons for both the reticence of the management experts and the continuing sway of the foremen. Management's interest in race science was necessarily abstract and conditioned by the labor market. Broad inquiries into race generally took a backseat to the judging of those who appeared at, or might easily be attracted to, the factory gates. As *Iron Age* noted, the prospective available employees in a city like Pittsburgh were confined to "certain races only," and management would have little interest in racial hierarchies beyond those. Employers had reasons to focus on the "betterment" of new immigrants rather than only on making invidious comparisons between groups. This emphasis on race development often directed attention to matters occurring away from the workplace, such as English classes, home visits, and citizenship programs. Its cheerful spin reflected the political necessity of defending relatively open immigration policies even for "lesser" European nationalities.[48]

Moreover, the case for "betterment" of immigrant races fit closely with some patterns of upward job mobility. A central goal of scientific management and assembly line production in these years was to erode the social position of skilled workers, typically native-born, by reengineering jobs to require more repetition and less craft skill. For the unskilled immigrant, this meant that a proliferation of "semiskilled" jobs in various grades opened the possibility of nominal and real upward mobility. The process is best studied in iron and steel, where management's institution of "minutely graded job ladders" enabled experts to point to acquisition of skills—albeit skills easily learned in a few weeks—to make a case for the racial development of white new immigrants. In one giant Pittsburgh mill in 1910, among recent immigrant workers the unskilled outnumbered the semiskilled almost six-fold in the group with less than two years of service. Among those with ten years or more of service the semiskilled almost equaled the unskilled in numbers, and the total of skilled plus semiskilled surpassed that of the unskilled. However dangerous, long, and alienating these jobs remained, as the immigrant rebellion in the steel strike of 1919 and 1920 registered, the changing job structure lent itself to management's narratives of progress. Although aware, as scientific management advocate Worman put it, of the desirability of "experience, brain power [and] adaptability" among the semiskilled, being attuned to the foreman's authority was considered just as vital. Management was therefore not interested in most cases in buying racial superiority, only competency and sometimes only brute strength. Commons himself expressed management's view: "The changing character of immigration is made possible by the changing character of industry. . . . Races wholly incompetent as pioneers and independent proprietors are able to find a place once manufactures, mines, and railroads have sprung into being, with their captains of industry to guide and supervise their semi-intelligent work."[49]

Also cutting against grand investigations of race at work was the reality that the personnel managers knew that the worker to be managed was an individual even as they sometimes reduced him or her to a racial type. Thus in one model employment questionnaire circulated in the management press "nationality" did form the subject of one question, but only one, among forty-four. Potential hires presented what have been termed "bodies of work" to employers and consciously showed off their own physical strength to the best advantage. Nonetheless, personnel managers regarded some racial and national types as "well-fitted" for hard jobs. "Hunkies" were especially likely to be regarded as "sturdy" and "insensitive to pain." They seemed "apparently insensible to the rigors of January" as well as to sweltering summers.[50]

The pulls both toward and away from making empirical investigation of race a central part of management reform emerged clearly in the brief vogue of the Blackford System. An attempt to bring together eugenics, climatologically based race theory, criminology, photography, and mail-order business, the theory of management was developed by Katherine Blackford, an Iowa-trained physician. Elaborated in her coauthored 1919 book *The Job, the Man, the Boss*, the system proposed to train managers to identify workers most fit for jobs by looking at their bodies, and especially faces, "reading character" from physical markers such as hair, shape of nose, color of eyes, and skin color. Blackford's theories, which made the consideration of "Why All Angels Are Blond" relevant to management theory, eventually came under withering assault in mainstream management literature as pseudoscience.[51] Yet for a time, one foundry in ten in Chicago reportedly made use of the system, as did such major national firms as Westinghouse and Scott Paper. During World War I the convention of the American Foundrymen's Association heard a leading advocate of "character analysis" detail the system at length. A mainstream investigation of labor turnover in 1917 apologized for lack of attention to differences between blondes and brunettes, Blackford's central managerial distinction.[52]

Blackford divided humanity into the categories "blondes" (or "blonds") and "brunettes" (or "brunets") not on the basis of hair color alone, but to be able to take into account the "totality" of racially associated physical traits—to manage groups without losing sight of individuals. The "white skins" were blonde and the "dark skins" brunette. The former were managerial, their ancestors having developed through surviving harsh conditions over centuries. Like the proslavery theorist and physician Dr. Samuel Cartwright, character analysts associated race with respiration, arguing, "In the savage races inhabiting the tropical countries, the noses are all broad and short, as there is less oxygen in warm air and they are therefore compelled to breathe in larger quantities of air in order to extract the same amount of oxygen from it." The analysis continued by insisting that the "snub or baby nose will be found amongst the lowest strata of society such as the Africans, Aboriginals, South Sea Islanders and most of the inhabitants of the Orient who are ignorant, worthless, low and indolent." The whole of humankind fit on a one-hundred-point pigmentation scale, to be used by employers; Africans defined the bottom at zero. Finely measured color differences could be used to discriminate among Europeans, and the facial analyses left room to judge individualized bodies as well as racial types. In many ways the system comported with past and ongoing attempts to theorize race within management, but it was soon discredited as unverifiable and arbitrary, an apt enough charge but one the journals publishing the critiques were hardly in a convincing position to make.[53]

That neither Blackford nor her detractors intensively investigated race and work left the "foreman's empire" less vulnerable to challenges by upper management and consultants. This reality was a major factor in ensuring that the power of foremen was not uprooted through the 1920s. Traditionally, "hiring and firing, assignment to tasks, setting the pay rate [and] determining who got laid off or told to stay over-time" defined that power. Scientific management only eroded such prerogatives, and the enormous arbitrary authority to judge new immigrants that they conferred, gradually and unevenly. As late as 1919, management scholar Sumner Slichter found the "coercive drive system" to thrive because "central management has been indifferent to the methods pursued by foremen in handling men" while it insisted on cost-cutting and greater output. Even as the unevenly developing trend toward personnel management identified the arbitrary and abusive behavior of lower management as a cause of the problem of labor turnover, foremen retained significant power over who got and kept jobs.[54]

Foremen could claim a time-tested ability to manage different nationalities and races, and through this skill an authority over workers and over other managers. John Fitch, a keen student of the iron and steel industry in the early twentieth century, once explained that foremen were called "pushers," because they "push the gang" through the use of "motions and profanity." His interviewer then asked if Fitch meant that famously abusive and profane "rolling-mill English" conveyed the urgency and threat many foremen sought. Fitch agreed that such foul language was what was used to "get a gang to get a move on."[55] Again and again, when the power of foremen was bemoaned or examined by management reformers, the seeming structural necessity of undermining their arbitrary "rough-and-tumble" production methods crossed into a discussion of race. This was particularly striking in a sustained series of *Industrial Management* articles on the roles of foremen in 1917. When, for example, Frank Rindge wrote under the striking title "From Boss to Fore-man," he regarded the foreman as either the grit smoothing production or the agent of disorder and waste. The old school practices of the foreman needed either to be reformed through "tact and education," or the offenders were to be removed. Among the offenses were widespread payoffs for jobs to foremen, "especially in case of foreigners," and extraction of sexual favors from "women and girls employed." Where race and nationality were concerned, Rindge's expert opinion stopped far short of solutions, or even conclusions. The foreman of "a different nationality than his men . . . is particularly apt to be unsympathetic, for he may not understand their habits and their slow mental processes," he thought. But the "Americanized foreman" would likely lack sympathy "for he may delight in his superiority over his one-time countrymen." The article wound its way to a discussion, likewise opaque, on whether "to mix nationalities."[56]

When more breathlessly hopeful prospects for reform of foremen appeared, the language of race also emerged. In a speech republished in *Industrial Management,* Meyer Bloomfield assured International Harvester foremen that their cultivation of workers' "good will" held the key to productivity—that they were "partners" and "upbuilders" of those working under them—"not slave drivers [but] educators." Nonetheless, nationality complicated matters and the audience needed reminding that such civility applied "no matter how backward, how crude, how ignorant, how illiterate are the workers and aliens who come to your shops." The foreman who dismissed such workers as "just wild" had not taken the trouble to "know them."[57] Harry Franklin Porter exalted the work of managers of the unskilled as producers of benefits for the "individual and the race," indeed as architects of "the upward trend of humankind." However, his ensuing paragraph summed up and sanitized the language of much management practice: "Here, Tony; take this shovel and get busy."[58]

Such combinations of high praise and mild reproach did not animate any campaign to supplant the foreman's claim to knowledge based on long experience of driving and mixing workers of varied races and nationalities. If management reform after Taylor sought to gather skilled workers' knowledge of the production process into management's hands, it largely settled on questions of race for gathering foremen's opinions or for simply leaving existing practice undisturbed. Thus well into the 1920s and '30s, foremen were the force behind the driving, bullying, and cajoling that typified managing immigrant workers. In the stockyards of Kansas City, workers suffered under foremen who refused to learn their names, opting for "Hunky" instead. In some Pennsylvania mines, commands were prefaced "Hey Polack" or "Hey Dago," much to the reported chagrin of those commanded. As Herman Feldman noted in 1931, the racial views of "supervisors, section heads, foremen and other minor functionaries" most mattered in the daily lives of ethnic and African American workers. Foremen in particular "vaunt[ed] their superiority by speaking of immigrant employees as 'wops,' 'bohunks,' or 'mutts.' " In the previous year, an article in *Personnel* personified the bad old days of management as ones when the foreman "hied himself immediately to the main gate of the plant where a crowd has gathered seeking employment. Hastily glancing over the throng, he would single out a likely looking prospect, beckon him with his finger, and say a few words." As the account continued, "When the timekeeper came around, the foreman told him the man's name, occupation and [pay] rate. If the name was too involved because of foreign sound or spelling," the new hire might be "re-christened on the spot" so that payrolls in steel still have names like "Joe Dollars and Frank Pennies." But the bad old days were continuing, their recurrence threatened more by immigration restriction, and later industrial unionism, than by the internal logic of management reform. When the sociologist Niles Carpenter interviewed Polish and Italian workers for his excellent study of Buffalo in 1925, he found more than twice as many complained of discrimination from foremen as reported mistreatment from fellow workers. As late as 1942, Louis Adamic's *What's Your Name?* recorded the "promiscuous changing" of names by workers who were trying to find favor with multiple bosses who possessed differing prejudices.[59]

Scientific management and race management coexisted because they worked on different levels to increase production and because they were not so utterly different after all. Scientific management was, as Bernard Doray wrote long ago, a "science" that could not escape "bear[ing] the scars of the social violence that characterized the society which gave birth to it." Replete with pro-management assumptions, it selectively drew on folk knowledge and self-interested observations of existing work patterns. Scientific management was therefore broadly compatible with that other great scar-bearing, scar-causing science of the early twentieth century—the continued elaboration of racial hierarchies.[60] Even attempts like those of Woofter and Feldman to cast race management as the exception to the general rationality of industry underlined the staying power of unscientific systems. Critics vacillated between ridiculing race management and calling for making its invidious race-based distinctions more scientifically systematic. The deep roots of the practice of race management go some distance to explaining its impressive durability. But to emphasize only such history risks seeing management by race as merely residual, even premodern, and therefore at odds with the longer rational logic of capitalism. To the contrary, it has been central to such logic.

The staying power of the "foreman's empire" in the face of scientific management was a triumph of one form of capitalist rationality intimately linked to reliance on deploying the irrationalities of race in order to manage labor. It is in this specific realm that Commons' remarks again become critical. Systems of modern management and race management coexisted cheek by jowl in the most advanced factories.[61] Such a system of racial competition did not rest on the fixing in place of a scientific chart of hierarchy but on the production, mostly by lower levels of management, of a series of contradictory and volatile managerial opinions. Since foremen often retained the ability to hire and fire in the 1920s in the face of challenges from personnel managers, their prejudices carried the power to keep racialized workers productively on edge. Indeed, on the rare occasion when the adequacy of the racial knowledge possessed by foremen was directly questioned by management experts, the framing of the issue was likely to be around the fear that the races were being too much pitted against each other, risking the possibility of fostering racial hatreds, political radicalism, and riots, particularly in the context of World War I and its aftermath.[62] If scientific management involved a "rational madness," management also long deployed the irrationalities of race in a calculating manner. Sometimes it did so by fixing categories and hierarchies, more often by leaving races unfixed in rankings and thus permanently in competition and flux, at the whim of lower management.[63]

6

The Crisis of Race Management

Immigrant Rebellions, Immigration Restrictions, and a New Focus on Black and Mexican Labor

UPTON SINCLAIR'S TWO GREAT NOVELS of mass production and the assembly line are separated by three dozen years and much more. The choices Sinclair made in writing them illuminate and evade how race management was transformed when the number of immigrants and the number of "races" to be managed declined dramatically as a result of World War I and the immigration restrictions of the early 1920s. The first and far more famous of Sinclair's two assembly line novels, *The Jungle*, represented the high tide of the "new immigration" from the poorest parts of Europe. It might be called, among other things, a story of race management at its most grand. The hero of the massive book, the Lithuanian immigrant Jurgis Rudkus, moved through the race-conscious world of Chicago's meatpacking plants in the first years of the twentieth century, facing the indignities of poverty and of being a "foreigner." He stood and waited to be picked to work by foremen in situations in which both workers and management thought in racial and national terms, even as he groped for socialist solutions to such divisions. After a strike and during an economic crisis, the labor market teemed with the "ten or fifteen thousand 'green' Negroes, foreigners, and criminals . . . now being turned loose to shift for themselves." Strikes allegedly were honored by the "better class of workingmen" and broken by "the criminals and thugs of the city, besides Negroes and the lowest foreigners—Greeks, Romanians, Sicilians, and Slovaks."[1] Since the southern and eastern European nationalities involved were at the time considered "races," those doing the hiring had, as the labor economist John R. Commons had put it while reflecting on the same stockyards at the same time, plenty of opportunities for "playing one race against the other."[2]

When Sinclair described the history of auto production in his 1937 novel *The Flivver King*, the period of mass immigration was long over, though eastern and southern Europeans remained a critical part of the working class. As the sweeping 1924 restrictions on immigration contained in the Johnson-Reed Act set quotas based on what numbers of national groups had arrived by 1890, dramatically slowing the arrival of new immigrants, the working class in this Sinclair novel faced a changed world. The novel alternated scenes of top management, in the person of the eponymous Henry Ford, and the working-class family led by Ford worker Abner Shutt. Ford's managerial innovations, from the assembly line to the five-dollar daily wage, from the use of sociological experts to remake workers to union busting and antilabor brutality, drive the plot. However, a literary imagination of race, management, and labor is absent. *The Flivver King* is as lacking a sustained ethnic presence as *The Jungle* was saturated with nationality and race.[3] Written as a contribution to the United Automobile Workers' organizing drives, the later novel's working-class heroes are portrayed, as is Ford, as without a racial identity. The move might have seemed to promise an end run around potentially divisive organizing problems or even to set aside cultural differences in order to highlight class. But Sinclair could make such a choice in *The Flivver King* precisely because race management had so radically narrowed after immigration restriction. Ford's own anti-Semitism is present for Sinclair, and the central working-class character briefly joins the Ku Klux Klan, but the company's interest in race development through Americanization is portrayed as part of a distant past.[4]

Sinclair's representation of post-1924 labor hardly exhausted the possible portrayals of race and management. Two alternative imaginations of the period after immigration restriction introduce themes vital to this chapter. In the 1935 proletarian novel *Marching! Marching!*, Clara Weatherwax fascinatingly made class both racial and transcendent of race, part of the past consequential in the present. In the novel's view class does not simply outweigh race but rather encapsulates it. Weatherwax writes, in something like a synthesis of Karl Marx and Carl Jung, that the miseries of labor "stayed etched in the worker-mind like carvings in stone. . . . All were simply present in him . . . Japanese, Filipinos, whites, Negroes, Mexicans [their] experiences hammered into them by clubs and toil."[5] William Attaway's *Blood on the Forge* suggests that through the Great Depression particular ethnic experiences within the emerging category of "white" still were being mobilized by management, partly to keep any unified "worker-mind" from being imaginable. Irish American lower management in that novel plays the black workers against the "hunky or a ginny [guinea],"[6] referring to eastern and southern Europeans. This chapter acknowledges the great changes caused by immigration restriction but pursues the leads of Weatherwax and Attaway as well. It emphasizes the titanic class struggles that forced management to give up on wide-open race management practiced on masses of newcomers, traces through the example of industrial psychology new attitudes towards race, and shows how increasing concentration on judging and bossing workers of color refocused race management.

Wanting and Suspecting Immigrants: Managerial Reform, Class Struggles, and the Troubles with Race Management

During the 1910s and '20s, management sometimes seemed willing to drop its reliance on the more brutal forms of racial competition in order to keep immigrant workers from leaving their jobs. At the time, some experts connected the desirability of more liberal labor-management regimes to the shortage of workers caused by the war, and projected to continue under anticipated postwar immigration-restriction laws. The scarcity of labor was understood as being connected to the war, even during the long period before U.S. entry into the conflict, as immigration was already largely cut off. As the old opportunities to manage by race and nationality gave way in the face of such realities, retaining immigrant workers appeared to become more critical than dividing them, especially since the latter strategy appeared perilously likely to spark ethnic conflict during wartime. Commons's remark that "when immigration suddenly stops we see a human being in those who are here and begin to ask them what they want" thus came well before immigration restriction and reflected on the experience of war production. If Commons overstated the extent of liberalization, he did identify one trend. Even in a city with relatively weak traditions of militant immigrant labor protest like Worcester, Massachusetts, engineers and Americanization experts identified the retention of workers and the prevention of labor militancy with the creation of "friendly, 'spirited' workplaces" during and after the war.[7]

Management quickly succeeded in combatting turnover, although for reasons not wholly attributable to the liberalization of managerial ideas. Separation rates, whether from firing, layoff, or quitting declined in manufacturing work from 123 for each 100 workers in 1920, to 100 in 1920 to 37 per 100 in 1928. In the 1920s workers lost the option of return migration to Europe, developed stronger U.S. family and community ties, and could expect progress up job ladders with multiple semiskilled gradations in industries like steel. Some went into installment-buying debt for consumer items which meant that loss of a paycheck threatened the loss of those items. Quitting jobs, which had accounted for 70 percent of all separations, plummeted. Moreover, some successful firms instituted private "welfare-capitalist" initiatives that provided new benefits and tied their workers to their jobs in expansive ways. Most important, huge technologically driven increases in productivity made the 1920s labor market into a "buyer's" one, well before the Great Depression. Such successes allowed management to de-emphasize turnover, as a problem already addressed, and to accept immigration restriction with some equanimity. Historians of management therefore argue that the moment in which personnel managers successfully attacked the foreman's power to arbitrarily drive workers proved brief indeed, unraveling by the early 1920s with "conservative" sections of personnel management learning anew to admire the foreman's authority.[8]

Were it not for such a speedy recrudescence of the foremen's arbitrary, race-managing sway over workers, it would be tempting to describe war labor and immigration restriction as the main context that permitted liberal managerial trends to triumph. There was certainly logic to liberalization. After all, Henry Ford's implementation of the five-dollar day (in order to retain workers whose Americanization his experts could monitor) happened before both World War I and immigration restriction. Perhaps management broadly learned during the war to imitate Ford, seeing advantages to cashing in its race development gains, adopting welfare capitalist strategies to retain Americanized European workers, increasingly seen as unambiguously "white" once so few of them were newly arriving.[9] Indeed, this was a story management sometimes tried to tell itself, with partial plausibility. The increased capitalization of industrial plants produced technologically advanced factories that saved labor, and assembly lines that paced workers. These developments ostensibly curbed the need for the arbitrary power of the "bellowing-bull type of foremanship" which pushed workers along racial lines. Less needed too was the "gorilla" type of unskilled worker. Frederick Winslow Taylor's foundational story of his system of scientific management had insisted that in 1898 he had to settle for Schmidt as the best-available pig iron handler but an ape might have served even better. A Taylor contemporary in the steel industry announced, "Gorilla men are what we need" in the mills. By the '20s so much was the "gorilla" type in retreat that when Eugene O'Neill described the lack of place in the modern economy and world of the simian-looking coal-handler at the center of his play *The Hairy Ape*, he concluded by placing the character in tragic proximity to apes displayed in a New York zoo.[10]

However, a story mainly emphasizing the triumph of managerial liberalism in new contexts clashes with not only the history of foremanship but also with the extent to which immigration restrictions of 1921 and 1924 were not simply foisted on employers by a nativist public. On the contrary, the examples of immigrant disloyalty, of what was seen as immigrant disability, and above all of immigrant labor rebellion during and after World War I made employers doubt whether race management should survive open immigration. The loss of faith in the new immigrant's fitness as a potential American citizen and as an industrial subject reached far past conservative politicians, disenchanted Progressive reformers, rural Protestant Americans, and the revived Ku Klux Klan. It took hold among industrial capitalist elites who resisted concessions to labor radicalism but acquiesced to anti-immigrant racism. The delicate balance in which prewar Progressives and industrialists might proclaim at once the need to recognize the racial and cultural problems with immigrants, the urgency of remaking newcomers, and the possibilities and benefits of their coming gave way to decidedly more negative and alarmed views. Industrialists did not so much give up on immigration as they proposed to make it "selective," and defensible, not only in political terms but also in terms of forestalling labor militancy.

Companies with a continuing material interest in the arrival of cheap, racially managed labor thus wavered on defending open immigration policies for Europeans. After the war and ensuing strike waves, capital backed even selective immigration only inconsistently and far less decisively than they might have within the pro-business climate of the 1920s. Before and after the 1924 restrictions, sectors of management thought continuing mass immigration to be untenable for the nation and for industry. This judgment stemmed not simply from the progress of technology and capitalist rationalization but from the actions of immigrant workers themselves—in mass strikes, in ethnic and racial fighting, and even in failing IQ tests given during the war to army recruits. The valuing of race management was not so much rejected in a burst of liberalism as it was retreated from in light of a period in which immigrants seemed undesirable and above all unmanageable.[11]

Such changes started small but grew quickly. When World War I was in its third year, but U.S. entry was still a year away, the U.S. Chamber of Commerce issued a report titled "The Americanization of Our Alien Workmen." The report presumed at the outset that debate over policy would center only on "the terms on which immigration will be resumed after the war," not whether it would pick up again. The chamber outlined formation of "Americanization Committees" framed around workplaces and participation in the labor force, seen as the key to acculturation.[12] Within five years, the workplace would seem instead to be a central site for the expression of a radicalism regarded as the antithesis of Americanism. By 1924, immigration from those countries producing the most prewar immigrants would be virtually shut down as sources of new Americans. What changed things was a war in which the fitness and loyalty of immigrants were sternly scrutinized. During and after the war came massive, militant strikes, concentrated in one of the largest waves in U.S. history between 1917 and 1922. In the year after the end of the war alone, a staggering four million workers struck. Although these strikes and campaigns for shorter hours and for workers' control over industries at times involved native-born craft unionists and even police as activists, the largest and most important ones, in steel, packing, mining, textiles, metal fabrication, lumbering, and the needle trades, involved "foreign," new immigrant workers.[13]

Old certainties quickly gave way. Management publications had posited that Slavs had a "temperamental tendency toward being easily managed," toward being antiunion, and toward preferring "the lowest wage scale" to any extra effort only until Slavic American militancy in the strike wave.[14] Slavs particularly assumed key positions in the Great Steel Strike of 1919 and 1920, a conflict the labor researcher David Saposs called at the time an "immigrant rebellion."[15] An antistrike graphic was splashed across the Pittsburgh press as an advertisement by employers attempting to play races against each other, using multiple immigrant languages, particularly Slavic ones, to sow suspicion among diverse groups.

The image likewise played on the fears and loyalty of the native-born, challenged not to join immigrants in fecklessly defying the back-to-work wisdom of Uncle Sam, still the key figure of patriotic conformity well into peacetime. As effective as such appeals doubtless were, raising the stakes in pathologizing the immigrant worker by setting him against the race-managing Uncle Sam complicated any subsequent turn to defending open immigration, especially when management believed its own anti-immigrant propaganda.[16]

With race management seeming to have failed, loyalty, labor, and immigration repeatedly came into conflict in ways that make more understandable the government's and industrial capital's unwillingness to defend against immigration restriction. Early in the steel strike, four immigrant steelworkers who had served in the war came before a Pittsburgh judge. He denied their request for naturalization because they were strikers, leading the Kansas City–based *Workers' World* newspaper to conclude that the real test of Americanism was willingness to serve the steel corporations, not in the military. Ford's Sociology Department, charged before the war with making certain that largely immigrant workers conformed to the company's standards of off-the-job discipline and morality, turned during the war to spying on potentially disloyal workers, checking that immigrants bought war bonds, for example. The

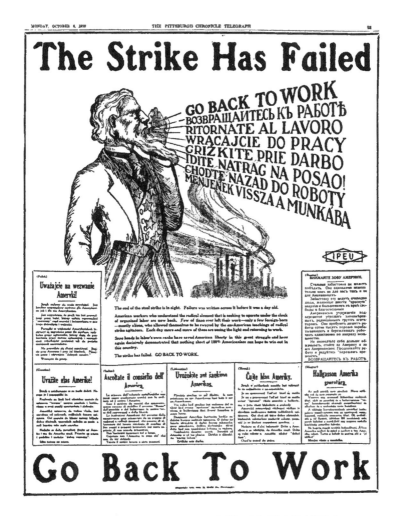

STEEL TRUST NEWSPAPER PROPAGANDA

Pittsburgh *Chronicle Telegraph*, October 6, 1919.

THE STRIKE HAS FAILED. Reproduced from William Z. Foster, *The Great Steel Strike and Its Lessons* (New York: Huebsch, 1920), unnumbered page following 188; originally appeared in the *Pittsburgh Chronicle-Telegraph*, October 6, 1919.

word "sabotage" was in the prewar years a labor tactic of undermining production by withdrawing efficiency and disrupting the work process, and even damging the means of production, sometimes in direct opposition to the exactions imposed by speedups and scientific management. During the war, "sabotage" became more clearly identified with the immigrant worker and was used to describe "un-American" destruction of property in order to help the nation's enemies.[17]

The general optimism of progressive reformers working with and for corporations to Americanize immigrants before 1917 was strong enough that it might have survived the brief period of U.S. involvement in the war were it not for immigrant labor militancy. Frances A. Kellor's work founding the Inter-Racial Council was a good barometer of such inter-sections of industry and reform. In 1915 Kellor wrote with breathless optimism for the Chamber of Commerce on "alien workmen" and their potential development through labor and the intervention of experts. The article featured a workplace photo captioned "The Imported American Always Starts in as a Worker." It promised "a more stable industrial body" through Americanization of immigrant bodies. Reform could counter "strikes and plots due to un-American agitators and foreign propaganda." Ford English School's graduation ceremony in Detroit had for a time expressed equally high hopes. It portrayed immigrant workers in "shabby rags" walking down a gangplank connected to the image of an ocean liner. They entered into a huge cauldron. The script labeled them with the racial slur "hunkie" as they entered the cauldron to, as a 1916 account in *Ford Times* put it, "see what the melting pot will do for them." After teachers from the school stirred vigorously, graduates emerged in "neat suits" as transformed. Workers entered the melting pot as "Irish Americans," "German Americans," and so on. They came out as just Americans, "having learned to view the hyphen as a minus sign."[18] Ford's efforts came in the context of more general "Detroit experiments" with Americanization, which drew national attention to the factory's role as the "real melting pot." Such emphases on "industrial Americanization" certainly had their coercive sides—Ford's Motion Picture Department made movies on the eve of World War I showing non-English speakers turned away from jobs—but the atmosphere was one of optimism. *Factory* touted the success of "hire-and-keep" employment plans and the development of "new men" out of immigrants through the war and reported on ingenious schemes to pay bonuses for staying with a company, but only "to Americans," thus coercing naturalization.[19]

By 1920, Kellor and others would sound very different notes. The project of race management now seemed threatened on two sides:

Workers might divide by national background or they might unite on class lines, each threatening the nation and production. Thus Kellor began one postwar article with alarms from the headlines of the day: "European labor chiefs plan to invade America" and "Riots in America between the Venizelosists and royalists over Greek election." Specifically tying immigration policy to capital accumulation, she complained that immigrant labor, and particularly immigrant war veterans, expected to get the same wage for half the work. Such a worker too often "brings with him the Bolshevist theory of 'working slowly on the job.'" Kellor worried further that "few businessmen realize the extent to which the war has accentuated the internationalism of the immigrant." Her proposals to combat "racial and international opinion and points of view" centered on redoubling surveillance of immigrants, specifically keeping records of labor turnover "by races" and undertaking "an inventory of racial solidarities." The Scovill Manufacturing Company shared Kellor's view that more zealous race management might cure labor militancy, keeping records on strikebreaking during the large 1920 brass workers' strike by race and nationality. The Carnegie Study of Methods of Americanization distributed a 1919 questionnaire asking "employment men" their sense of attitudes toward strikes and grievances of "foreign-born workers," compared to "native Americans." *Personnel*, which began in 1919 as avowedly THE EMPLOYMENT MANAGERS' BULLETIN, featured lengthy antiradical diatribes that veered into conspiracy theory and warned: "Social Diseases Spread Fast."[20] Such fears led experts to advocate efforts against racial bias in the workplace only occasionally and guardedly.[21]

In 1921 and 1924, years when the important legislative debates on immigration restriction occurred, industrial managers and reformers allied with them were insufficiently confident that race management and Americanization worked to present a united and coherent defense of open immigration from Europe. Business groups did continue to agitate episodically for relatively open labor markets, but from a chastened and defensive posture reflecting postwar experiences. In adopting cautious rhetoric and in proposing halfhearted pro-immigration arguments, industry meant to seem reasonable to the public. But such caution also reflected management's real anxieties. Thus in 1922 when *Barron's* opposed literacy tests, a favorite legislative device to limit immigration, that business journal both contested nativism and accepted that certain immigrants needed strict controlling. Assessing literacy was "no useful test. The agitators we are so anxious to keep out are literates to a man, often in more than one language. . . . But what we want is unskilled labor, and it is of small consequence to us whether it is literate." Some proposals for increased testing for physical able-bodiedness of immigrants did, on the other hand, excite managerial interest.[22]

In the debates leading up to the 1924 Johnson-Reed Act immigration restrictions, the steel industry took great care to portray itself as wanting only "selective immigration." In 1923 the industry journal *Iron Age* parried charges that steel "wanted to open wide the doors for all kinds of immigrants" including "more of the ignorant and vicious classes from southern Europe" by urging a turn to "selectivity." J. M. Larkin, assistant to the president of Bethlehem Steel, emphasized possibilities of race development to the House Committee on Immigration, but opposed the "wholesale admission of aliens." He favored regulating "numbers and quality," but not based on rigid quotas. *Iron Age* approvingly quoted the general counsel of the National Association of Manufacturers reporting that those whom he represented "favor selective immigration rather than lifting the bars to all classes of aliens, some of whom cannot be assimilated into American citizenship." Commitment to race management continued. Larkin held that in steel "the character of the work, being for the most part hot and heavy, attracts those people as contrasted with the Northern European races who in the main appear to have an aversion for this kind of work." But there would be no stirring appeals to the melting pot.[23]

Beyond steel, industry's lack of unity and commitment on the immigration issue was still more apparent. John Higham's classic account of the legislative victory of the restrictionists argues that industrialists "acquiesced" to the 1921 restrictions, but "clamored" for liberalization of restrictions in parts of the debates on the 1924 act, only to lack the "resoluteness" to push hard at key moments. The dithering of the National Industrial Conference Board (NICB) and other employer groups in 1923 and 1924 shaped outcomes. The head of U.S. Steel pronounced restrictions "one of the worst things" ever for the U.S. economy, but the NICB's head conceded to nativists the most important points by allowing that immigration was "essentially a race question," one speaking to the "kind of citizenship" a nation desired.[24]

At the level of presidential politics the doubts of capital regarding immigration registered impressively. Calvin Coolidge, who signed the 1924 restrictions into law and was perhaps the most extravagantly pro-business president ever, agreed to immigration restrictions that had long been seen as a "labor" (that is, craft union) demand. Coolidge, writing in *Good Housekeeping* while vice president, had professed to favor "the right kind of immigration" but stressed that "racial conditions too grave to be brushed aside" demanded that "the Nordics" be protected.[25] The towering figure in business-government cooperation in the 1920s, Herbert Hoover, impressively managed to almost avoid the immigration issue altogether as secretary of commerce during the Johnson-Reed immigration restriction debates and then during the law's early implementation. He received letters from industrialists asking for his support in combating or softening restrictions, but replied only on narrow technical grounds, apparently never tipping his hand on the decade's most vital political issue until as a presidential candidate he mildly opposed rigid "quotas" on immigration. As president during a depression, he then proved a vigorous advocate of restrictions, deportations, and repatriations.[26] As immigrant labor militancy was crushed, race management of existing new immigrants continued on the shop floor, but industrialists and management experts did not fight effectively or hard to continue to bring in new supplies of Europeans to be racially managed. New strategies and new subjects would have to be found if race management were to reinvent itself.

Servants of Power in War and Peace: The Growth of Industrial Psychology

The new field of industrial psychology attempted to premise its rise during the 1920s in significant measure on providing knowledge enabling race management to persist in a postimmigration-restriction context. It did so by offering ways to assess existing immigrants, by suggesting strategies to implement "selective" exceptions to immigration law, and by studying black and Mexican labor as alternatives to immigration from Europe. As science, industrial psychology inherited significant, even scandalous, practices from the World War I period and cannot be said to have overcome such practices in the 1920s. However, as ideology the new field is highly revealing, especially because its birth so clearly shows that even in the twentieth century, science could as readily be a distillation of the needs of race management as a solvent of its assumptions.

During World War I, the U.S. Army arranged to give soldiers IQ tests, tying a suspect regime of assessment to the national interest under the supervision of the president of the American Psychological Association. The infamous experiment featured questions wildly biased in terms of race, nationality, and class. Examples included "Why is tennis good exercise?" and "Where is Cornell University?" The *Atlantic Monthly* reported that almost half of white men tested as "morons" with a mental age between seven and twelve. The new immigrant took the blame for the test "failures."[27] Testers gave respondents a letter grade. Italians and Poles occupied the bottom rungs, often in the "D-group." Black Americans constituted a negative baseline against which the deficiencies of others were measured. Forty-six percent of Poles, 42 percent of Italians, and 39 percent of "Russians," often Jewish, were said to perform at levels equal or less than African Americans in a formulation demeaning all compared.[28] California tests, according to the psychologist Kimball Young, showed "excessive school retardation" among "Latin" students, who were Italian, Portuguese, and Mexican. Such "Latins" put the "the future standard of . . . high-grade citizenship" in "serious trouble." Indeed, patriotic racism, which Young later said he did not much believe in but regarded as necessary to get his "union card" in psychology, carried immigration policy implications.[29] Biologist Harry Laughlin, who speedily became the "Expert Eugenic Agent" to the House Committee on Immigration and Naturalization, used army test data to summarily categorize those assigned D and E grades: "Cost of supervision [is] greater than value of labor."[30]

The army IQ tests, designed in part to racially manage and develop immigrant military labor, underpinned efforts to yoke psychology to the needs of industry. The tests and their attendant publicity gave psychologists a foot in the door where industry was concerned. Indeed, the tests were so publicized that the sympathetic photographer of immigrant labor, Lewis Hine, proposed after the war that his photos be supplemented by Edward L. Thorndike's IQ tests to illustrate testing data. Never again would such tests be given so broadly in connection to work, but the testimony of psychologists became important as management considered immigration restriction. Typically, the historian Loren Baritz writes, "values and goals of managers were accepted as given," especially where profit was concerned.[31] As Elizabeth B. Messina argues in a profound essay on the tests, "The need to stratify the labor market to meet the needs of industrial capitalism gave rise to the moral and psychological justification of the subjugation and exploitation of Italian immigrants." One expert found that "men of the D class are physically well-developed. A large number of them are attractive and pass in a crowd as normal. In this class belongs the *moron*, whose intellectual level seldom exceeds that of eleven years . . . with pick and shovel [they] build roads." Thus they presented "a serious racial as well as social-economic problem."[32]

In attempting to solve such problems, industrial psychology intersected with management optimistically. Kimball Young helped to pioneer the idea of selective immigration when he wrote in 1922, "What we want . . . is such a selection of European peoples that they will add variety to our population but not lower its intelligence." When the journal *Industrial Psychology* began in 1926, it devoted much attention to questions of race, management, and immigration restriction. James S. Hunter titled a very early article "Can Psychology Offset Restricted Immigration?," pointing out that immigrants were now preponderantly "unskilled Mexicans and [French] Canadians" and endorsing "sounder psychological methods" to select and develop available workers.[33]

But it proved easier to volunteer to serve corporate power where immigration and management were concerned than to develop a stance, much less a science, from which to do so. Although its authors claimed to be able to measure everything from "tastes" to "moral traits" by race, they could not help but falter in building relationships with industrialists who had contradictory goals. The tellingly subtitled *Industrial Psychology Magazine: The Magazine of Manpower* reported findings from the insurance industry that "some races of people are more honest than others." The reader was left in suspense as to precise rankings by race, though it was specified that the "American man rides along in the middle of the races with regard to honesty."[34]

The title question of another early *Industrial Psychology* article, "Are We a Nation of Morons?," in particular opened a hornet's nest of problems. The "nation of morons" charge had undergirded immigration restriction. Reassurances as to the quality of immigrants were useful for management's continued campaigns for selective exemptions from immi-gration restriction, and there was no shortage of optimism that "mental tests" able to select for "a higher standard" of immigrant would improve matters. But *Industrial Psychology* authors also wanted to speak to a desire to admit those whose intelligence supposedly fit them for unskilled work that was said to attract "undesirables."[35] In its earliest pages, the journal reported that employment managers at a rubber shoe manufacturer believed that "the dumb-bells are the most reliable workers in our . . . department." The writer added, "Plants in increasing number are finding morons splendidly adapted for work of certain kinds . . . better than their more gifted employees." The quickening of interest in using the "feeble-minded" in unskilled jobs in the mid-1920s reflected at once humani-tarian impulses, the mania for talking about mental testing, the desire for new labor sources after immigration restriction, and the recognition that immigrant workers testing poorly already worked well in industry. On the immigration-restriction front, psychology provided no ready answer. Tailoring tests to specific job skills was desirable but proceeded slowly and could not really speak to the gap between what was seen as desirable in terms of citizenship and what was seen as profitable in terms of labor.[36]

Industrial Psychology ultimately split the difference between the fear of the immigrant worker felt by educated elites, panicked cultural con-servatives, craft-oriented labor unions, and some capitalists, on the one hand, and the desire of managers for plenty of choices among workers to hire, on the other. In the mid-1920s, this middle position left ample room for racism. The journal reprinted parts of *The Melting-Pot Mistake*, by the veteran anti-new-immigrant campaigner Henry Pratt Fairchild. Milder in victory than in the run-up to immigration restriction, Fairchild praised the 1924 immigration restriction law as "one of the most influen-tial and far-reaching pieces of legislation ever enacted in human history." The selection from his work that *Industrial Psychology* chose backed off of anti-immigrant hysteria as it encouraged Americanization among diverse "whites," now that the supposed flood of immigrants had been ended. It reserved its vitriol for the "black element" and the Japanese, with a section on "Color" championing the idea of a "white man's country" in which all Europeans could participate, though happily not all could come.[37]

Another early contributor to the journal, M. R. Trabue, had published the worst of the antiblack materials utilizing the army IQ data, leading W. E. B. Du Bois to offer Trabue as a specific example in asking in 1920 how elite universities could employ the authors of such "utter rot."[38] In featuring Carl C. Brigham's "Validity of Tests in Examination of Immigrants," *Industrial Psychology* offered a defense of the army IQ data by the expert who for a time drew some of the wildest conclusions from it. In his 1923 *A Study of American Intelligence*, Brigham had endorsed the notion that those in the central European "Alpine races" made the "perfect slave, the ideal serf." Nonetheless, Brigham concluded with a plea for the selective overriding of immigration quotas that important sectors of management sought, asking, "In closing may the writer be permitted to offer a constructive suggestion concerning our immigration legislation?" and urging nonquota exceptions for those tested to be "of outstanding promise and talent."[39]

Willing to venture, but not too far, away from eugenicist orthodoxies in pursuit of being useful to industry, early industrial psychologists were unable to let go of their suspicion of immigrants, which industry now often shared. Transferring such suspicion to immigrants of color was one possible move. F. H. Hankins's "Racial Differences and Industrial Welfare" began with a stern critique of the ideas of Madison Grant and other advocates of the centrality of racial hierarchies, including such hierarchy within European populations: "The general claim of Nordic superiority has not been established on a sound scientific basis." Hankins toyed with the idea that "race mixture" preceded significant cultural advances and organized material under the subhead "How the Immigrant Helps." He then retreated from such a pro-immigrant stance, turning to praising the 1924 restrictions, defending the army IQ tests, and writing that "lowgrade" stock complicated "problems of the present and future." Thus racebased bars on immigration remained sound policy, as the United States had no obligation to be "an asylum for the reckless breeding of the varied nationalities [of the] world." But exceptions for the "distinctly able" might be made, based on "mental tests" selecting for a "higher standard." On only one matter was Hankins an outspoken opponent of existing policy. Mexicans, he thought, should not be given freedom to cross the border as they were the "lowest grade of immigrants we have ever received."[40]

Kimball Young also adopted contorted positions in attempting to both support the race-based logic of the 1924 restrictions and to leave room for revisiting the issue. Writing in the inaugural volume of *Industrial*

Psychology, he too offered a stern critique of Madison Grant and of the notion of "the decay of our native stock." European "sub-races," significantly "overlapped" making stark hierarchies impossible. "Cultural differences," not "mysterious 'racial' qualities," were what mattered among Europeans. That out of the way, Young added, "To dismiss the absurdity of the 'Nordic Race Hypothesis' is not to go to the other extreme and hold that all persons in every race or sub-race or nationality group are equal in intellectual capacity." Soon the long article was rehearsing propensity to "intellectual retardation" and other deficiencies of new immigrants, especially within the "Latin race." In a continuation of the article in the next issue, Young continued by developing a "Mental Age Scale" broken down by European nationality and produced IQ scores arranged by sectors of the economy. Those in "agricultural pursuits" supposedly had an average IQ of 78. "Manufacturing, that particularly important field for the new immigrant," had workers with an average IQ of 79. Having first broken with and then exemplified all that was worst in studying the relationship of racism, testing, and policy, Young managed the slightest of possible conclusions: "The New Immigrant constitutes a genuine factor in our American industrial civilization."[41]

By 1927 *Industrial Psychology* reported on the study of "natio-racial mental differences" in a series on "genetic psychology" in a way that disaggregated the new immigrant population. Polish Jews did best on the tests and Russian Jews suddenly excelled over "Americans," but Greeks, Italians, Poles, French Canadians, and Portuguese joined "Negroes" at the bottom of the list.[42] Psychology, like industry, did not effectively argue to extend the life of a fullblown system of race management among Europeans. That system had been decisively called into question after immigrant labor rebellions. Instead, the weight of race management came to fall on growing numbers of African American and Mexican American workers.

Concentrating on Black Workers

Chastened by war and class conflict, capital could no longer dream of a system of endless competition and endless racial development among dozens of European immigrant laboring groups functioning in the same way it had before World War I. But it could still dream, reprocessing the actual experience of European immigration and fastening fantastic visions of race management increasingly onto nonwhite groups. In a 1930 article in a leading business journal, the steel industry became "The Beast That Nurtures Children." The "fabrication of metal," it argued, had pushed up successive waves of Irishmen, "dark Sicilians," and Slavic "hunkies" both "spiritually" and "materially," quickly freeing them from hard mill work so that even Slavs were supposedly gone from the plants' drudgery. By the time the article was written, all of them had supposedly become "foremen or assistant superintendents," if not self-employed. In this fanciful view, which reminds us how thoroughly race development coexisted with playing races against each other, it was time for the "uplifting forces of steel" to work their magic on "the last of the steel immigrants—southern negroes and Mexicans."[43]

High hopes and some reservations regarding black labor had coexisted for over a decade by 1930. Well before immigration restriction, Dwight Thompson Farnam's 1918 *Industrial Management* article "Negroes as a Source of Industrial Labor" saw a leading supervising engineer maintain that the potential African American supply of new labor doubled that of immigrants and declare that the management of black workers was the key to postwar productivity. Amidst wartime labor shortages and immigrant labor militancy, Farnam proposed a turn to black labor at an opportune moment. His double emphasis on the promise and the need for monitoring of African American industrial labor would prove widespread. Finessing questions of enduring biological inferiority by positing "inherited" characteristics of black workers as climate-based, Farnam left a large role for white managers. Describing the Great Migration to the North for war work as "trainloads of negro mammies, pickaninnies [with their] . . . pathetic paraphernalia of mysterious bundles and protesting household pets," Farnam compared black and immigrant workers' relative progress toward literacy, their rates of incarceration, and their reputations among foremen. He also developed an extended history and natural history of Africa as one "country," without "letters, art or science," with venomous snakes and diseases preventing herding everywhere, and above all with "luxuriant" food, "fit for kings," there for the taking. Further blunting the development of a work ethic was the "humid heat [that is] depressing and exhausting," with Farnam believing that all of West Africa from Senegambia to Angola somehow lay below the equator. Such misinformation became an explanation of the absence of any "feverish desire to work" among those more than a century removed from an imagined Africa.[44]

Thus, as a subheading from Farnam put it, only managers who realized that THE NEGRO IS DIFFERENT could develop black labor's potential. In many ways reprising literature on slave management, Farnam pronounced on the whole "negro race" as childlike and in dire need of a boss and then urged the individual selection of loyal, talented, and exemplary black workers. SOMEONE MUST THINK FOR THE NEGRO, another subheading stressed. The article described the foreman very much as an overseer, the figure doing such thinking. He needed a combination of "absolute firmness" and an ability to see the African American worker's "antics at first with assumed toleration."[45] At the same time, Farnam prized retention of black labor. He broached a discussion of the desirability of providing infrastructure to keep African American families near factories in order to decrease turnover, a strategy also developing in the postwar wood-products industry. While casting its subjects as a problem, the article sustained its hopeful tone through constant comparisons of them with increasingly unavailable new immigrants. Alarmed at increases in the African American prison population, for example, Farnam found the crime rates higher still for "some half dozen immigrant white races."[46]

The turn to black Southern labor as an alternative source of workers in the years of labor rebellion and decisive immigration restriction after the war registered in a series of extremely hopeful reports in the Department of Labor's *Monthly Labor Review*. That journal's 1924 summation of the record since World War I gave "Negro labor" very high marks in assessing "the relative faithfulness and efficiency of the colored and white workers." Though less enthusiastic about black female workers than about males in industry, it noted that African American workers could be paid less under the same conditions. The reports relied heavily on employer opinion, which sometimes included professed preference for African American labor. In Cleveland, for example, such workers were said to "check up well with the average for other workers who come as immigrants to help make up the great American industrial life." Employers found black workers understood "the language and the basic ideals of the country" and saw African Americans as doing well in skilled and machine-based work. Reports from Pennsylvania similarly glowed.[47] Nonetheless, even well after the 1920s and '30s such positive assessments coexisted with wholesale exclusion of African Americans from production jobs. A New Deal survey of fifteen hundred Phila-delphia workplaces, for example, saw black workers in production at only five. In Cleveland as late as World War II, integration into even unskilled positions had reached only a small minority of factories.[48]

Thus African American workers came partway into the factory, entering much more fully into the mix in which races and nationalities were played against each other than they had before 1917, but also being held in reserve to be brought in during periods of national emergency or labor militancy and prized for a supposed loyalty to the company. With job prospects still concentrated in agriculture and domestic service, Africans and Mexicans were available for industrial work. The role of black strikebreakers in the Great Steel Strike of 1919 and 1920 is a particularly well-studied example of the results of such structural inequalities. In meatpacking as well, the African American worker, valued for his or her vulnerability, was credited with being "immune" to radicalism and labor unionism, with exhibiting more "plant loyalty," and with being there when needed. In 1926 *Industrial Psychology* posed a "practical question" asking: "Is the Negro more loyal than the white worker?" At about the same time, a packinghouse manager provided one answer:

> You know the foreigners we had were Bolsheviki, dangerous, radical. . . . They made up all sorts of trouble by thinking up dan-gerous plots against the country. They were just the kind of foreigners who would go out and listen to agitators and create a big disturbance and strike in America. . . . Therefore, the big business men in the stockyards got together. We sent our agents into the South, to Missis-sippi, Georgia, Alabama, and we paid Negroes to come and work in the stockyards. We had a terrible time with them, but we pulled through the war and the last strike . . . because we could count upon the black man.

As the personal assistant to the magnate and philanthropist Julius Rosenwald put it, "Negroes" were seen to be "far more adjustable than the foreign-born."[49] The realities were always more complex with extensive "white" strikebreaking and, soon enough, great employer fears of the radicalism of African Americans, but the perception lingered.[50]

Workers of color found slots in the worst jobs and often the ones most central to keeping the plants running—the killing floor in packing, the foundries in auto, and the furnaces in steel. As historian Paul Street writes, they "were lumped in the dirtiest, wettest, lowest-paid, and least secure jobs and departments in the stockyards." However, they also "took an unusual number and share of prized and middling skilled and semiskilled production jobs . . . positions on the all-important killing floors [and] exhausting knife jobs vital to the packers' feverish pursuit of 'uninterrupted production.'"[51]

Employers differed as to how to place African American workers to optimize the weakening of labor unity. Sometimes having black workers in the city working in other places in degraded jobs, or a long train ride from the South away, seemed insufficient to provide what was called "strike insurance." Regarding St. Louis, as Lorenzo J. Greene and Carter G. Woodson wrote in a study combining history and contemporary observations, employers "fortified themselves against strikes by intermixing Negro workers among their white laborers." This made for labor forces as much as a quarter or even a third black. According to an investigator, "Every large foundry in St. Louis employs enough Negroes to offset the likelihood of a damaging strike." But only exceptionally, as at that city's Scullin Steel factory, did this practice lead to broad placement of African Americans in jobs across the plant, including many tasks involving machinery and seen as skilled. In Detroit, at his flagship Rouge plant, but only there, Henry Ford broke color barriers astonishingly after World War I, pegging black employment at least at the level of the African American population in the Detroit area. He dramatically placed at least a few black workers in every department, though preponderantly in the hot, deadly foundry, fashioning a temporarily successful insurance policy against labor organization.[52]

When black workers found themselves in the hottest and most dangerous jobs, management often cited "racial" reasons. At the Fairbanks Morse plant in Beloit, Wisconsin, for example, it was maintained that "the dark pigment of the negro's skin made him less susceptible to high temperatures than a white foundry worker." In West Virginia's coal mines, an employer argued, "The best points of the colored coal loader are that he will work in wet places and . . . where the air is bad with less complaint than the white man." Immigrants will only stay to work in best places in mines, another mine boss said, while "the colored man . . . will work anywhere," though over time African American miners came to reject dangerous work. Those "best places" were less subject to foul air, explosions, and collapses and also presented more favorable conditions for extraction of coal and therefore higher pay.[53] In western Pennsylvania, steel mills' proximity to dangerous chemicals as well as to heat predicted the position of the African American worker in industry. Indeed, in both steel and auto, observers found that even the statistical smattering of skilled black workers could be accounted for in large measure by the presence of heat, harmful fumes, and danger around a few jobs defined as skilled. Often enough the manager's description of jobs open to African American workers ran: "work white men won't do."[54]

Such brutal realities, shaped by foremen, found scant appreciation in the formal managerial literature. The first and one of the fullest accounts of the black worker to appear in *Industrial Psychology* offered elaborate study of "work curves." It found the "white" worker steady through the day and week while black workers had "very high and very low spots." The article elaborately purported to measure long-standing employer concerns regarding "recuperation to normality on a Monday after a pay day." Just a few years after the IQ scares of World War I so zealously fixed on differences among European workers, a single, stable "white" category appeared, describing an "energetic race both mentally and physically." An early contributor to the field of industrial psychology, Daniel DeNoyelles, charted workplace performance by race but missed the exclusionary impact of race management on the options of African American workers. He noted that in one workplace, "The men who do the boresome task of wheeling the brick to the kiln are more than 75 percent negroes," while "delicate" kiln building is done by native whites and mused: "The negroes for the most part choose work which requires primarily bodily strength" as if all options were open to all workers.[55]

DeNoyelles did realize that for all his elaborate graphing and expertise the arbitrary power of foremen decisively impacted African American productivity. "White gangs," he wrote, "with white bosses do the best . . . work. Next in line came negro gangs with white foremen. Last would come . . . negro gangs with negro bosses." Black supervision of white workers was not imagined in the research agenda. Moreover, he continued in particularizing whiteness-as-management: "The native whites seem to be the best leaders and under their guidance both whites and negroes do [the] best work."[56] Black workers agreed that the "driving" of the foreman made a deep impression on their lives and knew that lower management helped to make layoffs fall hardest on them. They not infrequently registered particular problems with immigrant foremen. "I just can't stand being Jim-Crowed by one of those fellows," one West Virginia miner explained.[57]

An African American social scientist and an African American foundry worker most fully captured the contradictory dynamics of a system that was both opening up to black workers and subjecting them to newly concentrated forms of race management. The best compilation of pro-black worker managerial opinion, a 1927 article by the African American reformer and sociologist Charles Johnson, also best registered the limits to the opportunities accruing to African Americans as race managers concentrated on black workers. The litany of favorable opinion Johnson found among at least some managers was useful: "loyalty," "they follow instructions," "they are steady husky, workers," "can stand heat," "can do hard work," "possess physical strength," and "are trustworthy." But the language carried its own limits too. Black workers were, Johnson wrote, "wanted for rough work because they are 'husky' and 'cheerful,' and fitting satisfactorily into this, it follows in reasoning that in the division of work they are best fitted for rough work, and frequently are held to it by a carefully reasoned process. Their success in one field thus limits prospects for advancement into others."[58]

The politicized African American foundry worker Charles Denby, writing as Matthew Ward in the memoir *Indignant Heart*, provided the perfect counterpoint to Johnson. In securing his first Detroit job in the 1920s, Ward "asked the man if there were any jobs. He said, yes. I told him I preferred to work somewhere else when he told me to work in the foundry." Ward explained, "I had worked in a foundry in Anniston [Alabama]. I knew what the work was like. He said there were no other jobs open. When white men came in he told them about other jobs and hired them." Poles were another story. As Ward continued, "As I looked around, all the men [in the foundry] were dirty and greasy and all smoked up. They were beyond recognition. These were Polish. Negroes told me later they were the only ones able to stand the work. Their faces looked exactly like Negro faces." Both groups contended with "raring and hollering" foremen, the last word regarding keeping the job, even as Poles and African Americans fought bitterly along "racial" lines. Ward ended up wondering with a friend how Americans could talk about freedom. "There was no one in the foundry but Negroes," he observed, either forgetting Poles or considering them blackened decisively, before concluding, "We didn't believe those men wanted to be in the foundry." Elsewhere too black workers puzzled over the positions of eastern and southern European workers who "were treated almost like blacks, to a certain degree." Putting immigrants in that position served race managers well, even as the available numbers of newcomers declined.[59]

Mexican Workers: Field, Factory, and the Changing Focus of Race Management

Equally dramatic was the turn to Mexican labor as a subject of race management. When the Dillingham Commission undertook its congressional inquiry into immigration between 1907 and 1911, Mexicans ranked only twenth-eighth in numbers among the thirty-nine groups listed by investigators. Amidst the sometimes histrionic reports of the commission on southern and eastern Europeans, Mexican Americans drew comparatively little attention and concern, provoking nothing like the anxiety that the descriptions of Asian migrants reflected. Instead, migrants from Mexico were seen as "providing a fairly acceptable supply of labor in a limited area in which it is difficult to secure others." They did so without the "same detriment to labor conditions as is involved in the immigration of other races who work at comparatively low wages." Although not "easily assimilated," Mexicans were on this view happily prone to "return to their native land in a short time," leaving the borderlands agricultural jobs in which they were highly concentrated. So sanguine was the commission regarding Mexican labor that its last volume mentioned the southern U.S. border only in connection with preventing movement of the Chinese across it.[60] The Mexicans remained a "local labor issue" largely beyond the purview of national investigators and forces of surveillance. Even popularizers of eugenics spent little ink on Mexicans early in the twentieth century.[61]

The border states and counties in which Mexican workers resided in the greatest numbers saw white employers proclaim both their value and their degradation—indeed their value because of their degradation. According to one Texas land development company in 1915, "The great advantage of Mexican labor is its dependability. The men are expert farmers, competent, willing and contented. They hold their place without attempting to mingle socially with the Americans, and are segregated in their own districts and have their own schools and churches. The Mexican women assist the housewives with their work." On the other hand, and especially in the expanding cotton culture of Texas, segregation became elaborated and hardened, alongside considerable anti-Mexican violence. In California, the *Pacific Rural Press* gloried in the natural inclination of Mexican labor to return home as soon as work became scarce, performing the "homing pigeon stunt."[62]

By 1924 much had changed from the time of the Dillingham report, making Mexicans seem both more promising and more in need of surveillance as workers. In that year the Border Patrol began, developing mechanisms for pursuing and policing Mexicans long after they had crossed into the United States. The "race" and the presumed "illegality" of Mexicans became linked. The various phases of the Mexican Revolution, some of them characterized by anarchist labor militancy, and of resulting U.S. incursions into Mexico joined the panic over possible German-Mexican alliances in World War I in raising suspicions of Mexicans. However, the war and the 1924 immigration restrictions so cut the supply of European labor that Mexicans simultaneously became increasingly desired as potential industrial laborers, as well as agricultural ones. In the 1920s, Mexicans came to account for 50 percent of all formal deportations and 80 percent of "voluntary," but often coerced, ones. At the same time, northern recruiters avidly sought their labor, encouraging their migration from Mexico and from the repressive conditions in Texas.[63] Cities like Chicago almost overnight became extensions of a North American borderlands labor market, even as they changed that market. When the Dillingham Commission did its work, for example, Chicago's giant packinghouses were without Mexican workers; by 1929 one worker in sixteen in the two giant

Chicago packinghouses Paul S. Taylor surveyed was Mexican, far more than the proportion of many southern and eastern European nationalities within the labor force. In the two large steel plants Taylor studied in the Chicago-Gary area, Mexicans went from no presence in 1912 to over one worker in eleven in 1929, only a third less in their proportion of workers in the plants than African Americans were.[64]

The transformation of Mexican laborers involved not simply the switch from their being a "local labor" problem in agriculture to their being players in a national industrial labor market but rather the convergence of the two systems. Regional variations gave form to the process in which labor markets opened. On nine surveyed major western railroads, one-seventh of maintenance-of-way employees were Mexican in 1909—already a significant proportion—but within twenty years that proportion increased to about three in five. The pull of better conditions (and car ownership) associated with labor in the Midwestern beet fields ensured that the terrible conditions of Texas agriculture were not all that workers could imagine. Beet workers in the Midwest then increasingly found jobs in industry, if only parts of the year. Alternative job opportunities in agriculture also developed in booming areas, such as California's Imperial Valley.[65]

In agriculture, and to some extent in expanding railway maintenance work, Mexicans were judged much as Asian labor had been in previous episodes of infrastructural work and farm labor in the West. The desideratum was often to arrive at a single best "race" to do the work. Experts strove to to develop a convincing lore showing why the one group most available and willing to work under extreme conditions was the best to do so and was capable of becoming even better under tutelage of whites. Alternatively, a handful, or even just a pair, of such possible groups, paid and exploited differently, might compete with each other, as had been true on the Great Northern Railroad and increasingly came to be the case on Imperial Valley farms.[66]

Charles Collins Teague, powerful banker, leader of California growers, initiator of irrigation projects, and conduit between academia and agribusiness, illustrated prevailing managerial views when he used the forum of the *Saturday Evening Post* in a 1928 justification for retaining and expanding Mexican labor in the fields. He found white labor "constitutionally" unable to withstand the rigors of California agricultural work, with only one white Oklahoma migrant in fifty finishing a season's work in cotton production. Teague parried the charge that "itinerant Mexican laborers" were "undesirables" by situating them as central to the full "development" of the Southwest, in mining and railroading, but above all in the many branches of agriculture. Such usefulness was allegedly inborn. "Mexican casual labor," Teague wrote, "filled the requirements of the California farm as no other labor has in the past" because "the Mexican withstands high temperatures" and moves to new locales readily. Mexicans were also said to be adapted to "stoop crops" and "knee crops," requiring bending, an argument Midwest sugar producers would reprise. Geography likewise "naturally" dictated that Mexicans do not need "to be supported through the periods when there was no work to do" since they could go home.[67]

For others, the fit of the Mexican with U.S. agriculture verged on the providential. Teague's associate, Dr. George P. Clements of the Los Angeles Chamber of Commerce's Agricultural Department, advocated both unrestricted Mexican immigration and limits on wholesale repatriations to Mexico during the Great Depression. Clements brought race, alleged physiology, and work insistently together in finding farm labor ideal for Mexicans "due to their bending habits." (Elsewhere Clements more soberly held that area growers had simply few choices, being "totally dependent" on Mexico as a source of labor.) The upright-standing white worker, he added, remained "physically unable to adapt himself" to such work demands. A 1930 article titled "The Mexican Laborer and You," in the Chamber of Commerce journal *Nation's Business*, credited Mexicans as "fond of outdoor life" and as workers who "easily enter a nomadic mode of living" making them almost "natural" farmworkers. These virtues ensured that the "average American wage earner" could have "fresh vegetables and fruits . . . the year around," furnishing "our essential vitamin supply."[68]

However, these grand claims remained brittle, premised on supposed Mexican passivity, and rather transparently designed to defend against nativist calls for controls on Mexican immigration. Mexicans were perfect on the farms because they regularly moved away, because they were more "loyal," and less "independent" or "sassy."[69] When they failed to live up to their reputation, the turn against them could be sharp and brutal. Alongside a reputation for quietude and a knowledge that forces of state repression of immigrants could be used to enforce such a stance, employers simultaneously fretted that Mexicans gravitated to the Industrial Workers of the World, were schooled in anarchism in Mexico, and even tended to informally "strike" each Monday in renegotiating the week's labor agreements. Teague, so certain of Mexican suitability in 1928, became—thirteen years and dozens of Mexican strikes later—the hardest of hardline growers refusing to bargain in a long, bitter 1941 lemon workers' strike.[70] Moreover, in a massive survey of farm operators for the California governor's "Mexican Fact-Finding Committee," more than half of listed responses to why "other than white" labor was used hinged on necessity or narrow calculation: "Available," "Not enough white help," "Willing," or "Cheaper." While only a fourth of respondents preferred white labor, the more soaring formulations of growers' public spokespersons regarding Mexicans were absent and even "constitutional" endorsements like "steady," "more efficient," and "stand heat better" appeared relatively rarely.[71]

As both the 1930 governor's study and Taylor's superb late 1920s research on Mexican labor in the Imperial Valley show, no overarching and permanent choice of Mexican labor occurred. The labor question in Southwest agriculture remained very much a multiple choice one, at least in the growers' hopes. Teague could raise the specter of importing "Porto Rican negroes or Filipinos" as labor if the idealized, denigrated Mexican supply were limited by the government. Indeed, growers like him in fact did bring in a variety of workers whom Teague would have insisted were more "undesirable" than the Mexican. By 1930 Taylor could report that Imperial Valley farm labor "has come to mean Mexican (and some Filipino)" laborers taking the place of declining proportions of white and Japanese workers. American Indian labor from Arizona had also been tried and deemed "unsatisfactory," alongside experiments with "Hindus" and U.S. Southerners, white and black, accustomed to cotton cultivation.[72]

Thus the Mexican farmworker was not so much heralded as weighed against a variety of potential competitors. In sugar beets in Colorado in 1909, Japanese were said to tend over twice the number of acres worked by "German-Russians" and Mexicans; two decades later, all groups exceeded 1909 norms, though immigration policies and patterns, and some upward mobility into the ranks of growers, limited Japanese supply. Taylor found employers warming to the Mexican-born over "Russian-Germans," as they were alternatively called, and even over Hispanic New Mexicans long in the United States. But some ratio-making suggested otherwise: "One white man will do the work of three Mexicans." Another Colorado employer suggested the low bar for paternalistic race-development ideology. With Mexicans, he advised, "the stricter the better" since they were as a people "shiftless and live like animals but they can be educated."[73] Mexican workers had potential, but "required herding" in order for them to realize it. Elsewhere the leeway given to the manager by the relative powerlessness of Mexican workers structured preferences. Bosses would not have to be "too mealy mouthed," as they supposedly were with white workers.[74]

Conceding that white workers would not typically stay in "unat-tractive" jobs and camps and avoided "stoop" labor, agribusiness management increasingly compared farmworkers of color to each other, before an influx of "Okie" migrants briefly changed matters during the Depression. Filipino-to-Mexican comparisons occurred with special frequency and passion. The former were said to be too militant, while the latter were loyal in comparison not only to whites but also to Filipinos. On the other hand, after anti-Filipino riots in the Watsonville area threatened use of that pool of labor, some growers trumpeted Filipinos as allegedly more accepting of the status quo, in comparison to whites. They were "steadier, more tractable, and more willing to put up with longer hours, poorer board, and worse lodging facilities," California Department of Industrial Rela-tions investigators were told. As Lloyd Fisher wrote in the middle of the twentieth century, "To be sure the farmer has preferences, but these are racial preferences. The Filipino is preferred because Fili-pinos are presumed to be skilled agricultural workers." The "race"-connected skill of Filipinos to which Fisher referred was at times tied to particular crops, especially lettuce and asparagus. While Japanese and Mexican workers won praise as especially desirable, only the former's pay at times reflected such desirability, episodi-cally exceeding that of white workers. Such was not the case with Mexican workers, whose desirability remained connected instead to low wages.[75]

Even when describing immigrants long accepted in agricultural jobs in California and the Southwest, the new attention of managers, nativists, and eugenicists to Mexican immigrants could be dramatic. The California economist Glenn E. Hoover, publishing in *Foreign Affairs* in late 1929, led off with the claim that in Mexico itself not one person in ten was of "unmixed white blood," making the country "an Indian civilization with but a thin veneer of European culture." The Indians in Mexico were "docile, musical, and pious in . . . an alcoholic way." Preferring a Chinese labor force, Hoover nonetheless allowed that Mexican labor underlay "agricultural specialization" in California. Hoover ridiculed the idea that "squatting" by "the peon" to pick crops could count as a "racial accomplishment," observed that Europeans did cultivate sugar beets in Europe, and extravagantly questioned whether it actually got hot in Mexico, in order to deny that Mexican labor might be accustomed to surviving the summer sun. Above all he feared social and sexual mixing of "gringo" and "greaser."[76] The formerly "local" issue of Mexican agricultural immigration was becoming a national one, though with local dimensions. In 1930, *Nation's Business* ran a nativist screed by longtime anti-Catholic and anti-immigrant campaigner Thomas Nixon Carver who fretted over migration by Filipinos, Cubans, Canadians, and "West Indian negroes" nationally. The journal's editors reasserted the Chamber of Commerce's own position in a boxed insert accompanying Carver's article, with the insert defending immigration in the specific interests of "growers and farmers in the Southwest."[77]

The signal moments in the nationalization of the question of Mexican immigration intersected fully with changes in the places of migrants in regimes of race management. A 1917 exemption allowing admission of Mexican workers with the requirement for a literacy test being waived infuriated critics who feared the precedents being set as much as they feared Mexicans. Opponents believed Asian immigration regulations might next be liberalized. Secretary of Labor William B. Wilson, a former leader of the United Mine Workers, justified the move in terms of wartime necessities and as a way to resist pressure to admit Chinese and "Filipinos, Hawaiians and other labor of a similar character." The framing of the issue suggested that agricultural labor in limited geographic areas lay at the problem's core, but during the war Mexicans moved unprecedentedly into wage work beyond agriculture. Taylor's work on Chicago finds a seventeen-fold increase in Mexican employment at surveyed steel plants and a great rise in the packing industry between 1916 and 1920. These increases, and similar ones in track work on Midwestern railroads, came from very low bases, and last-hired, first-fired patterns ensured that three-fourths or more of the gains would be rolled back in postwar depressions. However, Mexican employment in the surveyed plants soon again exceeded the 1920 levels and by 1928 dwarfed them. An initial generation of Mexican workers had proven able to occupy a valuable niche in schema of race management: available in war and the postwar strike wave, disposable by virtue of an ability to return to beet cultivation, to Texas, or to Mexico during downturns, and available again with recovery.[78]

As migration from Europe stalled, Bethlehem Steel began to seek Mexicans, recruiting aggressively in Texas to implant a Mexican "colony" in the Pittsburgh area after 1923. To do so necessitated a measure of hopefulness, relatively fair treatment, and good publicity. The corporation wanted it known that it was "interested in [Mexicans] as human beings" as well as for purposes of "good business and good morals." Managers viewed the "industrial qualities" of Mexicans as "favorable," though they were "not always in entire agreement." Engaging in a series of comparisons, they pronounced Mexicans better workers than "Negroes," though below Hungarians and Europeans generally. Some bosses spoke of the colony residents as "a good class of men as a whole"and even spoke of them as superior workers to the "Slavish." One manager perhaps humorously added, "If some people think our Mexicans are dumb, they should see some of our Irish."[79]

At Bethlehem Steel and elsewhere outside agriculture, Mexicans moved to jobs in workplaces often employing scores rather than a handful of races and nationalities. They fit into an overall structure shaped by the treatment of new immigrants from southern and eastern Europe, but important differences applied. If employers were coming to prize retention of new immigrants, they valorized the mobility of workers at Bethlehem, citing the presence of "birds of passage" moving seasonally to the South, and acknowledging that the industrially injured could be returned to Texas, or even to Michoacán. Moreover, as Paul S. Taylor's generally favorable account of the Bethlehem colony allows, even Mexicans who came with skills typically stayed in unskilled jobs.

Sometimes the agricultural stereotyping that Mexicans tolerated heat sent them to the hardest and hottest jobs in steel as well. The appreciation for Mexicans cultivated by recruiters and upper management did not extend to dismantling a system of discrimination by foremen. One immigrant held, "There is no discrimination in the work made by the company or employment department. The *mayordomos* discriminate. If they have fifteen of their own nationality, and are told to lay off three men, they tell three Mexicans to go." Another added, "The *mayordomos* give preference to their own race, but the company is fair."[80]

At the national level, the race management patterns like those at Bethlehem Steel recurred with some consistency and significant variations. Mexican labor came to mean "unskilled" so much so that an immigrant reported in one account, "If you are a mechanic, they won't believe you if you say you are a Mexican." The opposite was more often true, with skilled Mexicans placed in unskilled job categories.[81] It was said in California construction and industry that Mexicans alone would "stay" or "stick" as against "shifting" whites. As one Chicago Mexican steelworker had it, "They give Mexicans the heavy work and the Poles the *suave* [easy] work with better pay." Such associations kept Mexicans out of skilled and semiskilled positions in some factories and out of other factories altogether. One Chicago wire manufacturer reported, "We use no Mexicans. We have more refined work and have not had to resort to the greasers." He associated Mexican "greasers" with "rough work and [work] around the blast furnace." Another employer in the same city agreed: "We want intelligent labor; that is why we don't use Mexicans." The connection of Mexicans with heat proved especially widespread and long-standing, making up for a perceived lack of reliability and even for physical weakness, in some cases. On the latter score, the idea of race development could carry nutritional dimensions with the theory being that the Mexican was malnourished at home but could be "fed up" to greater industrial productivity. In meatpacking, sometimes Mexicans received credit for being good at all temperature extremes, working well in freezers as well as in extreme heat.[82] At Sherwin-Williams Paint, a company doctor floated the notion that Mexicans also "constitutionally" possessed resistances to poisons. Mexican "pigmentation" protected against occupational diseases caused by working with paint. Mexican skin color somehow "hid" the poisonous nature of the chemicals involved.[83]

Mexican "loyalty," conditioned by repression, by lack of choices, or by having already chosen to leave more oppressive social relations in the countryside, could seem a virtue to industrial employers, especially during strikes. "Many employers," according to historian Gabriela Arredondo, "saw Mexican disenfranchisement and lack of labor power as a bonus."[84] Foremen decisively shaped Mexican work lives, often attempting to exploit their powerlessness. In one instance a foreman "asked his Mexican workers to work in his home garden and clean up around the house." He reportedly did not ask Irish or Italian workers and took it out on those Mexicans who said no. Another Chicago workplace proceeded on the assumption that "if a foreman don't know how to rawhide [Mexican workers], they just stand around," though with brutal discipline their productivity was good. Others doubted that the "pick handle" could effectively manage Mexicans, though there was no disagreement as to the centrality of the foreman.[85]

The specific comparisons to which Mexican workers were subjected as they came onto the U.S. industrial scene mapped the contours of immigration restriction. The comparisons showed the continuing practice of race management directed toward Europeans and above all registered the increasing concentration of race management onto workers of color. Management informants in Taylor's massive research projects measured Mexicans against "old immigrants" from northern and western Europe infrequently, as befitted the fact that such immigrants rarely worked alongside such immigrants. These occasional comparisons of Mexicans to Germans, the Irish, and Swedes favored the old immigrant groups. More contradictory and purposeful were comparisons to new immigrant groups, whose ability to enter the country was decimated by the 1924 restrictions but who still constituted much of the industrial labor force. Mexicans were "not so clannish" or "demanding" as the Italians on some accounts, and better workers than the Greeks. At one Chicago area rolling mill, the superintendent found that "foremen are getting to like the Mexicans" who "use showers more" than Poles and are better workers than Italians, making Mexicans "the best class of labor we get now." Other managers made it the majority view around Chicago that Mexicans were "superior to . . . southern Europeans." Dissenters termed them "slow and dull" as well as accident-prone, with "more than their proportion of fatalities." Others figured them "about like boys," and "not very intelligent," but still likely to develop enough to "move up from menial labor like the rest." Taylor observed that the power of individual foremen left workplaces divided on whether segregation or mixed work gangs were best, though mixture was the rule. He enigmatically noted, "The preference of management for different nationalities among its employees, for variety's sake," and let a manager spell out why variety mattered: "We try to keep them balanced; we seem to get along better that way." Any single nationality, even "Scotch," was bad.[86]

As old and new patterns of race management dictated, Mexicans were most frequently measured as workers against African Americans. In the South Platte Valley of Colorado, where Mexicans worked in sugar beets and in industry, they were said to be childlike "rascals," and "like the plantation Negroes." In Chicago, Mexican life intersected with the fortunes of African American workers frequently as both arrived in the post–World War I city in increasing numbers. The powerful Irish street gang Ragen's Colts terrorized both groups at a time when some writers characterized Mexicans as being "eugenically as low-powered as the negro." Slight advantages for Mexicans left them worried at times about being mistaken for blacks. One Chicago steel plant employment manager claimed he could detect "Negro blood" in those passing as Mexicans, maintaining "they seem to be thicker through the temples." Mexicans in some "downtown" jobs meanwhile attempted to claim a Spanish identity. At the city's Wisconsin Steel plant, which did not hire black workers, the manager brought "in light-colored Mexicans to keep as far away from the color line as possible." The patterns were sufficiently varied to permit optimism, as in sociologist Charles Johnson's *The Negro in American Civilization* (1930), which found African American relations with Mexicans worthy of comment, though not alarm. According to Johnson, "As yet there is little [African American–Mexican] actual competition, the Mexicans taking the least desirable jobs, pushing up the Negroes one grade as the Negroes in turn pushed up the foreign born, who in turn pushed up the native whites."[87]

Increasingly competing with each other for what an official at Fisher Body, a division of General Motors, called the "hot dirty jobs," Mexicans and African Americans underwent constant comparative scrutiny as they were paired for judgment by managers who avoided both final positions and the kinds of set patterns Johnson's remarks suggested.[88]

In Midwestern track labor, Taylor's informants ranked Mexicans against and above "hoboes and Negroes." Those managers offering a comparison with "niggers" predictably favored Mexicans. In packing, Mexicans were said to be "not as adept with the knife as the colored," but their willingness to work amidst fertilizer counted as an advantage. In coke ovens, black workers seemed to some managers to withstand heat even better than Mexicans.[89] Here again diversity of opinion was not necessarily naïve or inapt. Variously treated and considered, black and Mexican workers competed for jobs in a system of concentrated race management designed to divide and drive them. One foundry specifically reported introducing Mexicans "to dilute colored labor." Management at the very plant that abjured segregated gangs nonetheless reported, "We have Negroes and Mexicans in competition with each other"—admittedly on the manager's own view a "dirty trick" but good policy.[90]

Such a formulation reflected long, destructive, and broad practices that had helped to produce the miracle of U.S. economic ascendancy between 1830 and 1930, newly concentrated in a particular way around narrower definitions of race. After 1924, such a system could not manage the world's workers against each other because it had given up on strategies to secure future supplies of European immigrants whose differences might be exploited. Given bars on most Asian immigration and the paucity of arrivals from Africa and elsewhere, new and broader systems of race management would be a long while in coming, though the idea of playing races against each other held tenaciously on, especially applying to workers of color.

AFTERWORD: THEN AND NOW

THROUGH MOST OF U.S. HISTORY, the act of discriminating was considered a hallmark of good judgment and even taste, positively applied to everything from aesthetic discernment, to moral choice, to financial prudence, to charitable giving, to intelligent shopping. Proslavery and antislavery advocates regularly accused the other side of lacking powers of discrimination with one advocate for slavery charging the abolitionists with being so lacking in the ability to discriminate that they could not separate "civilization and savagism." Elsewhere the defense of bondage took the form of the accusation that the North was "discriminating" against slave labor. The upper reaches of race management set out be discriminating, making calculating choices in the slave market and in the racialized markets for free labor. They had little reason to deny that they had such a goal.[1]

Today racial discrimination not only stands outside the law but also seemingly cuts against the grain of a vast managerial literature that preaches the virtues of diversity. Something changed but some things also have not.[2] Today's employers profess to reject discrimination not just because of the law, but because they see how diversity produces value.[3] Yet discussing the history of race and management with labor organizers and workers produces contemporary stories about how aptly race management describes the experiences of workers in meatpacking and hotel and restaurant service work—jobs where the workforce is now made of African American, African, Asian, Irish, Bosnian, West

Indian, eastern European, and Central American and Mexican workers. Activists relay stories of recent struggles in these workplaces in which management associates diversity with value in a far more traditional and troubling way, using difference and division to create surplus value, relying on the kind of methods described in this book's chapters on the early twentieth century.

This book is very much a work of history. It tells a story with a beginning and an end. There were compelling reasons for the choices regarding where the study was to start and where it was to conclude. The beginning, after some earlier background, is in the 1830s, with the rise of a slave management literature and a massive commodity-producing plantation economy that led to significant U.S. participation in world trade and to expanded industrial production. Our attempts to understand race management end with a discussion of the 1924 restriction of immigration and the impact of such restriction through about 1930. The tumultuous century under consideration, examined in every section and transnationally, makes the study a very ambitious one. At the start of the period, the United States was a secondary player in the world economy. At the end it was the world's largest producer. To restore slavery and especially race management to the story of this transformation is one aim of the book. The time frame further fits our scholarly expertise and allows for a compact book. Moreover, such an early end point does provide entry to some of the patterns with which we live. That is, it was during World War I and the two decades after it when management could no longer imagine itself as enduringly able to premise much of its activity on playing European "races" against each other, and began to "concentrate" race management onto African Americans and recently arrived immigrants of color, especially Mexicans.

But lines from past to present are not straight. While the early 1930s did resemble the 2010s in that race management overwhelmingly focused on people of color, the comparison also obscures differences. Such differences include the rise of managerial liberalism where race is concerned but also strong countervailing tendencies. In many ways, race management today more nearly resembles the high tide of new immigration of the European poor in the first fifteen years of the twentieth century than it does that of the late 1920s. As in that earlier period, management has not a handful but a host of racialized groups available to play against each other, groups also separated by citizenship status, religion, legality, and language.

Significant breaks came in the middle and later 1930s and the 1940s, when powerful industrial unions and the seniority systems for which they fought limited the arbitrary power of foremen to boss, curse, hire, and fire along most lines, including racial and ethnic ones. Especially protecting eastern and southern Europeans, with a far more uneven commitment to Latino and black workers, industrial unions helped solidify the idea that a large group of "whites" were being managed alongside African Americans, Mexicans, Filipinos, Puerto Ricans, and less populous immigrant groups.[4] The introduction of displaced persons after World War II, accompanied by much ideological work to establish their "whiteness," continued this pattern while the Bracero Program to bring in temporary Mexican workers ineligible for citizenship introduced new status distinctions within racial and legal categories. However, as late as the 1960s, it was still possible to imagine race management as a rather simple affair in terms of the groups involved. When a group of largely black workers organized against technologically driven speedups in automobile production around a sophisticated critique of what they called "niggermation," the shop-floor experience of race and management in industrial production could not have been shown more clearly. The cumulative results of 1965 legislative reforms accepting immigration without discrimination based on the race of people in the sending nation, along with openings to refugees, made the immigrant working class much larger, more divided in its relations to the state, and more plural in its origins. Unions likewise became far less present in private sector workplaces and less able to powerfully and effectively defend against the abuses of race management.[5]

Race management thus continues in the present and needs to be understood in terms of connections with, as well as distance from, the past. Such management is more than ever part of a global pattern and is especially favored in the most rapidly developing areas in the world, for example, the United Arab Emirates and Singapore. In such areas management draws on U.S. examples to get out production by recruiting from many nations and "races," producing what economist Nigel Harris has called the "instant cosmopolitan work force."[6] The work that goes into provisioning soldiers and building infrastructure during and after U.S. wars is no longer done by servicemen and women, having typically become the dangerous labor of divided workers from impoverished regions of the world. "Foreign contractors" have been one key to creating a "disposable army," which is more easily abandoned in adversity.[7] In the United States, the continuing and accelerating examples of race management's application—in agribusiness, in skilled jobs like nursing, laboratory, and computer work for which special exceptions are made in immigration law, in chemical plants, in meatpacking, in serving the U.S. armed forces, and in cleaning hotels and in working in restaurants and casinos—make it matter deeply today.[8] In many of these sectors the rhetoric of "diversity management" resonates with earlier twentieth-century claims by management to be able to "develop" immigrant and minority workers.

There is no better example of new realities for unions, management, and workers than the meatpacking industry, so long associated with race management. To take just one example, not long ago, Beardstown, Illinois, and nearby Rushville were "sundown towns," as well as meatpacking centers. Law enforcement, community practice and, according to oral history, a stark signboard warning off black visitors combined to keep African Americans out of these west-central Illinois towns after dark. The area's meatpacking industry, anchored by an Oscar Mayer factory, provided jobs to many of the white workers in the two towns. After Oscar Mayer decided to abandon the area in 1986, Beardstown courted the Cargill Corporation to run a giant pork-processing plant, attracting it with big tax breaks, a free enterprise zone, and a wage cut of over 25 percent. A much-chastened union further allowed a tremendous speedup on the pork-processing line. At first jobs went to local workers, including some formerly at Oscar Mayer. Beardstown mayor Bob Walters, a ham boner at Oscar Mayer and longtime United Food and Commercial Workers Union representative, took pride in keeping the jobs for "Americans," but not for African Americans. "Hispanics and blacks," he warned, undermined labor standards. A small number of workers of color had tried to work in Beardstown before 1989. As one white worker told a reporter, "There was [sic] very few coloreds and very few Mexicans. Every time we'd try to tell them to do something, they'd look at us stupid. So we'd start harassing them and they'd quit."[9]

But the very brutality of the factory did the work of multicultur-alism. With a hog being killed every 4.5 seconds, repetitive stress injuries and accidents sent labor turnover to 100 percent annually by the mid-1990s, as workers' compensation claims skyrocketed. Long associations of race management with dangerous work resurfaced. Latino and then African immigration accelerated in Beardstown as meatpacking became what Human Rights Watch has called the most dangerous U.S. factory job. As Reuters recently explained to its transnational audience, "A large portion of [U.S.] meat industry workers are immigrants, mainly Hispanics, because of difficulties filling positions that involve fast-paced and dirty work." By 2006 Cargill Meat Solutions slaughtered eighteen thousand hogs daily in Beardstown and at its twin plant in Ottumwa, Iowa—one every three seconds—with a Beardstown workforce that was 43 percent immigrant, aggressively recruited from multiple nations.[10] The corporation universalized labor and turned it into motions made in a frantic series in cold factories. Ottumwa or Beardstown, West African or Mexican, Honduran or Illinois farm boy, the "abstract labor," as Marx would have it, was interchangeable.[11]

Cargill increasingly sought not just impoverished workers but also divided ones. French-speaking West and Central Africans, mostly Togo-lese but also Senegalese, Congolese, Burkinabe, and Beninese, make up nearly 10 percent of Rushville's three thousand residents. Cargill's Latino workers, largely Mexican, but also Dominican, Cuban, and Central American, outnumber Africans in the plant by about 4 to 1. Vietnamese and Filipino workers also labor at Cargill. Language—French, Spanish, and English—religion, and legal status (Mexican workers are some-times undocumented and Africans typically are immigration lottery winners) further divide workers. Africans process some of their griev-ances regarding pace, danger, bathroom breaks, and cold in the factory as a problem with more experienced white and Latino workers and supervisors, even as remarkable solidarities develop in and out of work. In April 2007, immigration authorities raided the plant, arresting over sixty workers employed by a sanitation services subcontractor. Even with joblessness high in Illinois, the company still sends labor recruiters to far-flung areas of high unemployment overseas. Recently recruiting forays to Puerto Rico introduced a group of workers with yet another relation to citizenship and nationality.[12]

Such new and all-too-familiar dynamics apply in other sectors as well. There are signs of the erosion of race management, at least in its traditional forms. "Whiteness-as-management" no longer so literally applies as lower management is not infrequently African American or Latino from private employment to the armed forces. The white citizen-manager is no longer the ultimate authority at workplaces like Anheuser-Busch's large breweries, for example, where ownership is Belgian and important positions in upper management are overwhelmingly filled by Brazilians.[13] On the other hand, the messages conveyed by more diverse managers do not necessarily threaten the continued practice of race management. At one Chicago factory studied recently, a Mexican American manager appealed for obedience from a largely Latino labor force by balancing emphases on the pressures he got from whites above him in the company's hierarchy with references to the fate of black workers in the plant, who had made demands and lost jobs. Similarly marked by a new fluidity that often proved unable to dislodge old patterns was the position of trade unions. At least formally, organized labor moved to a much more pro-immigrant position after 1990. It connected workers' rights and immigrant rights, creating new possibilities for concerted actions against management attempts at dividing workers by race and nationality. Examples of such actions include the multinational Minneapolis hotel strike of 2000, and more recent union successes, after wildcat strikes against immigration raids and sexual harassment, unifying Latino and African American workers in hog processing at Smithfield's Tar Heel, North Carolina, plant. But such exemplary struggles remain few and far between.[14]

Compared to slavery or to the experiences of Chinese workers in the late nineteenth century, legally migrating workers now come to the United States with an expectation that they bear rights. Indeed, skilled workers and international students have had reason to believe that they are sought after and welcomed by the U.S. state. However, the suspicion and mass deportation of Mexican workers, and the numbers of deaths in the desert when they try to return, along with widespread suspicions of Arab and Islamic labor migrants and students after 9/11 complicate this picture. Indeed, even programs for educational diversity can prove uncomfortably close to government facilitation of race management by industry. In August 2011, hundreds of young people from all over the world walked off their jobs to protest long and disabling labor at a chocolate factory producing Hershey's products. From the Ukraine, Turkey, Nigeria, Romania, China, and elsewhere they held J-1 travel visas for cultural and educational exchanges but reportedly ended up doing cheap labor and little else in a telling meeting of diversity programs and race management.[15]

Above all, race management has changed, again in uncertain directions, with the increased velocity and ease with which capital moves and causes jobs—and thus people—to move in the world. The disciplining effect of playing races and nationalities against each other can now work across oceans and continents. In the first decade of the twenty-first century, for example, call centers addressing the customer-service needs of U.S. consumers moved in large measure to south Asia. The labor involved, often also well versed in technical matters bearing on servicing electronic products, was said to be cheaper and better. By 2010, the trend shifted as "burnout" of call-center workers spiked in India and as new opportunities for skilled workers there developed. Workers in the Philippines became one newly favored labor force in the industry and some call center jobs returned to the United States, now also offering low wages. Thus management succeeded not only in shifting jobs to cheaper areas but also in shifting conditions of jobs in the United States. Similarly, the use of race management during strikes now operates on new geographic scales and with increased velocity. The 2011 Communications Workers of America strike against Verizon saw management threaten almost immediately to send unionized customer-service jobs to India and to the Philippines.[16]

None of these realities suggest that great changes in the conditions and discourse of race management portend an end to that system. Arguably the most important legal decision on race and labor in the last thirty-five years protected its practice. Growing out of a dispute in Alaska in the salmon-canning industry, the landmark 1989 U.S. Supreme Court decision in *Wards Cove Packing Co. v. Atonio* saw a conservative 5–4 majority rule that the patterns of overwhelming concentration of Alaska Native, Filipino, Samoan, and Chinese labor in seasonal cannery work and of whites in "noncannery" white-collar and managerial jobs—a "racially stratified" pattern of "disparate impact"—lacked the probative value prior Title VII cases on discrimination had allowed. The court found in favor of a system of playing races against each other and endorsed an identification of whiteness with management as being no cause for suspicion of anything out of the ordinary.[17]

Given the increased transnational flows of work and of workers, and the advantages to powerful employers who were able to hire workers divided with regard to legality, race, and citizenship, it seems unlikely that there will be top-down policy changes that undermine race management. Such changes would require great transformations in the U.S. political economy and in structures of power. They are neither foreseeable nor likely to be possible if the movements involved spend energies attacking the ability of migrants to work. The localized examples of labor solidarity across racial and national lines during the last dozen years, and the large nationwide civil rights demonstrations by immigrant communities, are likely to define forward motion toward the dismantling of race management. The global economic and political realities that shape these struggles will continue to collide with the long and peculiar history of race, management, and the production of difference in U.S. capitalism.[18]

NOTES

———∞∞∞———

Introduction

1. The cartoon is included in Ernest Riebe, *Mr. Block: Twenty-Four IWW Cartoons*, Franklin Rosemont, ed. (Chicago: Charles H. Kerr, 1984), unpaginated and was published originally in Ernest Riebe, *Twenty-Four Cartoons of Mr. Block* (Minneapolis, MN: Block Supply Company, 1913), unpaginated. For the context of the cartoon, see David Roediger, *Towards the Abolition of Whiteness: Essays on Race, Politics, and Working Class History* (London: Verso, 1994), 143–45 and Michael Cohen, " 'Cartooning Capitalism': Radical Cartooning and the Making of American Popular Radicalism in the Early Twentieth Century," *International Review of Social History* 52 (2007): 35–58; for the multiple ways in which immigrant workers were kept "on trial" in this period, see David R. Roediger, *Working toward Whiteness: How America's Immigrants Became White* (New York: Basic, 2005), esp. 57–92.

2. *Lumberjack*, January 12, 1913.

3. John R. Commons, *Races and Immigrants in America* (New York: Macmillan, 1907), 150. Commons on scientific management is as quoted in Samuel Haber, *Efficiency and Uplift: Scientific Management in the Progressive Era, 1890–1920* (Chicago: University of Chicago Press, 1964), 148; see also Yngve Ramstad and James L. Starkey, "The Racial Theories of John R. Commons," *Research in the History of Economic Thought and Methodology* 13 (1195): 1–75; Chris Nyland, "Taylorism, John R. Commons, and the Hoxie Report," *Journal of Economic Issues* 30 (December 1996): 985–1016 provides an account of Commons's relations to scientific management and to Frederick Winslow Taylor himself, around the issues of trade unionism and restriction of output.

4. John R. Commons, *Industrial Goodwill* (New York: McGraw-Hill, 1919), 14 and 13–15.

5. Karl Marx and Friedrich Engels, *Manifesto of the Communist Party* (1848) at http://www.anu.edu.au/polsci/marx/classics/manifesto.html; Marx, "Notebook Three," *The Grundrisse* (1857) at http://www.marxists.org/archive/marx/works/1857/grundrisse/cho6.htm; Harry Braverman, *Labor and Monopoly Capital: The Degradation of Work in the 20th Century* (New York: Monthly Review Press, 1975); Antonio Gramsci, "Americanism and Fordism," in *Selections from the Prison Notebooks* (New York: International, 1971), 71, 287, and 279–318. Cf. C. L. R. James, *American Civilization*, Anna Grimshaw and Keith Hart, eds. (Cambridge, MA: Blackwell, 1993), 173–79 (on Ford) and 181–85. For the specific ways that this study emerges from parts of the Marxist tradition, see Elizabeth Esch and David Roediger, "Race and the Management of Labor in U.S. History," *Historical Materialism* 17 (2009): 3–43.

6. Edna Bonacich, "The Split Labor Market: A Theory of Ethnic Antagonism," *American Sociological Review* 37 (October 1972): 547–59; Bonacich, "Advanced Capitalism and Black/White Labor Relations in the United States: A Split Labor Market Interpretation," *American Sociological Review* 41 (February 1976): 34–51.

7. Selig Perlman in John R. Commons et al., *History of the Labour Movement in the United States*, 4 vols. (New York: Macmillan, 1918–1935), 2: 252–53. See also Andrew Gyory, *Closing the Gate: Race, Politics and the Chinese Exclusion Act* (Chapel Hill: University of North Carolina Press, 1998), 11–12.

8. On dating of the origins of management, see Daniel Nelson, *Managers and Workers: Origins of the Twentieth-Century Factory System in the United States, 1880–1920* (Madison: University of Wisconsin Press, 1996), 50 and passim.

9. Alexander Saxton, *The Indispensable Enemy: Labor and the Anti-Chinese Movement in California* (Berkeley: University of California Press, 1975); Ronald Takaki, *Pau Hana: Plantation Life in Hawaii, 1835–1920* (Honolulu: University of Hawaii Press, 1983); Bruce Nelson, *Divided We Stand: American Workers and the Struggle for Black Equality* (Princeton, NJ: Princeton University Press, 2001) and Moon-Kie Jung, *Reworking Race: The Making of Hawaii's Interracial Labor Movement* (New York: Columbia University Press, 2006); on the new South, see the acute work of Brian Kelly in his *Race, Class, and Power in the Alabama Coalfields, 1908–21* (Urbana: University of Illinois Press, 2001); Gerald David Jaynes, *Branches without Roots: Genesis of the Black Working Class in the American South, 1862–1882* (New York: Oxford University Press, 1986); Eric Arnesen, *Black Railroad Workers and the Struggle for Equality* (Cambridge, MA: Harvard University Press, 2002), 5–83; Joe Trotter, *Coal, Class, and Color: Blacks in Southern West Virginia, 1915–1932* (Urbana: University of Illinois Press, 1990); and Grace Hong, *The Ruptures of American Capital: Women of Color Feminism and The Culture of Immigrant Labor* (Minneapolis: University of Minnesota Press, 2006).

10. Dipesh Chakrabarty, "Universalism and Belonging in the Logic of Capital," *Public Culture* 12 (2000): 652–76; Michael A. Lebowitz, "The Politics of Assumption, the Assumption of Politics," *Historical Materialism* 14 (2006): 29–47, with quoted passage on 39.

11. Lisa Lowe, *Immigrant Acts: On Asian American Cultural Politics* (Durham, NC: Duke University Press, 1996), 27–28; Paul A. Silverstein, "Immigrant Racialization and the New Savage Slot: Race, Migration, and Immigration in the New Europe," *Annual Review of Anthropology* 34 (2005): 364. See also the commentary on what has been translated as "primitive accumulation" and the longer run of capitalism in Massimiliano Tomba, "Historical Temporalities of Capital: An Anti-Historicist Perspective," *Historical Materialism* 17 (2009): 51–56, esp. 55; Karen Brodkin, "Global Capitalism: What's Race Got to Do with It?" *American Ethnologist* 27 (2000): 238–56 and David Kazanjian's *The Colonizing Trick: National Culture and Imperial Citizenship in Early America* (Minneapolis: University of Minnesota Press, 2003), esp. 15 and 227, n33.

12. Roediger, *Working toward Whiteness*, esp. 2–34.

13. For Marx and the capitalist "personality" as against labor, see Karl Marx, *Pre-Capitalist Economic Formations* (New York: International, 2000), 118.

14. Karl Marx, *Capital: A Critique of Political Economy*, vol. 1 (Chicago: Charles H. Kerr, 1906), 364 (parenthetical additions in original).

15. James O. Breeden, ed., *Advice among Masters: The Ideal in Slave Management in the Old South* (Westport, CT: Greenwood, 1980), 44 for "scientifically" and passim; R. Keith Aufhauser, "Slavery and Scientific Management," *Journal of Economic History* 33 (December 1973): 811–24; Ken Lawrence, "Karl Marx on American Slavery" at http://www.sojournertruth.net/marxslavery.pdf.

16. William Cronon, *Changes in the Land: Indians, Colonists, and the Ecology of New England* (New York: Hill and Wang, 1983) and Carolyn Merchant, *Ecological Revolution: Nature, Gender, and Science in New England* (Chapel Hill: University of North Carolina Press, 1989).

17. Robert J. Miller and Jacinta Ruru, *An Indigenous Lens into Comparative Law: The Doctrine of Discovery in the United States and New Zealand* (Portland, OR: Lewis and Clark Legal Research Papers Series, no. 7, 2008); Robert J. Miller, "The Doctrine of Discovery in American Indian Law," *Idaho Law Review* 42 (2006): 1, 104–17; Cheryl Harris, "Whiteness as Property," *Harvard Law Review* 106 (1993): 1707–91.

18. Mechal Sobel, *The World They Made Together: Black and White Values in Eighteenth-Century Virginia* (Princeton, NJ: Princeton University Press, 1987), 48; Ira Berlin, "Time, Space, and the Evolution of Afro-American Society on British Mainland North America," *American Historical Review* 85 (February 1980): 55; Don Jordan and Michael Walsh, *White Cargo: The Forgotten History of Britain's White Slaves in America* (New York: New York University Press, 2007), 14–15 and 172–75. Theodore Allen, *The Invention*

of the White Race, 2 vols. (New York: Verso, 1994); Edmund Morgan, *American Slavery, American Freedom: The Ordeal of Colonial Virginia* (New York: Norton, 2003); Ethan A. Schmidt, "The Right to Violence: Customary Rights, Moral Economy, and Ethnic Conflict in Seventeenth Century Virginia" (PhD diss., University of Kansas, 2007).

19. The quotation is from Ira Berlin, "From Creole to African: Atlantic Creoles and the Origins of African American Society in Mainland North America," *William and Mary Quarterly* 53 (April 1996): 252; Barbara Jeanne Fields, *Slavery and Freedom on the Middle Ground: Maryland during the Nineteenth Century* (New Haven, CT: Yale University Press, 1985), 164.

20. See Ulrich Bonnell Phillips, "The Slave Labor Problem in the Charleston District," *Political Science Quarterly* 22 (September 1907): 419 and 422, wherein the "problem" and opportunity were seen as arising from the fact that so many slaves were "relatively intelligent," an insight Phillips cannot pursue.

21. John R. Commons et al., *A Documentary History of American Industrial Society*, 10 vols. (New York: Russell and Russell, 1909; repr. 1958), 2: 52–53 and 129; Berlin, "Time, Space, and the Evolution of Afro-American Society," 47; Judith Ann Carney, *Black Rice: The African Origins of Rice Cultivation in the Americas* (Cambridge, MA: Harvard University Press, 2001); Karen A. Bell, "Rice, Resistance, and Forced Transatlantic Communities: (Re)envisioning the African Diaspora in Low Country Georgia, 1750–1800," *Journal of African American History* 95 (Spring 2010): 166–82; Michael A. Gomez. *Exchanging Our Country Marks: The Transformation of African Identities in the Colonial and Antebellum South* (Chapel Hill: University of North Carolina Press, 1998); Lorena S. Walsh, *Motives of Honor, Pleasure, and Profit: Plantation Management in the Colonial Chesapeake, 1607–1763* (Chapel Hill: University of North Carolina Press for the Omohundro Institute of Early American History and Culture, 2010), 259–62 and 359; Stephanie E. Smallwood, *Saltwater Slavery: A Middle Passage from Africa to American Diaspora* (Cambridge, MA: Harvard University Press, 2007), esp. 153–81.

22. Paul Thomas Bonfiglio, *Race and the Rise of Standard American* (Berlin: Mouton de Gruyter, 2002), 75–78 contains a fine discussion and the Franklin quotations; Philip Gleason, "Trouble in the Colonial Melting Pot," *Journal of American Ethnic History* 20 (Fall 2000): 3–17.

23. Emma Christopher, *Slave Ship Sailors and Their Captive Cargoes, 1730–1807* (Cambridge: Cambridge University Press, 2006), 82–83; see also 52 and 72–73; Jeffrey Bolster, *Black Jacks: African American Seamen in the Age of Sail* (Cambridge, MA: Harvard University Press, 1997), 102–30; Kazanjian, *Colonizing Trick*, 39–47.

24. Tamara Spike, "St. Augustine's Stomach: Corn and Indian Tribute Labor in Spanish Florida" in Robert Cassanello and Melanie Shell-Weiss, eds.,

Florida's Working-Class Past (Gainesville: University Press of Florida, 2009), 25.

25. Martha C. Knack, *Native Americans and Wage Labor: Ethnohistorical Perspectives* (Norman: University of Oklahoma Press, 1996); Toni Morrison, *A Mercy* (New York: Knopf, 2008), 52; John Morris, "Capitalism into the Wilderness: Mountain Men and the Expansion of Capitalism into the Northern Rockies, 1807–1843" (PhD diss., University of Missouri, 1993); Daniel H. Usner, Jr., *Indian Work: Language and Livelihood in Native American History* (Cambridge, MA: Harvard University Press, 2009), 26 and 18–41. See also Matt Wray, *Not Quite White: White Trash and the Boundaries of Whiteness* (Durham, NC: Duke University Press, 2006), 21–46; Rachel Klein, *Unification of a Slave State: The Rise of the Planter Class in the South Carolina Back Country, 1760–1808* (Chapel Hill: University of North Carolina Press, 1990), 51–62.

Chapter 1

1. W. E. B. Du Bois, *Black Reconstruction in America, 1860–1880* (New York: Free Press, 1998, originally 1935), 38–41.

2. Ulrich Bonnell Phillips, *American Negro Slavery: A Survey of the Supply, Employment and Control of Negro Labor as Determined by the Plantation Regime* (New York: D. Appleton, 1918), 261.

3. John R. Commons et al., *A Documentary History of American Industrial Society*, 10 vols. (New York: Russell and Russell, 1958, originally 1909), 1: esp. 110–31; Ulrich B. Phillips, "The Central Theme in Southern History," *American Historical Review* 34 (October 1928): 30–43.

4. Phillips, *American Negro Slavery*, 52 and 261–90; Ulrich Bonnell Phillips, *Life and Labor in the Old South* (Boston: Little, Brown, 1963, originally, 1929), 305.

5. For a literature beginning to address this history, see Bill Cooke, "The Denial of Slavery in Management Studies," *Journal of Management Studies* 40 (December 2003): 1895–1918; Richard Fleischman and Thomas Tyson, "Accounting in Service to Racism: Monetizing Slave Property in the Antebellum South," *Critical Perspectives on Accounting* 15 (April 2004): 376–99; Alan Olmstead and Paul Rhode, "Biological Innovation and Productivity Growth in the Antebellum Cotton Economy," *Journal of Economic History* 68 (December 2008): 1123–71.

6. Thanks to Zachary Sell who did much of the digital searching here. The volumes included were *Farmer's Register* (1833–1843), *Southern Planter* (1841–1866), *De Bow's Review* (1850–1864), *Southern Cultivator* (1843–1866), and *American Cotton Planter* (1853, 1854, 1855, and 1857).

7. Weymouth T. Jordan, "Noah B. Cloud and the *American Cotton Planter*," *Agricultural History* 31 (October 1957): 44–49; James O. Breeden, ed., *Advice among Masters: The Ideal in Slave Management in the Old South* (Westport, CT: Greenwood, 1980); W. M. Mathew, "Edmund Ruffin and

the Demise of the *Farmers' Register*," *Virginia Magazine of History and Biography* 94 (January 1986): 3–24.

8. J. W. Pitts, "Best Method of Managing Negroes," *Southern Cultivator* [hereafter *SC*] 18 (October 1860): 325–26; S. A. "Management of Negroes," *SC* 18 (July 1860): 214; Hurricane, "The Negro and His Management," *SC* 17 (September 1860): 276–77; cf. Agricola, "Management of Negroes," *SC* 13 (June 1855): 171–74; Editor's note, *American Cotton Planter* [hereafter *ACP*] 1 (December 1853): 370. The black worker and cotton masthead begins with *ACP* 2 (August 1854), replacing one with a rake, a plough, and a plant."

9. Steve G. Collins, "System, Organization, and Agricultural Reform in the Antebellum South, 1840–1860," *Agricultural History* 75 (Winter 2001): 8–9 ("accountability"); Alan L. Olmstead and Paul W. Rhode, " 'Wait a Cotton Pickin' Minute!' A New View of Slave Productivity" (August 2005) at http://www.unc.edu/~prhode/Cotton_Pickin.pdf.

10. Edmund Ruffin, *Nature's Management: Writings on Landscape and Reform, 1822–1859*, Jack Temple Kirby, ed. (Athens: University of Georgia Press, 2000), 330.

11. Sally Hadden, *Slave Patrols: Law and Violence in Virginia and the Carolinas* (Cambridge, MA: Harvard University Press, 2001). The volumes were of *Farmers' Register* (1833, 1839, 1840, and 1841), *American Cotton Planter* (1854 and 1855), and *De Bow's Review* (1852, 1853, and 1860). The lone relevant citation is A. Roane, "The South, in the Union or out of It," *De Bow's Review* [hereafter *DR*] 29 (October 1860): 459. [Note that *De Bow's Review* slightly changed titles over the years but we cite all as *DR*.]

12. Robin Blackburn, *The Making of New World Slavery: From the Baroque to the Modern 1492–1800* (London: Verso, 1998), 565. Cf. Silvia Federici, *Caliban and the Witch: Women, the Body and Primitive Accumulation* (Brooklyn, NY: Autonomedia, 2004), 104, where Federici writes, "The plantation system was crucial for capitalist development not only because of the immense amount of surplus labor that was accumulated from it but because it set a model of labor management."

13. Walter Rodney, *How Europe Underdeveloped Africa* (Washington, DC: Howard University Press, 1974); Karen Brodkin, "Global Capitalism: What's Race Got to Do with It?" *American Ethnologist* 27 (2000): 245.

14. Robert Starobin, *Industrial Slavery in the Old South* (New York: Oxford University Press, 1971), 11–14; John Bezis-Selfa, "A Tale of Two Ironworks: Slavery, Free Labor, Work, and Resistance in the Early Republic," *William and Mary Quarterly* 56 (October 1999): 679; Seth Rockman, "The Unfree Origins of American Capitalism," in Cathy Matson, ed., *The Economy of Early America* (University Park: Pennsylvania State University Press, 2006), esp. 359–60.

15. Noel Ignatiev, *How the Irish Became White* (New York: Routledge, 1998); David R. Roediger, *The Wages of Whiteness: Race and the Making of the*

American Working Class (London: Verso, 1991); and Starobin, *Industrial Slavery*. For Strong, see Dale T. Knobel, *Paddy and the Republic: Ethnicity and Nationality in Antebellum America* (Middletown, CT: Wesleyan University Press, 1986), 82–99, and George Templeton Strong, *The Diary of George Templeton Strong: The Civil War, 1860–1865*, Allan Nevins and Milton Halsey Thomas, eds. (New York: Columbia University Press, 1952), 342 and 345.

16. Thomas Dublin, *Women at Work: The Transformation of Work and Community in Lowell, Massachusetts, 1826–1860* (New York: Columbia University Press, 1981); Mary Cain, "Race, Republicanism and Domestic Service in the Antebellum United States," *Left History* 12 (Fall/Winter 2007): 64–83; Eugene D. Genovese, *Roll, Jordan, Roll: The World the Slaves Made* (New York: Pantheon, 1974), 24.

17. Otto H. Olsen, "Historians and the Extent of Slave Ownership in the Southern United States," *Civil War History* 18 (June 1972): 101–16; Jonathan D. Martin, *Divided Mastery: Slave Hiring in the American South* (Cambridge, MA: Harvard University Press, 2004), esp. 1–8; Lisa Lowe, *Immigrant Acts: On Asian American Cultural Politics* (Durham, NC: Duke University Press, 1996), 27–28.

18. Phillips, *Life and Labor in the Old South*, 327; Susan Eva O'Donovan, *Becoming Free in the Cotton South* (Cambridge, MA: Harvard University Press, 2007), 26 ("managing negroes"); for an overseer being called a "manager," see Lewis Cecil Gray, *History of Agriculture in the Southern United States to 1860*, 2 vols. (Washington, DC: Carnegie Institution, 1933), 1: 547.

19. Sharla M. Fett, *Working Cures: Healing, Health, and Power on Southern Slave Plantations* (Chapel Hill: University of North Carolina Press, 2002), 183 and 188–92; Walter Fisher, "Physicians and Slavery in the Antebellum Southern Medical Journal," *Journal of the History of Medicine and Allied Sciences* 23 (1968): 36–48; Hadden, *Slave Patrols*, passim; Ariela Gross, *Double Character: Slavery in the Antebellum Southern Courtroom* (Athens: University of Georgia Press, 2006), esp. 132–37; John Hope Franklin, *The Militant South, 1800–1861* (Urbana: University of Illinois Press, 2002, originally 1956), 71, 72, and 68–73; Wm. S. Price, "Commercial Benefits of Slavery," *ACP* 1 (December 1853): 355; Peter H. Wood, "Slave Labor Camps in Early America: Overcoming Denial and Discovering the Gulag," in Carla Gardina Pestana and Sharon V. Salinger, eds., *Inequality in Early America* (Hanover, NH: University Press of New England, 1999), esp. 222–30; A YOUNG PLANTER, "Proper Regard to, and Management of Slaves," *Farmers' Register* [hereafter *FR*] (July 31, 1840): 426.

20. John Taylor of Caroline, "Labor," from his *Arator*, as reprinted in *FR* 13 (December 31, 1840): esp. 728 and 730; Jordan, "Cloud and the *American Cotton Planter*," 45; "J. H. Zimmerman to *ACP*," *ACP* 3 (February 1855):

57; Unsigned, "Plantation Book," *Southern Planter* [hereafter *SP*] 12 (August 1852): 251.

21. H. C. "On the Management of Negroes," *FR* 1 (February 1834): 564–65; Dr. R. W. Gibbes, "Proper Regard to, and Management of, Slaves," *FR* 13 (July 31, 1840): 426–27; Ulrich Bonnell Phillips, "The Slave Labor Problem in the Charleston District," *Political Science Quarterly* 22 (September 1907): 419 and 422.

22. Ruffin, *Nature's Management*, xvii–xviii.

23. Unsigned, "Laborers for the South," *SC* 16 (August 1858): 235.

24. Alisse Portnoy, *Their Right to Speak: Women's Activism in the Indian and Slave Debates* (Cambridge, MA: Harvard University Press, 2005).

25. "Address of the Hon. C.C. Clay," *ACP* 3 (July 1855): 195.

26. George Fitzhugh, *Sociology for the South, or the Failure of Free Society* (Richmond, VA: A. Morris, 1854), 286–87; "William S. Price to Freeman Hunt, Editor of the *Merchants' Magazine*: Moral Benefits of Slavery," *ACP* 1 (June 1853), 172–74. On the profound connections of proslavery thought to colonization and civilizationist racism, see also Brian Schoen, *The Fragile Fabric of Union: Cotton, Federal Politics, and the Global Origins of the Civil War* (Baltimore, MD: Johns Hopkins University Press, 2009), 163–66.

27. Alexander Saxton, *The Rise and Fall of the White Republic: Class Politics and Mass Culture in Nineteenth Century America* (New York: Verso, 2003, originally 1990), 390; Fitzhugh, *Sociology for the South*, 286–87.

28. Price, "Commercial Benefits of Slavery," 355; David A. Chang, *The Color of the Land: Race, Nation, and the Politics of Landownership in Oklahoma, 1832–1929* (Chapel Hill: University of North Carolina Press, 2010), 23.

29. Aziz Rana, *The Two Faces of American Freedom* (Cambridge, MA: Harvard University Press, 2010), 146–47 and passim; Left Quarter Collective, "White Supremacist Constitution of the U.S. Empire-State: A Short Conceptual Look at the Long First Century," *Political Power and Social Theory* 20 (2008): esp. 180–82.

30. Frederick Law Olmsted, *A Journey in the Seaboard Slave States: With Remarks on Their Economy* (New York: Dix and Edwards, 1856), 10, 90–91, and 550–51.

31. Phillips, *American Negro Slavery*, 301–3; Bernard Mandel, *Labor, Free and Slave* (Urbana: University of Illinois Press, 2007, originally 1955), 35; Roger W. Shugg, *Origins of Class Struggle in Louisiana: A Social History of White Farmers and Laborers during Slavery and After, 1840–1875* (Baton Rouge: Louisiana State University Press, 1939), 90. See also Todd L. Savitt, *Medicine and Slavery: The Diseases and Health Care of Blacks in Antebellum Virginia* (Urbana: University of Illinois Press, 2002, originally 1978), 104.

32. Kenneth M. Stampp, *The Peculiar Institution: Slavery in the Ante-Bellum South* (New York: Knopf, 1956), 80; see also Commons et al., *Documentary History of American Industrial Society*, 2: 182.

33. As cited, with further sources on Irish experience and skill, in Phillips, *American Negro Slavery*, 301–2; Peter Way, *Common Labour: Workers and the Digging of North American Canals, 1780–1860* (Cambridge: Cambridge University Press, 1993), 192–204.

34. Ronald L. Lewis, *Coal, Iron, and Slaves: Industrial Slavery in Maryland and Virginia, 1715–1865* (Westport, CT: Greenwood, 1979), 90–96; Seth Rockman, *Scraping By: Wage Labor, Slavery and Survival in Early Baltimore* (Baltimore, MD: Johns Hopkins University Press, 2008), esp. 94–95.

35. Richard Follett, *The Sugar Masters: Planters and Slaves in Louisiana's Cane World, 1820–1860* (Baton Rouge: Louisiana State University Press, 2005), 85; Fanny Kemble, *Journal of a Residence on a Georgian Plantation in 1838–1839* (New York: Harper and Bros., 1863), 88–89 and 90; Ulrich Bonnell Phillips and James David Glunt, eds., *Florida Plantation Records from the Papers of George Noble Jones* (St. Louis: Missouri Historical Society, 1927), 50–51; Commons et al., *Documentary History of American Industrial Society* 2: 181 ("whiskey"); Anderson as quoted in Charles B. Dew, *Ironmaker to the Confederacy: Joseph R. Anderson and the Tredegar Iron Works* (New Haven, CT: Yale University Press, 1966), 22–23; see also Richard B. Morris, "Labor Militancy in the Old South," *Labor and Nation* 4 (May/June 1948): 32–36.

36. Stampp, *Peculiar Institution*, 80; Charles Joyner, *Down by the Riverside: A South Carolina Slave Community* (Urbana: University of Illinois Press, 1984), 42; Lorena S. Walsh, "Slave Life, Slave Society, and Tobacco Production in the Tidewater Chesapeake, 1620–1820," in Ira Berlin and Philip D. Morgan, eds., *Cultivation and Culture: Labor and the Shaping of Slave Life in the Americas* (Charlottesville: University of Virginia Press, 1993), 186; see also Ruffin, *Nature's Management*, xviii; Phillips, "Charleston District," 418; and Chang, *Color of the Land*, 29.

37. On gender, see Gray, *History of Agriculture in the Southern United States to 1860*, 1: 551; John Hebron Moore, *The Emergence of the Cotton Kingdom in the Old Southwest, Mississippi, 1770–1860* (Baton Rouge: Louisiana State University Press, 1988), 87; Steven F. Miller, "Plantation Labor Organization and Slave Life on the Cotton Frontier: The Alabama-Mississippi Black Belt, 1815–1840," in Berlin and Morgan, eds., *Cultivation and Culture*, 158–59; Stampp, *Peculiar Institution*, 80; Starobin, *Industrial Slavery*, 215; John Musgrave, *Slaves, Salt, Sex and Mr. Crenshaw: The Real Story of the Old Slave House and America's Reverse Underground R.R.* (Marion, IL: IIllinoisHistory.com, 2004–2005), esp. 147–50.

38. Olmsted, *Seaboard Slave States*, 99–100 and 555; cf. J. S. "Slavery," *SP* 1 (September 1841): 157 for the view that the Negro slave was "at least twice as valuable" as the white hireling.

39. Starobin, *Industrial Slavery*, 11–14; Stampp, *Peculiar Institution*, 66, on textiles; Charles H. Wesley, *Negro Labor in the United States, 1850–1925* (New York: Vanguard Press, 1927), 16; Linda Upham-Bornstein, "Men of Families: The Intersection of Labor Conflict and Race in the Norfolk Dry

Dock Affair, 1829–1831," *Labor* 5 (Spring 2007): 65; "Slave Labor upon Public Works at the South," *DR* 17 (July 1854): 78; *Scientific American*, n.s., 9, no. 25 (December 19, 1863): 386, contains the Richmond quotation in an unsigned note.

40. Thomas C. Buchanan, *Black Life on the Mississippi: Slaves, Free Blacks, and the Western Steamboat World* (Chapel Hill: University of North Carolina Press, 2004), 12, 13, 68, and 75; Ira Berlin, *Slaves without Masters: The Free Negro in the Antebellum South* (New York: Vintage, 1976), 231; An American Citizen, "To the Editors of the *American*," *Baltimore American and Commercial Daily Advertiser*, April 11, 1827; Wilberforce, "Communication," *Baltimore American and Commercial Daily Advertiser* (April 2, 1827). Thanks to David Schley for alerting us to these citations. On "honorable competition," see Bernard Cook, "The Use of Race to Control the Labor Market in Louisiana" in Marcel van der Linden and Jan Lucassen, eds., *Racism and the Labour Market: Historical Studies* (Bern: Peter Lang, 1995), 154.

41. Berlin, *Slaves without Masters*, 231, 351 and passim, esp. tables at 220–21.

42. Walter Johnson, *Soul by Soul: Life in the Antebellum Slave Market* (Cambridge, MA: Harvard University Press, 1999), 142–62 and passim; Fett, *Working Cures*, 176; Edward Baptist, " 'Cuffy,' 'Fancy Maids,' and 'One-Eyed Men',' " in Johnson, ed., *The Chattel Principle: Internal Slave Trades in the Americas* (New Haven, CT: Yale University Press, 2005), 166–83; Wendell Holmes Stephenson, *Isaac Franklin: Slave Trader and Planter in the Old South, with Plantation Records* (Gloucester, MA: Peter Smith, 1968), 104 (enumeration by color); for the context of Franklin, see Sharony Green, " 'Mr. Ballard, I Am Compelled to Write Again': Beyond Bedrooms and Brothels, a Fancy Girl Speaks," forthcoming in the journal *Black Women, Gender, and Families*; William Kauffman Scarborough, *The Overseer: Plantation Management in the Old South* (Baton Rouge: Louisiana State University Press, 1966), 10–11. cf. Phillips, "Charleston District," 434–36 for continued use of black skilled urban labor despite "public dread of disorder" and "class dislike of negro competition."

43. Charles Dew, *Bond of Iron: Master and Slave at Buffalo Forge* (New York: Norton, 1994), esp. 106–7, 114 and 156; James Oakes, *The Ruling Race: A History of American Slaveholders* (New York: Knopf, 1982), 134 (for "driven"); Bezis-Selfa, "Tale of Two Ironworks," 679.

44. Dew, *Ironmaker to the Confederacy*, 24–26 and 29–31, quotes on 26; Dew, *Bond of Iron*, 259 ("not at work") and 260–63; Herbert Aptheker, *The Unfolding Drama: Studies in U.S. History by Herbert Aptheker*, Bettina Aptheker, ed. (New York: International, 1978), 29–47. For more on the Tredegar Iron Works and especially its transnational dimensions to its managerial strategies, see Daniel Rood's excellent dissertation, "Plantation Technocrats: A History of Science and Technology in the Slaveholding Atlantic World, 1830–1860" (PhD diss., University of California-Irvine, 2010).

45. Frederick Law Olmsted, *A Journey in the Back Country* (New York: Mason Brothers, 1860), 347.

46. Aptheker, *Unfolding Drama*, 38; Charles Lyell, *A Second Visit to the United States of North America*, 2 vols. (London: Spottiswoode and Shaw, 1855, originally, 1849), 2: 162–63.

47. Kenneth F. Kiple and Virginia Himmelstieb King, *Another Dimension to the Black Diaspora: Diet, Disease, and Racism* (Cambridge: Cambridge University Press, 1981), 183 ("Savannah").

48. Oakes, *Ruling Race*, 134 ("slave labour"); Joyner, *Down by the Riverside*, 35 ("thrived"); Follett, *Sugar Masters*, 90–91 ("agriculture").

49. Martineau in Genovese, *Roll, Jordan, Roll*, 299; Olmsted, *Seaboard Slave States*, 589. For the view in Alabama that "English servants" outworked enslaved Africans by a 2 to 1 ratio, see Commons et al., *Documentary History of American Industrial Society*, 2: 46.

50. Moon-Ho Jung, *Coolies and Cane: Labor and Sugar in the Age of Emancipation* (Baltimore, MD: Johns Hopkins University Press, 2006), 18–20; George Fitzhugh, *Cannibals All! Or, Slaves without Masters* (Richmond, VA: A. Morris, 1857), 337.

51. Genovese, *Roll, Jordan, Roll*, 295–98; Mechal Sobel, *The World They Made Together: Black and White Values in Eighteenth-Century Virginia* (Princeton, NJ: Princeton University Press, 1987), 47 ("sliding"); Olmsted, *Journey in the Back Country*, 228.

52. Ronald T. Takaki, *A Pro-Slavery Crusade: The Agitation to Reopen the African Slave Trade* (New York: Free Press, 1971), 70 (Fitzhugh), 227–43 and passim; Fitzhugh, *Cannibals All!*, 337; Unsigned, "Laborers for the South," *SC* 16 (August 1858): 233–36.

Chapter 2

1. Quoted in Eugene D. Genovese, *Roll, Jordan, Roll: The World the Slaves Made* (New York: Pantheon, 1974), 18.

2. John Spencer Bassett, *The Southern Plantation Overseer, As Revealed in His Letters* (Northampton, MA: Smith College, 1925), 264.

3. Walter Johnson, *Soul by Soul: Life in the Antebellum Slave Market* (Cambridge, MA: Harvard University Press, 1999), 142–62 and passim.

4. N. D. Guerry, "Management of Negroes—Duties of Masters," *Southern Cultivator* [hereafter *SC*] 28 (June 1860): 176–77; Philom, "Moral Management of Negroes," *SC* 7 (July 1849): 105; A. T. Goodloe, "Management of Negroes—Again," *SC* 18 (August 1860): 279; Marx as quoted in George P. Rawick, *From Sundown to Sunup: The Making of the Black Community* (Westport, CT: Greenwood, 1972), 138; on Marx on Southern slavery as a social system "grafted" onto capitalism, and Marx on "grafting" generally, see David Kazanjian, *The Colonizing Trick: National Culture and Imperial Citizenship in Early America* (Minneapolis: University of Minnesota Press, 2003), 17–27. For a colonial example of how "prudent management"

and barbarity coexisted, see Lorena S. Walsh, *Motives of Honor, Pleasure, and Profit: Plantation Management in the Colonial Chesapeake, 1607–1763* (Chapel Hill: University of North Carolina Press for the Omohundro Institute of Early American History and Culture, 2010), 486–88.

5. C. L. R. James, "The Making of the Caribbean People," *Radical America* 4 (May 1970): 40; William Howard Russell, *My Diary North and South* (Boston: Burnham, 1863), 273.

6. Dale Tomich as quoted in Charles Post, "Plantation Slavery and Economic Development in the Antebellum U.S.," *Journal of Agrarian Change* 3 (July 2003): 307; Willie Lee Rose, ed., *A Documentary History of Slavery in North America* (Athens: University of Georgia Press, 1999), 337–41.

7. John R. Commons et al., *A Documentary History of American Industrial Society*, 10 vols. (New York: Russell and Russell, 1958, originally 1909), 1: 124; "M. W. Philips to *ACP*," *American Cotton Planter* [hereafter *ACP*] (October 1853): 308; Chester McArthur Destler, "David Dickson's 'System of Farming' and the Agricultural Revolution in the Deep South, 1850–1885," *Agricultural History* 31 (July 1957): 31 and 32; Jonathan D. Martin, *Divided Mastery: Slave Hiring in the American South* (Cambridge, MA: Harvard University Press, 2004), 172 (Douglass) and 161–83; Unsigned, "Hiring Negroes," *Southern Planter* [hereafter, *SP*] 12 (December 1852): 376 likewise notes, but with alarm, the trend toward a situation in which "the negro is permitted to 'choose his master.' "

8. C. L. R. James, "The Atlantic Slave Trade and Slavery" in John A. Williams and Charles F. Harris, eds., *Amistad 1* (New York: Vintage, 1970), 153; Charles Joyner, *Down by the Riverside: A South Carolina Slave Community* (Urbana: University of Illinois Press, 1984), esp. 45, 59 ("managerial slaves"), 65. Robert W. Fogel, Ralph A. Galantine, and Richard L. Manning, eds., *Without Consent or Contract: The Rise and Fall of American Slavery: Evidence and Methods* (New York: Norton, 1992), esp. 84–86 and 106 suggests some of the extent to which assumptions shape conclusions on the extent of overseer and driver supervision, and argues for an increase in overseers in the late antebellum years.

9. William L. Van Deburg, *The Slave Drivers: Black Agricultural Labor Supervisors in the Antebellum South* (Westport, CT: Greenwood, 1979), 50 and passim; Mark M. Smith, *Mastered by the Clock: Time, Slavery, and Freedom in the American South* (Chapel Hill: University of North Carolina Press, 1997), 147; William Kauffman Scarborough, *The Overseer: Plantation Management in the Old South* (Baton Rouge: Louisiana State University Press, 1966), 19; and the excellent study by William E. Wiehoff, "Enslaved Africans' Rivalry with White Overseers in Plantation Culture," *Journal of Black Studies* 36 (January 2006): 429–55. On driving men like agricultural machinery, see Edward E. Baptist, "The Slave Labor Camps of Antebellum Florida and the Pushing System," in Robert Cassanello and Melanie Shell-Weiss, eds., *Florida's Working-Class Past: Current Perspectives on Labor,*

Race, and Gender from Spanish Florida to the New Immigration (Gainesville: University Press of Florida, 2009), 48.

10. Van Deburg, *Slave Drivers*, 50; A Subscriber, "Overseers," *ACP* 2 (May 1854): 150.

11. *Affleck's Southern Rural Almanac and Plantation and Garden Calendar for 1854* (Washington, MS: Affleck's Southern Nurseries, October, 1853), in the section for December at 51; Richard Fleischman and Thomas Tyson, "Accounting in Service to Racism: Monetizing Slave Property in the Antebellum South," *Critical Perspectives on Accounting* 15 (April 2004): 376–99.

12. Scarborough, *Overseer*, 70 quoting Affleck, cf. Ulrich Bonnell Phillips, *American Negro Slavery: A Survey of the Supply, Employment and Control of Negro Labor as Determined by the Plantation Regime* (New York: D. Appleton, 1918), 261–62.

13. Richard Follett, *The Sugar Masters: Planters and Slaves in Louisiana's Cane World, 1820–1860* (Baton Rouge: Louisiana State University Press, 2005), 69 (Raby and "demographic management"). The Weston text is included in Bassett, *Southern Plantation Overseer*, 31 and discussed in Joyner, *Down by the Riverside*, 51.

14. Sharla M. Fett, *Working Cures: Healing, Health, and Power on Southern Slave Plantations* (Chapel Hill: University of North Carolina Press, 2002), 15, 27 (Holmes) and 18. See also Amy Dru Stanley, "Slave Breeding: An Antebellum Argument over Commodity Relations, Love, and Personhood," unpublished paper presented at *Slavery's Capitalism: A New History of American Economic Development*, Brown University and Harvard University, April 7–9, 2011.

15. Agricola, "Management of Negroes," *SC* 13 (June 1855): 171; Guerry, "Management of Negroes—Duties of Masters," 176; Robert Collins, "Essay on the Management of Slaves," *De Bow's Review* [hereafter *DR*] 7 (January/February 1862): 155; James M. Towns, "Management of Negroes," *SC* 9 (June 1851): 87; P. T., "Judicious Management of the Plantation Force," *SC* 7 (May 1849): 69.

16. "MWP to *American Cotton Planter*: Plantation Economy," *ACP* 1 (December 1853): 377; A Subscriber, "Overseers," *ACP* 2 (May 1854): 150; John A. Calhoun et al., "Management of Slaves," *SC* 4 (August 1846): 113; Jacob Metzer, "Rational Management, Modern Business Practices, and the Economies of Scale in Ante-Bellum Southern Plantations," *Explorations in Economic History* 12 (April 1975): 125–27; on pay to overseers, Genovese, *Roll, Jordan, Roll*, 13–14; Unsigned, "The Duties of an Overseer," *ACP* (December 1854): 355; Editor, "Anonymous Communications," *ACP* 3 (September 1855): 274. Cf. Farmer and Planter, "The Duties of an Overseer," *SP* 17 (July 1857): 414 for evidence of internalizing the need for slave welfare and reproduction by one who had worked "in the harness" as an overseer.

17. John A. Calhoun et al., "Management of Slaves," *DR* 18 (June 1855): 713. Cf. Unsigned, "Management of Slaves and & c.," *Farmers' Register* [hereafter, *FR*] 5 (May 1, 1838): 32–33.

18. George Fitzhugh, *Sociology for the South, or the Failure of Free Society* (Richmond, VA: A. Morris, 1854), 287.

19. Jno. W. Pitts, "Best Method of Managing Negroes," *SC* 18 (October 1860): 325; Towns, "Management of Negroes," 87.

20. Frederick Law Olmsted, *The Cotton Kingdom: A Traveler's Observations on Cotton and Slavery in the American Slave States, 1853–1861* (New York: Da Capo Press, 1996, originally 1861), 248; Ulrich Bonnell Phillips and James David Glunt, eds., *Florida Plantation Records from the Papers of George Noble Jones* (St. Louis: Missouri Historical Society, 1927), 154–55.

21. Unsigned, "Revolutionizing a Plantation," *SC* 16 (November 1858): 346.

22. Phillips, *American Negro Slavery*, 261–62; Stephanie M. H. Camp, *Closer to Freedom: Enslaved Women and Everyday Resistance in the Plantation South* (Chapel Hill: University of North Carolina Press, 2004), 63; Pamela D. Bridgewater, "Ain't I a Slave: Slavery, Reproductive Abuse and Reparations," *UCLA Women's Law Journal* 14 (2005): 122, n. 166 ("cat") and 89–162. On advertisements as a public discourse in which capacity for reproductive was prominently mentioned, see Gerald Norde, "From Genesis to Phoenix: The Breeding of Slaves during the Domestic Slave Era, 1837–1863, and Its Consequences" (PhD diss., University of Delaware, 1985), esp. 109.

23. Fred Moten, *In the Break: The Aesthetics of the Black Radical Tradition* (Minneapolis: University of Minnesota Press, 2003), 16 and 1–24. Joyner, *Down by the Riverside*, 45; Scarborough, *Overseer*, 70; Fett, *Working Cures*, 176; John Hebron Moore, *The Emergence of the Cotton Kingdom in the Old Southwest, Mississippi, 1770–1860* (Baton Rouge: Louisiana State University Press, 1988), 84; Elizabeth Fox-Genovese, *Within the Plantation Household: Black and White Women of the Old South* (Chapel Hill: University of North Carolina Press, 1988), 187–90; on sucklers' gangs, see Phillips, *American Negro Slavery*, 264; Marie Jenkins Schwartz, *Birthing a Slave: Motherhood and Medicine in the Antebellum South* (Cambridge, MA: Harvard University Press, 2006), 17–20, 189–91, and 224–25 establishes how mixed the record of making postnatal concessions regarding labor could be as does Angela Davis, "Reflections on the Black Woman's Role in the Community of Slaves," in Joy James, ed., *The Angela Davis Reader* (Malden, MA: Wiley-Blackwell, 1998), 117; Commons et al., *Documentary History of American Industrial Society*, 1: 122 [emphasis original]; Bridgewater, "Ain't I a Slave: Slavery," 122, n. 168 ("dozen") and 89–162.

24. James L. Huston, *Calculating the Value of the Union: Slavery, Property Rights, and the Economic Origins of the Civil War* (Chapel Hill: University of North Carolina Press, 2003), esp. 116 (Lincoln), 28–32 and 292, n.7; Douglass C. North, *The Economic Growth of the United States, 1790–1860*

(Englewood Cliffs, NJ: Prentice Hall, 1961), 233; Gavin Wright, *Slavery and American Economic Development* (Baton Rouge: Louisiana State University Press, 2006), 67; Roger L. Ransom, "The Economics of the Civil War," EH.Net Encyclopedia, Robert Whaples, ed., August 24, 2001, at http://eh.net/encyclopedia/article/ransom.civil.war.us.

25. Adrienne Davis, " 'Don't Let Nobody Bother Yo' Principle': The Sexual Economy of American Slavery," in Sharon Harley and the Black Women and Work Collective, eds., *Sister Circle: Black Women and Work* (New Brunswick, NJ: Rutgers University Press, 2002), 103–27; See also Zillah Eisentein, *Against Empire: Feminisms, Racism, and the West* (London: Zed Press, 2004), 85–91.

26. Hurricane, "The Negro and His Management," *SC* 17 (September 1860): 276–77; for the patterns of usage, see e.g., Agricola, "Management of Negroes," 171–74; John A. Calhoun, "Management of Slaves," *DR* 18 (June 1855): 713; Collins, "Management of Slaves," *DR* 17 (October 1854): 421–23; A Small Farmer, "Management of Negroes," *DR* 11 (October 1851): 369–72; A. T. Goodloe, "Management of Negroes," *SC* 18 (April 1860): 130–31; Goodloe, "Management of Negroes—Again," 279–80; A. T. Goodloe, "Management of Negroes—Caution!," *SC* 18 (October 1860): 305; Guerry, "Management of Negroes—Duties of Masters," 176–77; Towns, "Management of Negroes," 87–88; Arkansas River, "Dickson's Planting—Overseers—Negroes Etc.," *SC* 18 (October 1860): 304–5; Pitts, "Best Method of Managing Negroes," 325–26; A Tennesseean, "Management of Negroes—Bathing Feet," *SC* 11 (October 1853): 302.

27. Phillips in Commons, *Documentary History of American Industrial Society,* 2: 31–35 (Phillips heads the section "NEGRO SLAVE LABOR"; cf. Phillips, *Life and Labor in the Old South* (Boston: Little, Brown, 1963, originally, 1929), 243; Genovese, *Roll, Jordan, Roll,* 13–24, Grimball quotation at 18; see also Lewis Gray, *History of Agriculture in the Southern United States to 1860,* 2 vols. (Washington, DC: Carnegie Institution, 1933), 1: 559.

28. Calhoun et al., "Management of Slaves" [*DR* version], 713 and 716–17; Floyd, "Management of Servants," *SC* 11 (October 1853): 301; Wendell Holmes Stephenson, *Isaac Franklin: Slave Trader and Planter in the Old South, with Plantation Records* (Gloucester, MA: Peter Smith, 1968), 138–70; Rose, ed., *Documentary History of Slavery in North America,* 337–44.

29. Collins, "Essay on the Management of Slaves," (1862 version), 156; Ira Berlin, *Slaves without Masters: The Free Negro in the Antebellum South* (New York: Vintage, 1976), 234–40; Todd L. Savitt, *Medicine and Slavery: The Diseases and Health Care of Blacks in Antebellum Virginia* (Urbana: University of Illinois Press, 2002, originally 1978), 163 (Ramsay); Fett, *Working Cures,* 135–46 ("mothers").

30. Gray, *History of Agriculture in the Southern United States to 1860,* 1: 547 ("breakfast"); Eugene D. Genovese, *The Political Economy of Slavery:*

Studies in the Economy & Society of the Slave South (New York: Pantheon, 1965), 54–55.

31. Scarborough, *Overseer*, 104; Goodloe, "Management of Negroes," 130–31; Guerry, "Management of Negroes—Duties of Masters," 176–77; cf. Thavolia Glymph, *Out of the House of Bondage: The Transformation of the Plantation Household* (Cambridge: Cambridge University Press, 2008), 49–51.

32. Goodloe, "Management of Negroes—Caution!," 305. Samuel Cartwright, "Dr. Cartwright on the Caucasians and the Africans," *DR* 1 (July 1858): 46–47 and 52 ("like the mule"); Robert Collins, "Essay on the Management of Slaves," *SC* 12 (July 1854): 205–6 and the citations in the note above.

33. Gray, *History of Agriculture in the Southern United States to 1860*, 1: 551–52; Geoff Burrows, "The Interface of Race and Accounting: A Comment and an Extension" and Fleishman and Tyson, "Interface of Race and Accounting: A Reply to Burrows," *Accounting History* 7 (May 2002): 7–32; Richard Fleischman and Thomas Tyson, "Accounting in Service to Racism: Monetizing Slave Property in the Antebellum South," *Critical Perspectives on Accounting* 15 (April 2004): 376–99; Ulrich Bonnell Phillips, "The Slave Labor Problem in the Charleston District," *Political Science Quarterly* 22 (September 1907): 418 and 428; Post, "Plantation Slavery and Economic Development," esp. 316; Rose, ed., *Documentary History of Slavery in North America*, 337–44; James O. Breeden, ed., *Advice among Masters: The Ideal in Slave Management in the Old South* (Westport, CT: Greenwood, 1980), 69–74. See also Genovese, *Roll, Jordan, Roll*, 61, 310, 361, and 371; Ira Berlin, *Generations of Captivity: A History of African-American Slaves* (Cambridge, MA: Belknap Press, 2004), 132, 149, 178, and 212; Joseph P. Reidy, "Obligation and Right: Patterns of Labor, Subsistence, and Exchange in the Cotton Belt of Georgia" and Steven F. Miller, "Plantation Labor Organization and Slave Life on the Cotton Frontier: The Alabama-Mississippi Black Belt, 1815–1840," both in Ira Berlin and Philip Morgan, eds., *Cultivation and Culture: Labor and the Shaping of Slave Life in the Americas* (Charlottesville: University of Virginia Press, 1993), 140–41 and 164–65 as well as 15 of the editors' introduction to the volume. On race and driving, see Robert Fogel and Stanley Engerman, *Time on the Cross: The Economics of American Slavery* (New York: Norton, 1989, originally 1974), 204–5, including the quotation; Frederick Law Olmsted, *A Journey in the Seaboard Slave States: With Remarks on Their Economy* (New York: Dix and Edwards, 1856), 204–6 and Olmsted, *Cotton Kingdom*, 153 and 452. See also Mark M. Smith, *Mastered by the Clock: Time, Slavery, and Freedom in the American South* (Chapel Hill: University of North Carolina Press, 1997), 133–50 for dramas eventuating when masters attempted to uses clock time to impose work discipline on slaves holding to "African" conceptions of time.

34. Alan Olmstead and Paul Rhode, "Biological Innovation and Productivity Growth in the Antebellum Cotton Economy," *Journal of Economic History* 68 (December 2008): 1123–71; Fleischman and Tyson, "Accounting in Service to Racism," 376–99; Gray, *History of Agriculture in the Southern United States to 1860*, 1: 552.

35. Eugene D. Genovese, "The Medical and Insurance Costs of Slaveholding," *Journal of Negro History* 45 (July 1960):148; Savitt, *Medicine and Slavery*, 36 ("medical extremist").

36. Kenneth F. Kiple and Virginia Himmelstieb King, *Another Dimension to the Black Diaspora: Diet, Disease, and Racism* (Cambridge: Cambridge University Press, 1981), 179–83; William J. Cooper, Jr., *Jefferson Davis, American* (New York: Vintage, 2001), 233; Mary Louise Marshall, "Samuel A. Cartwright and States' Rights Medicine," *New Orleans Medical and Surgical Journal* 90 (1940–1941), esp. 74–76; Warren Sawyer, "Brickell v. Cartwright: Confrontations in the Antebellum Medical Literature," *Southern Medical Journal* 81 (June 1988): 774–80; James Denny Guillory, "The Pro-Slavery Arguments of Dr. Samuel A. Cartwright," *Louisiana History* 9 (Summer 1968): 225, 226 ("first place") and 209–27; Savitt, *Medicine and Slavery*, 10.

37. W. E. B. Du Bois, *Black Reconstruction in America, 1860–1880* (New York: Free Press, 1998, originally 1935), 39. Cartwright's views on race and the Bible are laid out in "Unity of the Human Race Disproved by the Hebrew Bible," *DR* 4 (August 1860): 131 and 129–36; "Dr. Cartwright on the Serpent, the Ape, and the Negro," *DR* 31 (December 1861), 507–16; Cartwright, "Ethnology of the Negro or Prognathous Race: A Lecture Given November 30, 1857, before the New Orleans Academy of Science," (n.p.: Samuel A. Cartwright and Family Papers, Printed Pamphlets, Special Collections, Louisiana State University Library, n.d.), esp. 14 (Indians); Guillory, "Pro-Slavery Arguments of Cartwright," 224 ("belly").

38. George Fredrickson, *The Black Image in the White Mind* (Middletown, CT: Wesleyan University Press, 1987), 87–88; Colin Kidd, *The Forging of Races: Race and Scripture in the Protestant Atlantic World, 1600–2000* (Cambridge: Cambridge University Press, 2006), 147 ("humanity") and 134–49; Savitt, *Medicine and Slavery*, 7–8; Guillory, "Pro-Slavery Arguments of Cartwright," 224. For the most spirited critical response, see Editor, "Dr. Cartwright on the Negro," *DR* 8 (May–August, 1862), esp. 62–64; see also Agricola, "Management of Negroes," 171–74.

39. E. G. on the "Africans in America" website at http://www.pbs.org/wgbh/aia/part4/4h3106.html and in Arthur L. Caplan, James J. McCartney, Dominic A. Sisti, eds., *Health, Disease, and Illness: Concepts in Medicine* (Washington, DC: Georgetown University Press, 2004), 28–39.

40. Kiple and King, *Another Dimension to the Black Diaspora*, 179; Guillory, "Pro-Slavery Arguments of Cartwright," 211–14.

41. Samuel Cartwright et al., "Report on the Diseases and Physical Pecu-liarities of the Negro Race," *New Orleans Medical and Surgical Journal* 7 (May 1851): 703 and 691–715; cf. Kenneth M. Stampp, *The Peculiar Insti-tution: Slavery in the Ante-Bellum South* (New York: Knopf, 1956), 309.

42. Cartwright et al., "Report on the Diseases and Physical Peculiarities of the Negro Race," 691–715; William E. Wiehoff, "Enslaved Africans' Rivalry with White Overseers in Plantation Culture: An Unconventional Interpre-tation," *Journal of Black Studies* 36 (January 2006): 429–55; Breeden, ed., *Advice among Masters*, esp. 81–86, 170–78, and 291–304; Van Deburg, *Slave Drivers*, esp. 3; Genovese, *Roll, Jordan, Roll*, 366–67; Robert Starobin, *Industrial Slavery in the Old South* (New York: Oxford University Press, 1971), 168–73.

43. Sheldon Watts, *Epidemics and History: Disease, Power, and Imperialism* (New Haven, CT: Yale University Press, 1997), 242 ("drudgery"), and Guillory, "Proslavery Arguments of Cartwright," 222–23 for the quotations.

44. Cartwright et al., "Report on the Diseases and Physical Peculiarities of the Negro Race," 723; John S. Haller, Jr., "The Negro and the Southern Physician: A Study of Medical and Racial Attitudes, 1800–1860," *Medical History* 16 (1972): 239–42; Guillory, "Pro-Slavery Arguments of Cartwright," 224 ("dust").

45. As quoted in Haller, "Negro and the Southern Physician," 242.

46. Cf. Cartwright, "Report on the Diseases and Physical Peculiarities of the Negro Race," 691–715 and Samuel Cartwright, "Diseases and Peculiarities of the Negro Race, Concluded" *DR* 1 (September 1851): 331–35.

47. Cartwright, "Ethnology of the Negro or Prognathous Race," 6, 9, and 14 ("fist," "ethnological peculiarity," and "cowhide"). On consumption see Dr. S. Cartwright, "The Diseases of Negroes—Pulmonary Congestions, Pneumonia, &c.," *DR* 11 (August 1851): 212; Cartwright, "Diseases and Peculiarities of the Negro Race, Concluded," 332, 333 ("negro liberty"), and 331–35. Also see "Dr. Cartwright on the Serpent, the Ape, and the Negro," 507–16 and Dr. S. Cartwright, "Negro Freedom an Impossibility under Nature's Laws," *DR* 30 (May/June 1861): 648–59; Fett, *Working Cures*, 150; on sleep and night, see Mechal Sobel, *The World They Made Together: Black and White Values in Eighteenth-Century Virginia* (Princeton, NJ: Princeton University Press, 1987), 32–33; Guillory, "Proslavery Arguments of Cartwright," 222 ("mule" and "overwork"), 215 ("mysterious love"), and 216 ("leather strap").

48. On Cartwright's use of work as a cure and on his managerial impulses for ethnology, see his "Diseases and Peculiarities of the Negro Race," 335 ("*bi-pedum nequissimus*") and 333–35 passim. On brain size, see Haller, Jr., "Ne-gro and the Southern Physician," 248 and 238–53; Dr. Samuel Cartwright, "How to Save the Republic," *DR* 11 (August 1851): 186–87. On Cartwright and disability, see Douglas Baynton, "Disability and the Justification of

Inequality in American History," in Paul K. Longmore and Lauri Umansky, eds., *The New Disability History: American Perspectives* (New York: New York University Press, 2001), 37.

49. Du Bois, *Black Reconstruction in America*, 55; Johnson, *Soul by Soul*, 142–62 and passim.

50. "Samuel Adolphus Cartwright," *A Dictionary of Louisiana Biography*, 2 vols. (New Orleans: Louisiana Historical Association, 1988), 1: 157; David F. Allmendinger, *Ruffin: Family and Reform in the Old South* (New York: Oxford University Press, 1990), 171–76; Weymouth T. Jordan, "Noah B. Cloud and the *American Cotton Planter*," *Agricultural History* 31 (October 1957): 46–49; on the limits of slaveholder support for immigration, see Gavin Wright, *The Political Economy of the Cotton South: Households, Markets, and Wealth in the Nineteenth Century* (New York: Norton, 1978), 121–25. On the Freedmen's Bureau, see "Chairman of the Orangeburg, South Carolina, Commission on Contracts to the Freedmen's Bureau Commissioner, Enclosing a Speech to the Freedpeople; and the Commissioner's Reply" (June 12, 1865) at Freedmen & Southern Society Project at http://www.history.umd.edu/Freedmen/Soule.htm.

51. J. D. B. De Bow, "Letter from the Editor to Gov. Perry, of South Carolina," *DR* 1 (January 1866): 6; cf. E. Q. B. "In Lieu of Labor," *DR* 4 (August 1867): 69.

52. George Fitzhugh, "The Negro Imbroglio—Farms for the Freedmen" *DR* 3 (June 1867): 518–19 and 521 ("single negro"); Unsigned, "Virginia—New Spirit and Development" *DR* 2 (July 1866): 56.

53. Moon-Ho Jung, *Coolies and Cane: Labor and Sugar in the Age of Emancipation* (Baltimore, MD: Johns Hopkins University Press, 2006), 202–3 ("situation"); Unsigned, "A Picture of the West Indies," *DR* 3 (June 1860): 729–38. Cf. Lucy M. Cohen, *The Chinese in the Post-Civil War South* (Baton Rouge: Louisiana State University Press, 1984), 53; Paul Ashdown and Edward Gaudill, *The Myth of Nathan Bedford Forrest* (Lanham, MD: Rowman and Littlefield, 2006), 61–64. See also: Matthew Guterl, "Asian Labor, The American South, and the Age of Emancipation," *Journal of World History* 14 (June 2003): 223 and esp. 221–41 and, for the varied ways experiences of Southerners with Chinese workers in Cuba influenced the debates, 211–21.

54. On Forrest and on the KKK in the Piedmont, see Ashdown and Gaudill, *Myth of Nathan Bedford Forrest*, 62–63 and Scott Reynolds Nelson, *Iron Confederacies: Southern Railways, Klan Violence, and Reconstruction* (Chapel Hill: University of North Carolina Press, 1999), 135–37; Chad Pearson, " 'The South Wants to Be Free': N. F. Thompson, The KKK, and the Origins of the Southern Open-Shop Drive" (Unpublished paper, c. 2009, in the possession of David Roediger); on convict leasing, Alex Lichtenstein, *Twice the Work of Free Labor: The Political Economy of Convict Labor in the New South* (London: Verso, 1996), 134 (for the quoted

material). See also 52 and 184 and Matthew J. Mancini, *One Dies, Get Another: Convict Leasing in the American South, 1866–1928* (Columbia: University of South Carolina Press, 1996), 40–41; Douglas A. Blackmon, *Slavery by Another Name: The Re-Enslavement of Black People in America from the Civil War to World War II* (New York: Doubleday, 2008), 55 and 107. For the story of "boss," see David R. Roediger, "Gaining a Hearing for Black-White Unity: Covington Hall and the Complexities of Race, Gender, and Class," in *Towards the Abolition of Whiteness: Essays on Race, Politics, and Working Class History* (New York: Verso, 1994), 138 and 173 and David R. Roediger, *The Wages of Whiteness: Race and the Making of the American Working Class* (New York: Verso, 1991), 54, 63, and 69.

55. Inspector, "The Negro as a Molder," *Foundry* 19 (September 1901): 17–18. Thanks go to Zach Sell for this source. See also, e.g., Brian Kelly, *Race, Class, and Power in the Alabama Coalfields, 1908–21* (Urbana: University of Illinois Press, 2001), 7, 12, 22–24, 49, 56.

Chapter 3

1. Herman Melville, *The Confidence Man: His Masquerade* (Evanston, IL: Northwestern University Press, 1984, originally 1857), esp. 115–28; Carolyn Karcher, *Shadow over the Promised Land: Slavery, Race, and Violence in Melville's America* (Baton Rouge: Louisiana University Press, 1979).

2. Melville, *Confidence Man*, 156, 194 and 195–223. On "coon," see David R. Roediger, *The Wages of Whiteness: Race and the Making of the American Working Class* (New York: Verso, 1991), 97–99.

3. Moon-Ho Jung. *Coolies and Cane: Labor and Sugar in the Age of Emancipation* (Baltimore, MD: Johns Hopkins University Press, 2006).

4. Frederick Jackson Turner, *The Frontier in American History* (New York: Henry Holt, 1920), 3–4 and 12. See also 3–4.

5. On western film and fiction as myth and in history, see Richard Slotkin, *Gunfighter Nation: The Myth of the Frontier in Twentieth Century America* (New York: Atheneum, 1992).

6. Howard Lamar's important work on these matters is brilliantly summarized by Steven Hahn and Jonathan Prude in the introduction to their edited collection *The Countryside in the Age of Capitalist Transformation: Essays in the Social History of Rural America* (Chapel Hill: University of North Carolina Press, 1985), 17. In that same volume, see Howard Lamar, "From Bondage to Contract: Ethnic Labor in the American West," 300–313; see also Shelton Stromquist, "Railroad Labor and the Global Economy: Historical Patterns," in Jan Lucassen, ed., *Global Labour History: A State of the Art* (Bern: Peter Lang, 2006), 630 and 623–48.

7. Donald Worster, *Rivers of Empire: Water, Aridity, and the Growth of the American West* (New York: Pantheon Books, 1985), 217, 218 (quoting Davis), 219 and 220–22. Among bracing recent works on race and class in western history, see Tomás Almaguer, *Racial Fault Lines: The Historical*

Origins of White Supremacy in California (Berkeley: University of
California Press, 1994) and Alexander Saxton, *The Rise and Fall of the
White Republic: Class Politics and Mass Culture in Nineteenth Century
America* (New York: Verso, 1990), esp. 269–91.

8. John Hoyt Williams, *A Great & Shining Road: The Epic Story of the
Transcontinental Railroad* (New York: Times Books, 1988), 46; Stephen
Ambrose, *Nothing Like It in the World: The Men Who Built the Transconti-
nental Railroad* (New York: Simon and Schuster, 2000), 126–27.

9. Christian Wolmar, *Blood, Iron, and Gold: How Railroads Transformed the
World* (New York: Public Affairs, 2010), 135; Wesley S. Griswold, *A Work of
Giants: Building the Transcontinental Railroad* (New York: McGraw-Hill,
1962), 216; Ambrose, *Nothing Like It in the World*, 361, 209, 279 ("befriend"
and Grant), 296–97 ("befriend"), 340, 346, and 218 (quoting Grant).
Grenville M. Dodge, *How We Built the Union Pacific Railway and Other
Railway Papers and Addresses* (Washington, DC: Government Printing
Office, 1910), 14 ("Mormon question") and 13–25. See also Edwin L. Sabin,
Building the Pacific Railway (Philadelphia, PA: J. B. Lippincott, 1919),
231–34; and John Debo Galloway, *The First Transcontinental Railroad: Cen-
tral Pacific, Union Pacific* (New York: Simmons-Boardman, 1950), 292–97.

10. James McCague, *Moguls and Iron Men: The Story of the First Transcontinental Railroad* (New York: Harper and Row, 1964), 103; Oscar Lewis, *The
Big Four: The Story of Huntington, Stanford, Hopkins, and Crocker, and of
the Building of the Transcontinental Railroad* (New York: Knopf, 1966), 59
and 69; Galloway, *First Transcontinental Railroad*, 75; Crocker's testimony
in *Report of the Joint Special Committee to Investigate Chinese Immigration, 44th Congress, 2d Session. Senate Report No. 689, February 27, 1877*
(Washington, DC: Government Printing Office, 1877), posted on Central
Pacific Railroad Photographic History Museum website at http://cprr.org/
Museum/Chinese_Immigration.html, 11.

11. Ambrose, *Nothing Like It in the World*, 134–35; Williams, *Great & Shining
Road*, 94, discusses Poor's proposal.

12. William Dobak, "Fort Riley's Black Soldiers and the Army's Changing
Role in the West," in Bruce A. Clasrud and Michael A. Searles, eds.,
Buffalo Soldiers in the West (College Station: Texas A&M University Press,
2007), 46–47; in same volume see also Frank N. Schubert, "Black Soldiers on the White Frontier: Some Factors Influencing Race Relations,"
178; Manu Vimalassery, "Skew Tracks: Racial Capitalism and the First
Transcontinental Railroad" (PhD diss., New York University, 2010), 166
and 335 and 113-369 passim. On the effort to so massively recruit black
strikebreakers, see Ping Chiu, *Chinese Labor in California, 1850–1880: An
Economic Study* (Madison: State Historical Society of Wisconsin, 1963),
47. On Mexican labor, see Lewis, *Big Four*, 69; McCague, *Moguls and
Iron Men*, 103; Victor Clark, *Mexican Labor in the United States, U.S.
Labor Bulletin* 78 (September 1908): 478–81.

13. Maxine Hong Kingston, *China Men* (New York: Vintage, 1989), 139.
14. Crocker and Strobridge, in *Report of the Joint Special Committee to Investigate Chinese Immigration*, esp. 5–11.
15. Williams, *Great & Shining Road*, 96 and 97; Crocker and Strobridge in *Report of the Joint Special Committee to Investigate Chinese Immigration*, 6 and 23–24; see also Stan Steiner, *Fusang: The Chinese Who Built America* (New York: Harper and Row, 1979), 129.
16. George Kraus, *High Road to Promontory: Building the Central Pacific (now the Southern Pacific) across the High Sierra* (Palo Alto, CA: American West, 1969), 107 and 110 ("nearly"); Williams, *Great & Shining Road*, 96 and 97 ("vindicated"); Ambrose, *Nothing Like It in the World*, 322 ("whole work"); Crocker in *Report of the Joint Special Committee to Investigate Chinese Immigration*, 6 ("favor" and Cornish miners). Cf. Strobridge in ibid. at 23–25. For an earlier account of a similar "race" between Chinese and white graders, with the same result, see Steiner, *Fusang*, 131–32. On "teamwork," see Chiu, *Chinese Labor in California*, 46.
17. Crocker, in *Report of the Joint Special Committee to Investigate Chinese Immigration*, 7; for Strobridge's view see, 24 in ibid. On the complexities of pay rates, see the important work of William F. Chew, *Nameless Builders of the Transcontinental Railroad: The Chinese Workers of the Central Pacific Railroad* (Victoria, BC: Trafford, 2004), 51–55.
18. Crocker, in *Report of the Joint Special Committee to Investigate Chinese Immigration*, 6–7 and 11; Crocker in U.S. Senate, *Testimony Taken by the United States Pacific Railway Commission*, 9 vols. (Fiftieth Congress, First Session, Executive Document 51, part 8, 1887), 7: 3660.
19. Crocker, as quoted in Williams, *Great & Shining Road*, 96; Central Pacific Railroad [Stanford], *Statement Made to the President of the United States, and the Secretary of the Interior of the Progress of the Work*, October 10, 1865 (Sacramento, CA: H.S. Crocker, 1865), 7–8. Chew, *Nameless Builders of the Transcontinental Railroad*, 129.
20. Alexander Saxton, *The Indispensable Enemy: Labor and the Anti-Chinese Movement in California* (Berkeley: University of California Press, 1971), 61 ("over-age"); [Stanford], *Statement Made to the President of the United States, and the Secretary of the Interior of the Progress of the Work*, 7.
21. Kraus, *High Road to Promontory*, 134; Galloway, *First Transcontinental Railroad*, 86 and 89; Williams, *Great & Shining Road*, 94 ("persuader"); Saxton, *Indispensable Enemy*, 61.
22. Clement quoted from Galloway, *First Transcontinental Railroad*, 144.
23. Chiu, *Chinese Labor in California*, 43–44.
24. U.S. Senate, *Testimony Taken by the United States Pacific Railway Commission*, 7: 3660.
25. See Ronald Takaki, *A Different Mirror: A History of Multicultural America* (Boston: Little, Brown, 1993), 197–98.

26. U.S. Senate, *Testimony Taken by the United States Pacific Railway Commission*, 7: 3660; Chew, *Nameless Builders of the Transcontinental Railroad*, 50–51; Saxton, "The Army of Canton in the High Sierra," *Pacific Historical Review* 35 (May 1966): 149; [Stanford], *Statement Made to the President of the United States, and the Secretary of the Interior of the Progress of the Work*, 7: 3660.

27. U.S. Senate, *Testimony Taken by the United States Pacific Railway Commission*, 7: 3660; "Tunnels of the Pacific Railroad," reprinted from *Van Nostrand's Eclectic Engineering Magazine* (1870) Central Pacific Railroad Photographic History Museum website at http://cprr.org/Museum/Tunnels.html#Laborers; Steiner, *Fusang*, 134.

28. Hong Kingston, *China Men*, 130–31; Ambrose, *Nothing Like It in the World*, 251; Iris Chang, *The Chinese in America* (New York: Penguin, 2003), 59–60. For controversy on the wicker baskets story, see "Cape Horn: Ropes or Baskets" at http://cprr.org/Museum/Chinese.html#baskets.

29. Saxton, "Army of Canton in the High Sierra," 149 and 141–52; Lewis, *Big Four*, 69–70; Jung, *Coolies and Cane*, passim.

30. Lewis, *Big Four*, 69; McCague, *Moguls and Iron Men*, 103.

31. Ambrose, *Nothing Like It in the World*, 391–93 and 532–33; Hong Kingston, *China Men*, 141; McCague, *Moguls and Iron Men*, 198; Chiu, *Chinese Labor in California*, 47; Dodge, *How We Built the Union Pacific Railway*, 24; Sabin, *Building the Pacific Railway*, 196–97; for the press on strike demands, see David Montgomery, *The Fall of the House of Labor: The Workplace, the State, and American Labor Activism, 1865–1925* (Cambridge: Cambridge University Press, 1987), 67–68; Vimalassery, "Skew Tracks," 485–111 and esp. 100 (on the right to quit).

32. Vimalssery, "Skew Tracks," 72 ("price of labor") and 85–112; and; Chiu, *Chinese Labor in California*, 45–46; on meanings of "coolie" and the problem of its implications for idea of near-total lack of freedom to postbellum Chinese workers in the West, see Committee of the Senate of the State of California, *Chinese Immigration: The Social, Moral, and Political Effect of Chinese Immigration* (Sacramento, CA: State Printing Office, 1876), esp. 26–36; Mary Roberts Coolidge, *Chinese Immigration* (New York: Henry Holt, 1909), 41–68; Ambrose, *Nothing Like It in the World*, 395 ("price of labor"); See also Saxton, "Army of Canton in the High Sierra," 150–51. On Nevada, see Loren B. Chan, "The Chinese in Nevada: An Historical Survey, 1856–1970," in Arif Dirlik, ed., with the assistance of Malcolm Yeung, *Chinese on the American Frontier* (Lanham, MD: Rowman and Littlefield, 2001), 91–92.

33. John C. Lammers, "The Accommodation of Chinese Immigrants in Early California Courts," *Sociological Perspectives* 31 (October 1988): esp. 452–53; Coolidge, *Chinese Immigration*, 26–141.

34. Saxton, "Army of Canton in the High Sierra," 51–52; Steiner, *Fusang*, 128–29 and 138.

35. Sabin, *Building the Pacific Railway*, 176–77; Erle Heath, "A Railroad Record That Defies Defeat," *Southern Pacific Bulletin* 16 (May 1928): 3–5.

36. Crocker in *Report of the Joint Special Committee to Investigate Chinese Immigration*, 15.

37. Ambrose, *Nothing Like It in the World*, 251–53, 323 and 382; Chew, *Nameless Builders of the Transcontinental Railroad*, 51.

38. For controversies on the numbers of deaths, cf. "Dead Chinese" at CPRR Discussion Group. Central Pacific Railroad Photographic History Museum website at http://cprr.org/CPRR_Discussion_Group/2007/01/dead-chinese.html (2007) and William F. Chew, "Author's Rebuttal" Central Pacific Railroad Photographic History Museum website at http://cprr.org/Museum/Rebuttal_William_Chew.html (2004); Chew, *Nameless Builders of the Transcontinental Railroad*, 94, 97–98 (on Ambrose and historiography), and 94–101; on Chinese death rates in British colonial mines, see Vimalassery, "Skew Tracks," 94–95. On "race," immigration, and the toleration of industrial accidents, see Michael K. Rosenow, "Injuries to All: The Rituals of Dying and the Politics of Death among United States Workers, 1877–1910" (PhD diss., University of Illinois, 2008), 32–33 and 81. On snow and danger, see Saxton, *Indispensable Enemy*, 64–65.

39. Crocker, in *Report of the Joint Special Committee to Investigate Chinese Immigration*, 6 on prejudice; Stanford quoted in Williams, *Great & Shining Road*, 97.

40. Crocker in *Report of the Joint Special Committee to Investigate Chinese Immigration*, 7–8; Ambrose, *Nothing Like It in the World*, 391–93; Vimalassery, "Skew Tracks," 98 ("Chinese quiet") and 99.

41. Crocker in *Report of the Joint Special Committee to Investigate Chinese Immigration*, 18 and 12; Strobridge, in ibid., 24–26; Kraus, *High Road to Promontory*, 204–8; Ambrose, *Nothing Like It in the World*, 507 (*Chronicle* and "herders"); Chiu, *Chinese Labor in California*, 89 ("Riding Bosses"). On gangs and pay, see David Montgomery, *Workers Control in America* (Cambridge: Cambridge University Press, 1979), 11–12. When Chinese names were listed by CP management, they often featured "generalized honorifics," not individual first names. See Vimalassery, "Skew Tracks," 71.

42. Crocker in *Report of the Joint Special Committee to Investigate Chinese Immigration*, 8 and 15.

43. Wolmar, *Blood, Iron, and Gold*, 145; W. Thomas White, "Race, Ethnicity and Gender in the Railroad Work Force: The Case of the Far Northwest, 1883–1918," *Western Historical Quarterly* 16 (July 1985): esp. 266–67; Edward J. M. Rhoads, "The Chinese in Texas," in Dirlik, ed., *Chinese on the American Frontier*, 171–72.

44. Erika Lee, *At America's Gates: The Exclusion Era, 1882–1943* (Chapel Hill: University of North Carolina Press, 2003) 1–46; Roger Daniels, *The*

Politics of Prejudice: The Anti-Japanese Movement in California and the Struggle for Japanese Exclusion (Berkeley: University of California Press, 1977, originally 1962), esp. 31–45; Chang, *Chinese in America*, 116–56.

45. Kornel S. Chang, "Transpacific Borderlands and Boundaries: Race, Migration, and State Formation the in North American Pacific Rim, 1882–1917," 2 vols. (PhD diss., University of Chicago, 2007), 1: 28, 33 n. 10, 28–34, and 52–54. Professor Chang has generously shared research materials.

46. "[I. Hirota] Hirota and Son to R. Harding, Gen. Supt. G.N.R." (October 8, 1898) and "R. Harding to J. J. Hill" (September 8, 1898) both in *Great Northern Railway Collection*, Minnesota Historical Society, Saint Paul, Microfilm, part 1, 1862–1922, series B (Labor), [hereafter GNRC], reel 1; Chang, "Transpacific Borderlands and Boundaries," 53–67 and the unpublished chapter "The Next Wave: Colonial Expansion and Japanese Migrant Labor" from his forthcoming book provisionally titled *Pacific Connections: Race, Migration, and Empire in the U.S.-Canadian Borderlands* (Berkeley: University of California Press) inform our account of the GN and OTC as does Yuji Ichioka, "Japanese Immigrant Labor Contractors and the Northern Pacific and the Great Northern Railroad Companies, 1898–1907," *Labor History* 21 (Summer 1980): 325–50.

47. "General Superintendent [F. E. Ward] to Geo. T. Ross" (March 21, 1900) GNRC, reel 1, for the quotation. In the same collection, see also "P. T. Downs to Mr. F. E. Ward" (December 20, 1899, and February 15, 1900) and "P. T. Downs to Unknown" (undated) GNRC, reel 1, Image 645.

48. "General Superintendent to P. T. Downs" (June 7, 1900) for "further East" and "Oriental Trading Company to Mr. F. E. Ward" (November 23, 1902), all in GNRC, reel 1; Chang, "Transpacific Borderlands and Boundaries," 64.

49. For Hill on Swedes, see e.g., William H. Rehnquist, "Reflections on Swedish Immigration to the United States," *Scandinavian Review* 89 (Winter 2002) at http://findarticles.com/p/articles/mi_qa3760/is_200201/ai_n9078884/pg_3/; "C. T. Takahashi to Geo. T. Slade" (December 9, 1903), GNRC, reel 1; Albro Martin, *James J. Hill and the Opening of the Northwest* (New York: Oxford University Press, 1976), 431; "General Manager to Mr. George T. Slade" (July 18, 1903); "H. A. Kennedy to General Superintendent G. T. Slade" (June 24, 1903); "H. A. Kennedy to J. R. W. Davis" (March 17, 1905); "G. H. Emerson to Mr. Geo. T. Slade" (April 9, 1906) for a 25 percent pay premium to Italians over Japanese; "H. Elliott to G. T. Slade" (March 27, 1905) and "General Superintendent Russell Harding to P. T. Downs" (June 7, 1900), all from GNRC, reel 1; Chang, *Pacific Connections*, forthcoming.

50. Claire Strom, *Profiting from the Plains: The Great Northern Railway and Corporate Development of the American West* (Seattle: University of Washington Press, 2003), 88–89; "C. T. Takahashi to F. E. Ward" (October 10,

1905), GNRC, reel 1; Joseph Gilpin Pyle, *The Life of James J. Hill*, 2 vols. (Garden City, NY: Doubleday, 1917), 2: 52 ("thief"); Chang, "Transpacific Borderlands and Boundaries," 59–60 and "Next Wave," forthcoming.

51. Hill as quoted in Chang, "Transpacific Borderlands and Boundaries," 64; "H. A. Kennedy to F. E. Ward" (December 13, 1902), on tensions with "book-men" see"Oriental Trading Company to F. E. Ward" (November 23, 1902), GNRC, reel 1.

52. "H. A. Kennedy to F. E. Ward" (December 13, 1902) and "Russell Harding to Oriental Trading Company" (January 22, 1905) both GNRC, reel 1; on the lawsuits, see "F. E. Ward to Mr. George T. Slade" (July 6, 1903) and "General Superintendent to H. A. Kennedy" (July 9, 1903) GNRC, reel 1; see also "C. T. Takahashi to F. E. Ward" (December 9, 1902 and January 23, 1902) GNRC, reel 1 for disputes on how to racially classify jobs. On snow and railway work, see Saxton, *Indispensable Enemy*, 64–65.

53. "G. T. Slade to H. A. Kennedy" (December 15, 1901); "C. T. Takahashi to George T. Slade" (October 11, 1906); "L. W. Hill to Mr. Howard Elliott, President, Northern Pacific Railway Company" (October 26, 1905); "H. A. Kennedy to R.W. Bryan" (July 1, 1907) and "H. A. Kennedy to G. H. Emerson" (June 5, 1907) all GNRC, reel 1; Chang, "Transpacific Borderlands and Boundaries," 83 and 84 for the quotations and 65 and 80–85.

54. "H. A. Kennedy to J. R. W. Davis" (March 17, 1905) and "Oriental Trading Company to F. E. Ward" (October 10, 1905) both GNRC, reel 1; "Proof of Japanese Plot: Takahashi Reported to Yamaoka and Told Him to Agitate," *New York Times*, June 11, 1907, 4; Ichioka, "Japanese Immigrant Labor Contractors," esp. 327–35; Chang, "Transpacific Borderlands and Boundaries," 64–76. See Daniels, *Politics of Prejudice*, esp. 31–45 for a fine account of exclusion at the national level.

55. Chang, "Transpacific Borderlands and Boundaries," 65; White, "Race, Ethnicity and Gender in the Railroad Work Force," 278–78. On the cross-border traffic, see Kornel Chang, "Enforcing Transnational White Solidarity: Asian Migration and the Formation of the U.S.-Canadian Boundary," *American Quarterly* 60 (September 2008): esp. 671–88.

56. We take "miner's frontier" from Turner, *Frontier in American History*, 12. See also 3–4.

57. For "white citizen-worker," see Eric Meeks, *Border Citizens: The Making of Indians, Mexicans and Anglos in Arizona* (Austin: University of Texas Press, 2007); for "citizen-miner" and "questionably white" see Katherine Benton-Cohen, *Borderline Americans: Racial Division and Labor War in the Arizona Borderlands* (Cambridge, MA: Harvard University Press, 2009), 146 and passim.

58. Turner, *Frontier in American History*, 3–4 and 279; Charles Howard Shinn, *Mining Camps: A Study in American Frontier Government*, Rodman Wilson Paul, ed. (Gloucester, MA: Peter Smith, 1970, originally 1884), xvii and 212.

59. "Sociology in Mining Camps," *Camp and Plant* 2 (November 22, 1902): 573 and 574, reprinted from *Springfield Daily Republican*, September 27, 1902.

60. Frank J. Weed, "The Sociological Department at the Colorado Fuel and Iron Company, 1901–1907: Scientific Paternalism and Industrial Control," *Journal of the History of the Behavioral Sciences* 41 (Summer 2005): 269, n. 1 and 269–84; Montgomery, *Fall of the House of Labor*, 237–38.

61. Weed, "Sociological Department," 272 and 73 ("mixed") and passim; Ross, *The Old World in the New: The Significance of Past and Present Immigration to the American People* (New York: Century, 1914), 209. For *Camp and Plant* on the races, hierarchies, and subdivisions of workers, see Alexander Toman, "Austrian Slavs of Pueblo," *Camp and Plant* 2 (December 27, 1902): 622–23.

62. Weed, "Sociological Department," 269, 273 quote from *Engineering* and 271–84; Sarah Deutsch, *No Separate Refuge: Culture, Class, and Gender on an Anglo-Hispanic Frontier in the American Southwest, 1880–1940* (New York: Oxford University Press, 1987), 94–99; Rick J. Clyne, *Coal People: Life in Southern Colorado's Company Towns, 1890–1930* (Denver: Colorado Historical Society, 1999), 20–24.

63. Scott Martelle, *Blood Passion: The Ludlow Massacre and Class War in the American West* (New Brunswick, NJ: Rutgers University Press, 2007), esp. 2 and 146–218; Zeese Papanikolas, *Buried Unsung: Louis Tikas and the Ludlow Massacre* (Salt Lake City: University of Utah Press, 1982), 39–238; Weed, "Sociological Department," 281; Anthony Destefanis, "Violence and the Colorado National Guard: Masculinity, Race, Class, and Identity in the 1913–1914 Southern Colorado Coal Strike," in Jaclyn J. Gier and Laurie Mercier, eds., *Mining Women: Gender in the Development of a Global Industry, 1670 to 2005* (New York: Palgrave Macmillan, 2006), 203–5 and Turner, *Frontier in American History*, 319.

64. John Reed, *The Education of John Reed: Selected Writings* (New York: International, 1955), 116.

65. Upton Sinclair, *King Coal: A Novel* (New York: Macmillan, 1917), 1, 91, 266–67, 153, 64, 66–67 and, for the excerpts from the testimony, 384–96.

66. Sinclair, *King Coal*, 55–56, 21, 23, and 91–201. See also Rick Clyne, *Coal People: Life in Southern Colorado's Coal Towns* (Denver: Colorado Historical Society, 2000).

67. Walter Schroeder and Howard Marshall, eds., *Missouri: The WPA Guide to the "Show-Me" State* (Saint Louis: Missouri Historical Society Press, 1998), xii; "Why Is Missouri Called the 'Show-Me' State?" in the "Missouri History" section of the website of the Missouri Secretary of State at http://www.sos.mo.gov/archives/history/slogan.asp; Mark Wyman, *Hard Rock Epic: Western Miners and the Industrial Revolution, 1860–1910* (Berkeley: University of California Press, 1979), 45–51 and 57; Ronald C. Brown, *Hard-Rock Miners: The Intermountain West, 1860–1920* (College

Station: Texas A&M University Press, 1979), 128; on Du Bois, see David
Roediger, "Afterword: Du Bois, Race, and Italian Americans," in Jennifer
Guglielmo and Salvatore Salerno, eds., *Are Italians White? How Race Is
Made in America* (New York: Routledge, 2003), 259–64; on contemporary
apprehensions of mining, race, and strikebreaking, see Ross, *Old World in
the New*, 207–8.

68. James Whiteside, *Regulating Danger: The Struggle for Mine Safety in the
Rocky Mountain Coal Industry* (Lincoln: University of Nebraska Press,
1990), 48–49; Deutsch, *No Separate Refuge*, 94–85; Wyman, *Hard Rock
Epic*, 57; Allan Kent Powell, *The Next Time We Strike: Labor in Utah's
Coal Fields, 1900–1933* (Logan: Utah State University Press, 1985), 46–47;
David M. Emmons, *The Butte Irish: Class and Ethnicity in an American
Mining Town, 1875–1925* (Urbana: University of Illinois Press, 1990), 369.

69. Destefanis, "Violence and the Colorado National Guard," 200; Benton-
Cohen, *Borderline Americans*, 106; Wyman, *Hard Rock Epic*, 118–48;
Richard E. Lingenfelter, *The Hardrock Miners: A History of the Mining
Labor Movement in the American West, 1863–1893* (Berkeley: University
of California Press, 1974) 23–24; Thomas G. Andrews, *Killing for Coal:
America's Deadliest Labor War* (Cambridge, MA: Harvard University Press,
2008), 172–73.

70. Michael Rosenow, "Injuries to All: The Rituals of Dying and the
Politics of Death Among United States Workers, 1877–1910" (PhD diss.,
University of Illinois, 2008), 30–41; Tom Vaughan, "Everyday Life in
a Copper Camp," in Carlos Schwantes, ed., *Bisbee: Urban Outpost on
a Frontier* (Tucson: University of Arizona Press, 1992), 61; Emmons,
Butte Irish, 368; William M. Leiserson, *Adjusting Immigrant and Industry*
(New York: Harper and Bros., 1924), 134; David Roediger, *Working
toward Whiteness: How America's Immigrants Became White* (New York:
Basic, 2005), 44.

71. Whiteside, *Regulating Danger*, 83, 49, and 80–105; Rosenow, "Injuries to
All," 31–40; Powell, *Next Time We Strike*, 33–35.

72. Quoted in Whiteside, *Regulating Danger*, 105; see also 61 and 93; Andrews, *Killing for Coal*, 151–52.

73. Whiteside, *Regulating Danger*, 82 and 83 ("holocausts"); Emmons, *Butte
Irish*, 182 and 364–86; Arnon Gutfeld, "The Speculator Disaster in 1917:
Labor Resurgence in Butte, Montana," *Arizona and the West* 11 (Spring
1969): 27–38. On smelting, danger, and race, see Laurie Mercier, *Ana-
conda: Labor, Community, and Culture in Montana's Smelter City* (Urbana:
University of Illinois Press, 2001), 31–32; Matthew Basso, "Man-Power:
Montana Copper Workers, State Authority, and the (Re)Drafting of
Manhood during World War II," in Matthew Basso, Laura McCall, and
Dee Garceau, eds., *Across the Great Divide: Cultures of Manhood in the
American West* (New York: Routledge, 2001), 188–91; Benton-Cohen,
Borderline Americans, 109.

74. Philip J. Mellinger, *Race and Labor in Western Copper: The Fight for Equality, 1896–1916* (Tucson: University of Arizona Press, 1995), 160–61 and 192–203; Benton-Cohen, *Borderline Americans*, 201–4 and 229–30.

75. Emmons, *Butte Irish*, 182 and 368 ("kaleidoscopic") and 364–66; Whiteside, *Regulating Danger*, 48; Theodore Jesse Hoover, *The Economics of Mining (Non-Ferrous Metals): Valuation—Organization—Management* (Stanford, CA: Stanford University Press, 1933), 143 and 468–70; on the "white man's camp" and other axes of division, see Benton-Cohen, *Borderline Americans*, 87 ("peon") and 80–119; Brown, *Hard-Rock Miners*, 133 and 134 ("peon"); Phylis Cancilla Martinelli, *Undermining Race: Ethnic Identities in Arizona Copper Camps* (Tucson: University of Arizona Press, 2009), 108–10.

76. Emmons, *Butte Irish*, 368; Terry Boswell and John Brueggeman, "Labor Market Segmentation and the Cultural Division of Labor in the Copper Mining Industry," in Patrick Coy, ed., *Research in Social Movements, Conflicts and Change*, vol. 22 (Stamford, CT: JAI Press, 2000), 200–201; Whiteside, *Regulating Danger*, 48 ("turbulent"); Deutsch, *No Separate Refuge*, 94–95; Lingenfelter, *Hardrock Miners*, 5–6; Mellinger, *Race and Labor in Western Copper*, 74–79, 181, and 184. On wholesale changes of employer opinion on hiring preferences, see also Brown, *Hard-Rock Miners*, 132.

77. Wyman, *Hard Rock Epic*, 55 and 58; Gunther Peck, *Reinventing Free Labor: Padrones and Immigrant Workers in the North American West, 1880–1930* (Cambridge: Cambridge University Press, 2000), 167–69; Linda Gordon, *The Great Arizona Orphan Abduction* (Cambridge, MA: Harvard University Press, 1999), 57–59.

78. Whiteside, *Regulating Danger*, 49 ("no two"); Brown, *Hard-Rock Miners*, 132 (for Siringo) and 119.

79. Powell, *Next Time We Strike*, 129; Mellinger, *Race and Labor in Western Copper*, 242, n. 57; Roediger, *Working toward Whiteness*, 89; Philip D. Dreyfus, "The IWW and the Limits of Inter-Ethnic Organizing: Reds, Whites, and Greeks in Grays Harbor, Washington, 1912," *Labor History* 38 (Fall 1997): 454–69; Meeks, *Border Citizens*, 103.

80. Powell, *Next Time We Strike*, 46–47 (band); Wyman, *Hard Rock Epic*, 158; Lingenfelter, *Hardrock Miners*, 103–5; Brown, *Hard-Rock Miners*, 147; Emmons, *Butte Irish*, 145.

81. James W. Byrkit, *Forging the Copper Collar: Arizona's Labor-Management War of 1901–1921* (Tucson: University of Arizona Press, 1982), esp. 219–26; Meeks, *Border Citizens*, 107–8; Martinelli, *Undermining Race*, esp. 121; Emmons, *Butte Irish*, 398 and 340–86.

82. Boswell and Brueggeman, "Labor Market Segmentation and the Cultural Division of Labor in the Copper Mining Industry," 205, 208, and 209; Wyman, *Hard Rock Epic*, 267, n. 27; Carlos Schwantes, "Toil and Trouble: Rhythms of Work Life," in Schwantes, ed., *Bisbee*, 117; Martinelli, *Undermining Race*, 52; Lingenfelter, *Hardrock Miners*, 5–6; Geoff Mann,

"Race, Skill, and Section in Northern California," *Politics and Society* 30 (September 2002): 465–96.

83. Meeks, *Border Citizens*, 29–30; Boswell and Brueggeman, "Labor Market Segmentation and the Cultural Division of Labor in the Copper Mining Industry," 205–11; Martinelli, *Undermining Race*, 108–9; Lingenfelter, *Hardrock Miners*, 107–8; Vaughan, "Everyday Life in a Copper Camp," 61; Liping Zhu, *A Chinaman's Chance: The Chinese on the Rock Mountain Mining Frontier* (Niwot: University Press of Colorado, 1997), 104–8 and 123; Boswell and Brueggeman, "Labor Market Segmentation and the Cultural Division of Labor in the Copper Mining Industry," 201; David H. Stratton, "The Snake River Massacre of Chinese Miners," in Dirlik, ed., *Chinese on the American Frontier*, 215–30. On how the success of militant and violent insistence on Chinese exclusion by white miners could win political battles and even acquiescence from management in ways that class-wide demands could not, and the tragedies attending this reality, see esp. Brown, *Hard-Rock Miners*, 114–27; Wyman, *Hard Rock Epic*, 39; Chan, "Chinese in Nevada," 106–8. Benton-Cohen, *Borderline Americans*, 85–86 very astutely connects Chinese exclusion, anti-Mexican discrimination and the "white man's camp" as a site of class collaboration through white manliness.

84. Brown, *Hard-Rock Miners*, 134 ("greasers"); Martinelli, *Undermining Race*, 68–69 and 131; Benton-Cohen, *Borderline Americans*, 99–101.

85. Benton-Cohen, *Borderline Americans*, 167, 184, 202, and 229–37: Schwantes, "Toil and Trouble," 117; Antonio Rios Bustamante, "As Guilty as Hell: Mexican Copper Miners and Their Communities in Arizona, 1920–1950," in John Mason Hart, ed., *Border Crossings: Mexican and Mexican-American Workers* (Wilmington, DE: Scholarly Resources, 1998), esp.170; Meeks, *Border Citizens*, 184.

Chapter 4

1. Herman Melville, "The 'Gees," in *Great Short Works of Herman Melville*, Warner Berthoff, ed. (New York: Harper and Row, 1969, originally 1856), 355–61.

2. Ibid.; Carolyn L. Karcher, "Melville's 'The 'Gees': A Forgotten Satire on Scientific Racism," *American Quarterly* 27 (October 1975): 421–22; Melville, "Benito Cereno," in *Great Short Works*, 238–315, originally from 1854 and 1855.

3. Gerald Horne, *The White Pacific: U.S. Imperialism and Black Slavery in the South Seas after the Civil War* (Honolulu: University of Hawaii Press, 2006), 77–91, esp. 78–80.

4. Frenise A. Logan, "A British East India Company Agent in the United States, 1839–1840," *Agricultural History* 48 (April 1974): 267–78; Andrew Zimmerman, *Africa in Alabama: Booker T. Washington, the German Empire, and the Globalization of the New South* (Princeton, NJ: Princeton

University Press, 2010), esp.173, 167 and 166–72; Donald C. Simmons, Jr., *Confederate Settlements in British Honduras* (Jefferson, NC: McFarland, 2001), 54–57, 77, 96, and 95–103 passim.

5. George Cary Eggleston, *Love Is the Sum of It All* (Boston: Lothrop, Lee and Shepard, 1907), 35, 94–95, 110, 117–18, and 175 for quoted passages. See also 36–37, 50, 64, 118, 138, 176–77, 193, 211–15, 300, 325, 383, and 385. We thank Professor Jeremy Wells of Southern Illinois University for alerting us to the novel and sharing his excellent work on it in his forthcoming study of white Southern men and the "burdens of empire."

6. James E. Brittain and Robert C. McMath, Jr., "Engineering and the New South Creed," *Technology and Culture* 18 (April 1977): 195–97; Robert C. McMath, Jr., Ronald H. Bayor, James E. Brittain, Lawrence Foster, August W. Giebelhaus, and Germaine M. Reed, *Engineering the New South: Georgia Tech, 1885–1985* (Athens: University of Georgia Press, 1985), 81; Eggleston, *Love Is the Sum of It All*, 35, 94–95, 110, 117–18, and 175 for quoted passages. See also 36–37, 50, 118, 138, 176–77, 193, 211–15, 300, 325, 383, and 385.

7. Ronald Takaki, *Iron Cages: Race and Culture in 19th-Century America* (New York: Oxford University Press, 2000), 161.

8. Andrew Carnegie, "The Venezuelan Question," *North American Review* 471 (February 1896): 133. Cf. "Lo, the Poor Indian," *Barron's* 4 (November 10, 1924), 9 for an even more extreme sense that, whether in Australia, New Zealand, Canada, or the United States, when an "aboriginal race" is exterminated "it is hard to see more than a sentimental reason for deploring its extinction. People die anyway."

9. Shelley Streeby, *American Sensations: Class, Empire, and the Production of Popular Culture* (Berkeley: University of California Press, 2002), 183–91; Reginald Horsman, *Race and Manifest Destiny: The Origins of American Anglo-Saxonism* (Cambridge, MA: Harvard University Press, 1981), 208–28.

10. Aims McGuinness, *Paths of Empire: Panama and the California Gold Rush* (London: Cornell University Press, 2008), 192 and 58. For background, see also 54–83 and 150.

11. McGuinness, *Paths of Empire*, 54–55, 62 and 56–83; Fesseden Nott Otis, *Isthmus of Panama: History of the Panama Railroad and of the Pacific Steamship Company* (New York: Harper and Bros., 1867), 76 and 35.

12. McGuinness, *Paths of Empire*, 62, 70–71, 66, and 54–83; Otis, *Isthmus of Panama*, 35–36; Lancelot S. Lewis, *The West Indian in Panama: Black Labor in Panama, 1850–1914* (Washington, DC: University Press of America, 1980), 17–18. For a leering medical view of the suicides, see Robert Tomes, *Panama in 1855: An Account of the Panama Rail-Road* (New York: Harper and Bros., 1855), 120–21.

13. On the canal and its pay system, see Julie Greene's masterful *The Canal Builders: Making America's Empire in the Panama Canal* (New York: Penguin Press, 2009), esp. 64–67 and 37–158.

244   NOTES TO PAGES 103-107

14. Harry A. Franck, *Zone Policeman 88: A Close Range Study of the Panama Canal and Its Workers* (New York: Century, 1913), 30; Michael Conniff, *Black Labor on a White Canal: Panama, 1904–1981* (Pittsburgh, PA: University of Pittsburgh Press, 1985), 32–33.

15. Franck, *Zone Policeman*, 119 and 124; Velma Newton, *The Silver Men: West Indian Labour Migration to Panama, 1850–1914* (Mona, Jamaica: Institute of Social and Economic Research: University of the West Indies, 1984), 92–93.

16. For the deaths, see Conniff, *Black Labor on a White Canal*, 30–31; Franck, *Zone Policeman*, 119 and 84; see also Greene, *Canal Builders*, 134–41.

17. Franck, *Zone Policeman*, 84, 38, 119, and 225; William L. Sibert and John Frank Stevens, *The Construction of the Panama Canal* (New York: D. Appleton, 1915), 115; Joseph Buchlin Bishop, *Goethals: Genius of the Panama Canal: A Biography* (New York: Harper and Bros., 1930), 62–64; Sydney Bacon Williamson Papers (Virginia Military Institute) at http://www.vmi.edu/archives.aspx?id=14125; Conniff, *Black Labor on a White Canal*, 35, 43, and 31–38.

18. Michael P. Malone, *James J. Hill, Empire Builder of the Northwest* (Norman: University of Oklahoma Press, 1996), 131–33; John F. Stevens, *An Engineer's Recollections* (n.p.: Engineering News-Record reprint, 1935), 22–25; Greene, *Canal Builders*, 43 and 44–53. For Stevens's central importance to James J. Hill, see Albro Martin, *James J. Hill and the Opening of the Northwest* (New York: Oxford University Press, 1976), 379, 381–83, 507–8, and 566–67.

19. Greene, *Canal Builders*, 48; Sibert and Stevens, *Construction of the Panama Canal*, 115–16.

20. Greene, *Canal Builders*, 50–52 and 408, n. 28.

21. Conniff, *Black Labor on a White Canal*, 25 ("excuse") and 35; Lewis, *West Indian in Panama*, 46, 34, and 48; Sibert and Stevens, *Construction of the Panama Canal*, 113–15; Greene, *Canal Builders*, 50, 51, 52, 39–53, and 160–65; David McCullough, *The Path Between the Seas: The Creation of the Panama Canal, 1870–1914* (New York: History Book Club, 2002, originally 1977), 474–77. On Guatemala, see Frederick Douglass Opie, *Black Labor Migration in Caribbean Guatemala, 1882–1923* (Gainesville: University Press of Florida, 2009), 17–35.

22. Greene, *Canal Builders*, 50; John Foster Carr, "The Panama Canal, Fourth Paper: The Silver Men," *Outlook*, May 19, 1906, 120 and 117–19.

23. Michael O'Malley, "Specie and Species: Race and the Money Question in Nineteenth-Century America," *American Historical Review* 99 (April 1994): 369–95. For "semiwhite" see Greene, *Canal Builders*, 470.

24. Greene, *Canal Builders*, 146–47 [quoting Stevens on West Indians], 164, and 160–79; Frederic J. Haskin, *The Panama Canal* (Garden City, NJ: Doubleday, 1914), 157; Lewis, *West Indian in Panama*, 36; Conniff, *Black Labor on a White Canal*, 33 and 36.

25. Greene, *Canal Builders*, 163; Lewis, *West Indian in Panama*, 49; Conniff, *Black Labor on a White Canal*, 38.

26. Sibert and Stevens, *Construction of the Panama Canal*, 118; Stevens, *Engineer's Recollections*, 45.

27. Tomes, *Panama in 1855*, 112 and 80–81. Our treatment of Tomes, and of Mary Jane Megquier, benefits greatly from Jake Mattox's "Claiming Panama: Genre and Gender in Antebellum U.S. Isthmiana," under review at *American Studies*. On Tomes's biography, here and below, see "Inventory of the Francis and Robert Tomes Papers" from Midwest Manuscript Collection at Newberry Library (Chicago) at http://www.newberry.org/collections/FindingAids/tomes/Tomesf.html.

28. Tomes, *Panama in 1855*, 40–41, 44, 202, 186, 173–74, 91,151, 228, 151, 230, and 215.

29. Tomes, *Panama in 1855*, 116 and 207. See also 68.

30. Tomes, *Panama in 1855*, 112; Robert Glass Cleland, ed., *Apron Full of Gold: The Letters of Mary Jane Megquier from San Francisco, 1849–1856* (San Marino, CA: Huntington Library, 1949), vi, 11, and 15; Polly Welts Kaufman, ed., *Apron Full of Gold: The Letters of Mary Jane Megquier from San Francisco, 1849–1856* (Albuquerque: University of New Mexico Press, 1994), 15 and 140; Amy S. Greenberg, *Manifest Manhood and the Antebellum American Empire* (Cambridge: Cambridge University Press, 2005), 205, 211–15.

31. Kaufman, *Apron Full of Gold*, 18, 12, 100–101, and 122; Cleland, *Apron Full of Gold*, 59; Mattox, "Claiming Panama" is especially acute on Megquier in California.

32. Kaufman, *Apron Full of Gold*, xv, 12, 25, 47, 100–101, and 122. Cleland, *Apron Full of Gold*, 11 and 19.

33. Greene, *Canal Builders*, 259 and 230–60; Lewis, *West Indian in Panama*, 62–66.

34. Tomes, *Panama in 1855*, 218; Greene, *Canal Builders*, 292, 293, and 292–95 passim.

35. Greene, *Canal Builders*, 59, 69, and 58–75; Vicente Rafael, *White Love and Other Events in Filipino History* (Durham, NC: Duke University Press, 2000), 69 and 58–74.

36. Committee of the Senate of the State of California, *Chinese Immigration: The Social, Moral, and Political Effect of Chinese Immigration* (Sacramento, CA: State Printing Office, 1876), 35, 59, 62, 81, 88, 101, 102, 107, 109, 112–13, 116, 118, 125–26, and 131; on prostitution and slavery in the report, see e.g., 33, 47–48, 55, 59 69, 80, 89, 93, 99, 100, 108–9, 115, 120, 126, 128, 136, and 142; Najia Aarim-Heriot, *Chinese Immigrants, African Americans, and Racial Anxiety in the United States, 1848–82* (Urbana: University of Illinois Press, 2003), 174–82; Ronald Takaki, *Strangers from a Different Shore: A History of Asian Americans* (New York: Penguin, 1989), 40. On "hoodlums," and for a good account of the 1876 hearings, see Hiroyuki

Matsabara, "Stratified Whiteness and Sexualized Chinese Immigrants in San Francisco: The Report of the California Special Committee on Immigration in 1876," *American Studies International* 41 (October 2003): 43 and 32–59.

37. Greenberg, *Manifest Manhood*, 123 and 112–34. Streeby, *American Sensations*, esp. 100–144; Tomás Almaguer, *Racial Fault Lines: The Historical Origins of White Supremacy in California* (Berkeley: University of California Press, 1994), 58–59; Katherine Benton-Cohen, *Borderline Americans: Racial Division and Labor War in the Arizona Borderlands* (Cambridge, MA: Harvard University Press, 2009), 36–40.

38. Margaret Lynch-Brennan, *The Irish Bridget: Irish Immigrant Women in Domestic Service in America, 1840–1930* (Syracuse, NY: Syracuse University Press, 2009), 119, 118, and 163–68; Martha M. Gardner, "Working on White Womanhood: White Working Women in the San Francisco Anti-Chinese Movement, 1877–1890," *Journal of Social History* 33 (Fall 1999): 73–95. Bee as quoted in Andrew Theodore Urban's invaluable "An Intimate World: Race, Migration, and Chinese and Irish Domestic Servants in the United States, 1850–1920" (PhD diss., University of Minnesota, 2009), 105; Faye E. Dudden, *Serving Women: Household Service in Nineteenth Century America* (Middletown, CT: Wesleyan University Press, 1983), 64–65; Almaguer, *Racial Fault Lines*, 48–50, 130, 142, and 185; Evelyn Nakano Glenn, "The Dialectics of Wage Work: Japanese-American Women and Domestic Service, 1905–1940," *Feminist Studies* 6 (Fall 1980): 432–71. For trends in the service labor force's composition over time, see David Katzman, *Seven Days a Week: Women and Domestic Service in Industrializing America* (Urbana: University of Illinois Press, 1981), 44–94; Priscilla Wegars, "Entrepreneurs and 'Wage Slaves': Their Relationship to Anti-Chinese Racism in Northern Idaho's Mining Labor Community, 1880–1910," in Marcel van der Linden and Jan Lucassen, eds., *Racism and the Labour Movement: Historical Studies* (Bern: Peter Lang, 1995), 471; Benton-Cohen, *Borderline Americans*, 75.

39. Nerissa S. Balce, "The Filipina's Breast: Savagery, Docility, and the Erotics of the American Empire," *Social Text* 87 (Summer 2006): 103; Paul Taillon, *Good, Reliable White Men: Railroad Brotherhoods, 1877–1917* (Urbana: University of Illinois Press, 2009), 32–33 and Taillon, " 'By Every Right and Tradition': Racism and Fraternalism in the Railway Brotherhoods, 1880–1910," Unpublished paper delivered to the American Studies Association, Baltimore, 1991, for white skilled workers exacting personal service from workers of color on the job.

40. Cleland, *Apron Full of Gold*, 76–77.

41. Almaguer, *Racial Fault Lines*, 158–61; Robert G. Lee, *Orientals: Asian Americans in Popular Culture* (Philadelphia, PA: Temple University Press, 1999), 82–105; Takaki, *Iron Cages*, 227.

42. The survey is quoted in David F. Noble, *America by Design: Science, Technology and the Rise of Corporate Capitalism* (New York: Oxford University Press, 1979), 172, which also is acute on management and nationality at 57–58. See Graham Adams, Jr., *Age of Industrial Violence, 1910–1915: The Activities and Findings of the United States Commission on Industrial Relations* (New York: Columbia University Press, 1966), 228 for the line (quoted by Noble at 57) of immigration and "developing management techniques."

43. Clark C. Spence, *Mining Engineers & the American West: The Lace-Boot Brigade, 1849–1933* (New Haven, CT: Yale University Press 1970), 165–87 and 278–317; Monte A. Calvert, *The Mechanical Engineer in America, 1830–1910: Professional Cultures in Conflict* (Baltimore, MD: Johns Hopkins University Press, 1967), 211. Shula Marks and Stanley Trapido, "Lord Milner and the South African State," *History Workshop Journal* 8 (Spring 1979): 61; Yvette Huginnie, "A New Hero Comes to Town: The Anglo Mining Engineer and 'Mexican Labor' as Contested Terrain in Southeastern Arizona, 1880–1920," *New Mexico Historical Review* 69 (October, 1994), 323–44; David R. Roediger, *Working toward Whiteness: How America's Immigrants Became White* (New York: Basic, 2005), 74–75. See also Steven G. Vick, *Degrees of Belief: Subjective Probability and Engineering Judgment* (Reston, VA: ASCE Press, 2002), 342; See esp. N. K. Nkosi, "American Mining Engineers and the Labor Structure of South African Gold Mines," *African Journal of Political Economy* 2 (August 1987): 69 on training in mines in the western United States. For a vivid example of larger patterns, with important and precocious South African ties, see the biography of John Hays Hammond in *Cyclopaedia of American Biography* (New York: Press Association Compilers, 1915), 56–61; see also ibid., 249–50 for the adventure/romance/engineering transnational biography of Frederick Russell Burnham, from Indian Wars to South Africa; ibid. on Eben Erskine Olcott at 558–60, and Richard Harding Davis, "Soldiers of Fortune," *Scribner's Magazine* 21 (January 1897): 29–47.

44. On Joralemon, see his interview with Henry Carlisle, "Arizona Characters and the Ajo Mine" from November 1959 and included in the Mining Engineer Project, vol. 1, part 1, in the Columbia University Oral History Project, Butler Library, Columbia University. It is unclear from context whether Joralemon meant "squaw men" to refer to the Indian miners or, as was more common usage, white men cohabiting with Indian women. See Angela Wanhalla, "Rethinking 'Squaw Men' and 'Pakeha-Maori': Legislating White Masculinity in New Zealand and Canada, 1840–1900" in Leigh Boucher, Jane Carey, and Katherine Ellinhaus, eds., *Re-Orienting Whiteness* (New York: Palgrave Macmillan, 2009), 219–34. On Tohono O'odham miners, see Eric V. Meeks, *Border Citizens: The Making of Indians, Mexicans, and Anglos in Arizona* (Austin: University of Texas Press, 2007), 29–30, 62, and 70.

45. Herbert A. Megraw, "The Mines of Mexico," *Engineering Magazine* 46 (October 1913): 44–45; Casper L. Redfield, "Industrial Ascendancy of the Anglo-American Peoples," *Engineering Magazine* 20 (February 1901): 847–52; Honnold as quoted in John Higginson, "Privileging the Machines: American Engineers, Indentured Chinese and White Workers in South Africa's Deep-Level Mines, 1902–1907," *International Review of Social History* 52 (2007): 10 and 15; see also James T. Campbell, "The Americanization of South Africa" in Reinhold Wagnleitner and Elaine Tyler May, eds., *"Here, There and Everywhere": The Foreign Politics of American Popular Culture* (Hanover, NH: University Press of New England, 2000), 38–41. On Jennings, see Nkosi, "American Mining Engineers," esp. 69–74 and 75 and Elaine Katz, "The Role of American Mining Technology and American Mining Engineers in the Witwatersrand Gold Mining Industry, 1890–1910," *Economic History of Developing Regions* 20 (September 2005): 48–82. On social Darwinism and competing theories of engineering education, see James Brittain and Robert McMath, Jr., "Engineers and the New South Creed: The Formation and Early Development of Georgia Tech," *Technology and Culture* 18 (April 1977): 177.

46. Bruce Cumings, *The Origins of the Korean War*, vol. 2, *The Roaring of the Cataract, 1947–1950* (Princeton, NJ: Princeton University Press, 1990), 142 and 141–45; Fred Harvey Harrington, *God, Mammon, and the Japanese* (New York: Arno Press, 1980, originally 1944), 161–65 and 186–87.

47. Brittain and McMath, Jr., "Engineers and the New South Creed," 195–97; Robert C. McMath, Jr., Ronald H. Bayor, James E. Brittain, Lawrence Foster, August W. Giebelhaus, and Germaine M. Reed, *Engineering the New South: Georgia Tech, 1885–1985* (Athens: University of Georgia Press, 1985), 81; Spence, *Mining Engineers*, 278; Jeremy Mouat and Ian Phimester, "The Engineering of Herbert Hoover," *Pacific Historical Review* 77 (2008): 555; Joan Hoff Wilson, *Herbert Hoover: Forgotten Progressive* (Prospect Heights, IL: Waveland Press, 1992, originally 1975), 33–37. On Janin, see the guide to his papers, held by the Huntington Library (San Marino, CA) at http://www.oac.cdlib.org/data/13030/b0/tf3b69n6b0/files/tf3b69n6b0.pdf; for "highest-salaried," see *San Francisco Chronicle*, December 8, 1901.

48. George H. Nash, *The Life of Herbert Hoover: The Engineer, 1874–1914* (New York: Norton, 1983), 72–73 and 330–33; Herbert Hoover Scrapbooks (Hoover Presidential Library, hereafter HL, West Branch, IA); "Extracts from Letters Home" (Western Australia, 1897?) in HL, box 50, Pre-Commerce Papers.

49. See, for example, "Rand Native Labor Committee" (1903) in HL, box 56, Pre-Commerce Papers; "Notes on Stopping on the Rand During 1907" in HL, box 55, Pre-Commerce Papers; Herbert Hoover, *Principles of Mining: Valuation, Organization and Administration* (New York: Hill, 1909), 161–65; "Hoover to Dear Mr. Congressman [John Baker]" (February 19,

1924) in HL, box 289, Commerce Papers and the draft dated February 13, 1924, in the same box; Herbert Hoover, "The Keeping Coal Mines and Coal Field, Chile Province, North China" in "Eighth Ordinary Meeting" proceedings of the Institute of Mining and Metallurgy (London, 1902), 419 and 426–27 in HL, box 50, Pre-Commerce Papers.

50. See the 1902 paper above and Hoover, "Metal Mining in the Provinces of Chi-lid and Shantung, China" printed in the proceedings of the Sixth Ordinary Meeting of the Institute of Mining and Metallurgy (London, 1900) in HL, box 50, Pre-Commerce Papers and the clipping in box 56 of the same collection defending Chinese miners.

51. Cf. the Hoover papers given in 1900 and 1902 and cited in note 27 and 28 above and the comment appended to (page 427) the 1902 paper.

52. Herbert Hoover, *The Memoirs of Herbert Hoover: Years of Adventure, 1874–1920* (New York: Macmillan, 1951), 69–71 and Hoover, *Principles of Mining*, 161–65. For a provocative exploration of the relationship of the use of race to organize management to more contemporary concerns about technology and the control of workers see Michael Perelman, "Preliminary Notes on Technology and Class Struggle," *Labor Tech: Bringing Technology to Serve the Labor Movement*, http://www.labortech.net/Papers.htm.

53. T. A. Rickard, ed., *The Economics of Mining* (New York, 1905), 388 reprints material from the *Engineering and Mining Journal*; Hoover, *Principles of Mining*, 162; H. G. Prout, "The Economic Conquest of Africa," *Engineering Magazine* 18 (February 1900): 657 and 680; Theodore Jesse Hoover, *The Economics of Mining (Non-Ferrous Metals): Valuation—Organization—Management* (Stanford, CA: Stanford University Press, 1933), 143 and 469.

54. John Higginson, "Privileging the Machines: American Engineers, Indentured Chinese and White Workers in South Africa's Deep-Level Mines, 1902–1907," *International Review of Social History* 52 (2007), 16 and 12–26; Kornel Chang, "Transpacific Borderlands and Boundaries: Race, Migration, and State Formation the in North American Pacific Rim, 1882–1917," 2 vols. (PhD diss., University of Chicago, 2007), 1: 101. See also Nkosi, "American Mining Engineers," 76; Mouat and Phimester, "Engineering of Herbert Hoover," 581, n. 87 and Peter Richardson, "Coolies and Randlords: The North Randfontein Chinese Miners' 'Strike' of 1905," *Journal of Southern African Studies* 2 (April 1976): 151–77. On Matthews and the transnational patterns of labor reform and Chinese exclusion that he was part of, see Marilyn Lake and Henry Reynolds, *Drawing the Global Colour Line: White Men's Countries and the International Challenge of Racial Equality* (Cambridge: Cambridge University Press, 2008), 221 and passim.

55. William Edward Leuchtenburg, *Herbert Hoover* (New York: Henry Holt, 2009), 13–14; Hoover, *Memoirs of Hoover*, 48–53; David C. King, *Herbert*

Hoover (Tarrytown, NY: Marshall Cavendish, 2010), 26–31. Cf. Friedrich Katz, *Life and Times of Pancho Villa* (Stanford, CA: Stanford University Press, 1998), 567–76 on the murders of eighteen mining engineers by Villa's forces in 1916 as one factor leading to the subsequent U.S. incursion into Mexico.

56. Wilson, *Hoover*, 32–33; Hoover, *Memoirs of Hoover*, 71; on Ford, see Stephen Meyer, III, *The Five-Dollar Day: Labor Management and Social Control in the Ford Motor Company, 1908–1921* (Albany: SUNY Press, 1981), esp.156–92. See also Elizabeth Esch, "Shades of Tarzan! Ford on the Amazon," *Cabinet: A Quarterly Journal of Art and Culture* 7 (Summer 2002): 76–79.

57. Paul A. Kramer, *The Blood of Government: Race, Empire, the United States and the Philippines* (Chapel Hill: University of North Carolina Press, 2006), 124–30, 181 (for Taft) and 313 ("capacity"); Richard Drinnon, *Facing West: The Metaphysics of Indian-Hating and Empire-Building* (New York: New American Library, 1980), 281 ("utter unfitness") and 279–332; Rafael, *White Love*, 34 ("imitation"). See also Paul A. Kramer, "The Water Cure: Debating Torture and Counterinsurgency a Century Ago," *New Yorker*, February 25, 2008, 5. See also the beautifully researched American Social History Project Film, *Savage Acts: on Wars, Fairs and Empire* (American Social History Project, 1994.)

58. Beveridge as quoted in Cynthia H. Tolentino, *America's Experts: Race and the Fictions of Sociology* (Minneapolis: University of Minnesota Press, 2009), 47. On differing inflections, see Julian Go, " 'Racism' and Colonialism: Meanings of Difference and Ruling Practices in America's Pacific Empire," *Qualitative Sociology* 27 (2002) at http://www.bu.edu/sociology/files/2010/04/Jgo-QualSoc.pdf, esp. 47–50. Drinnon, *Facing West*, 298–99 (Rooosevelt quotations), 317 ("homogeneity"), and 279–332; Balce, "Filipina's Breast," 101–2; José de Olivares, *Our Islands and Their People, Seen with Camera and Pencil*, 2 vols. (New York: N. D. Thompson, 1899), 2: 559 and 555; Kramer, *Blood of Government*, 124–27 and 143–44.

59. Frederic Sawyer, *The Inhabitants of the Philippines* (London: Sampson Low, Marston, 1900), 164; Drinnon, *Facing West*, 283; Warwick Anderson, *Colonial Pathologies: American Tropical Medicine, Race, and Hygiene in the Philippines* (Durham, NC: Duke University Press, 2006), 41 ("underwater"); Robert R. Reed, *City of Pines: The Origins of Baguio as a Colonial Hill Station and Regional Capital* (Berkeley, CA: Center for South and Southeast Asian Studies), 67 (1903 report) and 64–68; Daniel Bender, *American Abyss: Savagery and Civilization in the Age of Industry* (Ithaca, NY: Cornell University Press, 2009), 49–50; Kristin L. Hoganson, *Fighting for American Manhood: How Gender Politics Provoked the Spanish-American and Philippine-American Wars* (New Haven, CT: Yale University Press, 1998), 180–99.

60. George Steinmetz, "Imperialism or Colonialism? From Windhoek to Washington, by Way of Basra," in Craig Calhoun, Frederick Cooper, and Kevin W. Moore, eds., *Lessons of Empire: Imperial Histories and American Power* (New York: New Press, 2006), 144 and 143–45; Rafael, *White Love*, 22; Kimberly Alidio, "Between Civilizing Mission and Ethnic Assimilation: Racial Discourse, U.S. Colonial Education and Filipino Ethnicity, 1901–1946" (PhD diss., University of Michigan, 2001), 62 (Barrows) and 60–84.

61. Drinnon, *Facing West*, 291 ("jumble" and "ethnologist") and 279–306; Dean C. Worcester, *The Philippines: Past and Present* (New York: Macmillan, 1921), 21, 532, 635. On Worcester, see also Rodney J. Sullivan, *Exemplar of Americanism: The Philippine Career of Dean C. Worcester* (Ann Arbor, MI: Center for South and Southeast Asian Studies, 1991).

62. Drinnon, *Facing West*, esp. 294–99; Worcester, *Philippines*, 938–39; David Barrows, *History of the Philippines* (Indianapolis, IN: Bobbs-Merrill, 1905), esp. 28–36; W. Cameron Forbes, *The Philippine Islands*, 2 vols. (Boston: Houghton Mifflin, 1928), 1: 586–604. On Worcester, "disdain," and "race prejudice," see Sullivan, *Exemplar of Americanism*, 139, 137, 148, and passim; cf. Gerard A. Finin, *The Making of the Igorot: Ramut ti Panagkaykaysa dagiti taga Cordillera (Cotours of Cordillera Consciousness)* (Manila: Ateneo se Manila University Press, 2005), 33 on Worcester's affection for Luzon workers. On romantic racialism, see George Fredrickson, *The Black Image in the White Mind: The Debate on Afro-American Character and Destiny, 1817–1914* (Middletown, CT: Wesleyan University Press, 1987, originally 1971), 97–129.

63. See Worcester, *Philippines*, 938–39; Barrows, *History of the Philippines*, esp. 28–36; Forbes, *Philippine Islands*, 1: 586–604; Kramer, *Blood of Government*, 229–31; Robert W. Rydell, *All the World's a Fair: Visions of Empire and American International Expositions, 1876–1916* (Chicago: University of Chicago Press, 1984), 167 and 171, and on Jenks, Mark Soderstrom, "Family Trees and Timber Rights: Albert E. Jenks, Americanization, and the Rise of Anthropology at the University of Minnesota," *Journal of the Gilded Age and Progressive Era* 3 (April 2004): 176–204.

64. Rafael, *White Love*, esp. 29–34; Barrows, *History of the Philippines*, 25 and 317; Forbes, *Philippine Islands*, 603–4; Dean C. Worcester, *Slavery and Peonage in the Philippine Islands* (Manila: Bureau of Printing, 1913), 31–33; Sullivan, *Exemplar of Americanism*, 142; Oscar V. Campomanes, "The New Empire's Forgetful and Forgotten Citizens: Unrepresentability and Unassimilability in Filipino-American Postcolonialities," *Hitting Critical Mass: A Journal of Asian American Cultural Criticism* 2 (1995): 148–49.

65. Rydell, *All the World's a Fair*, 164 and Drinnon, *Facing West*, 317 ("annex"); Kramer, *Blood of Government*, 254 and 237–61; Glenn May, *Social Engineering in the Philippines: The Aims, Execution, and Impact of American Colonial Policy, 1900–1913* (Westport, CT: Greenwood, 1980).

66. Drinnon, *Facing West*, 292 ("anthropoid") and 154–83; Rydell, *All the World's a Fair*, 163, 175, and 154–83; Benedict Burton, "Rituals of Representation: Ethnic Stereotypes and Colonized Peoples at World's Fairs" in Robert W. Rydell and Nancy Guinn, eds., *Fair Representations: World's Fairs and the Modern World* (Amsterdam: VU University Press, 1994), 46.

67. Soderstrom, "Family Trees and Timber Rights," 176-204; "Albert E. Jenks" at the University of Minnesota Department of Anthropology website at http://anthropologylabs.umn.edu/wlana/history/academic/; Albert Ernst Jenks, *The Bontoc Igorot* (Manila: The Ethnological Survey, 1905), 17–18 and n. 1; on the lessons imparted by Igorot display and their context, see also Rydell, *All the World's a Fair*, 167, 175–76, and 154–83 and Nancy Parezo and Don Fowler, *Anthropology Goes to the Fair: The 1904 Louisiana Purchase Exposition* (Lincoln: University of Nebraska Press, 2007), 167–71.

68. Rydell, *All the World's Fair*, 176–77; Forbes, *Philippine Islands*, 1: 611–12; Worcester, *Philippines*, 635 (Moro); Anderson, *Colonial Pathologies*, 76–95; Thomas Dyer, *Theodore Roosevelt and the Idea of Race* (Baton Rouge: Louisiana State University Press, 1980).

69. Wilson as quoted in Rafael, *White Love*, 23; Rydell, *All the World's a Fair*, 168–69; Anderson, *Colonial Pathologies*, 49 (Munson); *Third Annual Report of the Philippine Commission to the Secretary of War, 1902* (Washington, DC: Government Printing Office, 1903), vol. 10, part 1: 175, 173, 174, and 169–75.

70. *Report of the Philippine Commission to the Secretary of War, 1902*, vol. 10, part 1: 177, 178; *Fourth Annual Report of the Philippine Commission, 1903* (Washington, DC: Government Printing Office, 1904), part 1: 54; Sawyer, *Inhabitants of the Philippines*, 139; see also 144 and 152 on labor shortages in mining.

71. *Fourth Annual Report of the Philippine Commission, 1903*, part 1: 379 (Holmes) and part 3: 192 and 263-70; Worcester, *Philippines*, 508.

72. T. Thomas Fortune, "Politics in the Philippines," *Independent* 55 (September 24, 1903): 2266–68 and Fortune, "The Filipino: A Social Study in Three Parts," *Voice of the Negro* 1 (March, 1904): 94 and 95 for the quotations. On Fortune within the civil rights movement of the late nineteenth and early twentieth centuries, see Shawn Leigh Alexander, *An Army of Lions: The Struggle for Civil Rights before the NAACP*, forthcoming from University of Pennsylvania Press. We thank Professor Alexander for sharing these and other articles by Fortune on the Philippines.

73. Drinnon, *Facing West*, 286 (Worcester); Butt in *Report of the Philippine Commission to the Secretary of War, 1902*, 174; Worcester, *Philippines*, 886, 508 and 934; Barrows, *History of the Philippines*, 28 and 34 contain the tribal assessments; Kramer, *Blood of Government*, 216–17 and 314–16; Catherine Ceniza Choy, *Empire of Care: Nursing and Migration in Filipino American History* (Durham, NC: Duke University Press, 2003), 17–40;

Anderson, *Colonial Pathologies*, 194–204. On schooling, see May, *Social Engineering in the Philippines*, esp. 92; Alidio, "Between Civilizing Mission and Ethnic Assimilation," 60–71; David P. Barrows, "What May Be Expected from Philippine Education?" *Journal of Race Development* 2 (October 1911): 156–58 and 167.

74. The secondary accounts from which we draw here include Robert R. Reed, *City of Pines: The Origins of Baguio as a Colonial Hill Station and Regional Capital* (Berkeley, CA: Center for South and Southeast Asian Studies, 1970), 89 on comparisons to New England and esp. 97–104; Erlyn Ruth Alcantara, "Baguio: Between Two Wars: The Creation and Destruction of a Summer Capital," , in Angel Velasco Shaw and Luis H. Francia, eds., *Vestiges of War: The Philippine-American War and the Aftermath of the Imperial Dream, 1899–1999* (New York: New York University Press, 2002), 207–23, esp. 214–16 on gold. In the same volume see also, Patricio Abinales, "An American Colonial State: Authority and Structure in Southern Mindanao," esp. 91–93; Sullivan, *Exemplar of Americanism*, 146–47; Lewis E. Gleeck, Jr., *Americans on the Philippine Frontiers* (Manila: Carmelo and Bauermann, 1974), 216–20, esp. on engineering deficiencies; and Patricia Okubo Afable, ed., *Japanese Pioneers in the Northern Philippine Highlands: A Centennial Tribute* (Baguio City, Philippines: Filipino-Japanese Foundation of Northern Luzon, 2004), 13–28. See also Anderson, *Colonial Pathologies*, 143 ("champagne") and 142–47; for Baguio as a center of exoticizing and eroticizing of Filipinas and sometimes Filipinos, see Gerald M. Gems, "Anthropology Days, the Construction of Whiteness, and American Imperialism in the Philippines," in Susan Brownell, ed., *The 1904 Anthropology Days and the Olympic Games: Sport, Race, and American Imperialism* (Lincoln: University of Nebraska Press, 2008), 212.

75. Kramer, *Blood of Government*, 201 ("education") and 316 ("preoccupations"); Worcester, *Philippines*, 571 ("wild man's territory"); Rafael, *White Love*, 33; Bender, *American Abyss*, 51 and Afable, *Japanese Pioneers in the Northern Philippine Highlands*, 15 (porters); *Fourth Annual Report of the Philippine Commission, 1903*, part 3: 192 and part 1: 54 ("great works"). On the proposed drafting of labor for building roads, see May, *Social Engineering in the Philippines*, 144 and *Fifth Annual Report of the Philippine Commission, 1904* (Washington, DC: Government Printing Office, 1905), part 3: 256–57. For later implementation of such a scheme, see Finin, *Making of the Igorot*, 58.

76. Reed, *City of Pines*, 109–11 on the work force; *Fourth Annual Report of the Philippine Commission, 1903*, part 3: 192 (foremen), 248–49 ("easily managed") and 263–70 for the statistics and part 1: 379 on managing tribal workers; Gleeck, Jr., *Americans on the Philippine Frontiers*, 217; Afable, *Japanese Pioneers in the Northern Philippine Highlands*, 15 (Igorots and Christians); May, *Social Engineering in the Philippines*, 144.

77. Kramer, *Blood of Government*, 314–16; *Fourth Annual Report of the Philippine Commission, 1903*, part 1: 54 ("wages considered") and part 3: 263 and for the investigation into starvation of Benguet Road workers from Manila, part 1: 358–91; *Fifth Annual Report of the Philippine Commission, 1904*, part 1: 11 ("very gradually") and part 3: 249.
78. *Fourth Annual Report of the Philippine Commission, 1903*, part 3: 263–70 and Afable, *Japanese Pioneers in the Northern Philippine Highlands*, 12–23.
79. Butt in *Third Annual Report of the Philippine Commission to the Secretary of War, 1902*, part 1: 171; Forbes, *Philippine Islands*, 2: 394; for Worcester, Drinnon, *Facing West*, 286 and Worcester, *Philippines*, 714.
80. *Eighth Annual Report of the Philippine Commission, 1907* (Washington, DC: Government Printing Office, 1908), part (idiosyncratically titled "volume") 2: 998 and 1007–8.

Chapter 5

1. Harry Braverman, *Labor and Monopoly Capital: The Degradation of Work in the 20th Century* (New York: Monthly Review Press, 1975).
2. The best account of the "foreman's empire," and of scientific management's challenges to it, is Daniel Nelson, *Managers and Workers: Origins of the Twentieth-Century Factory System in the United States, 1880–1920* (Madison: University of Wisconsin Press, 1996), 35–78.
3. Arthur Conan Doyle, "Silver Blaze" (1893), online at *The Complete Sherlock Holmes* at http://files1-christoph-ender.de/Sherlock_Holmes/pdf-latex-a4-1/silv.pdf, 11.
4. On "nigger driver," Taylor as extracted in Frank Barkley Copley, *Frederick W. Taylor: Father of Scientific Management*, 2 vols. (New York: Augustus Kelley, 1969, originally 1923), 1: 163; Flint's remark is from a "Conference on Labor and Capital," covered in *Iron Age* in May of 1901 and as quoted in Michael K. Rosenow, "Injuries to All: The Rituals of Dying and the Politics of Death Among United States Workers, 1877–1910" (PhD diss., University of Illinois, 2008), 26. On Stone, see James Hollandsworth, Jr., *Portrait of a Scientific Racist: Alfred Holt Stone of Mississippi* (Baton Rouge: Louisiana State University Press, 2008), esp. 127–76. See also Matthew Frye Jacobson, *Barbarian Virtues: The United States Encounters Foreign Peoples at Home and Abroad, 1876–1915* (New York: Hill and Wang, 2000), 151.
5. Frederick Jackson Turner, *The Frontier in American History* (New York: Henry Holt, 1920), 299–300. See Jacobson, *Barbarian Virtues*, 151, for Hoover.
6. John R. Commons, *Races and Immigrants in America* (New York: Macmillan, 1907), 150; Charles W. Mills, "White Ignorance," in Shannon Sullivan and Nancy Tuama, eds., *Race and Epistemologies of Ignorance* (Albany: State University of New York Press, 2007), 13 and 13–38, with thanks to Sundiata Cha-Jua for the reference.

7. We adapt freely here from Williams on oppositional forms in his "Base and Superstructure in Marxist Cultural Theory," in *Problems in Materialism and Culture* (London: Verso, 1980), 40 and 31–49.

8. Leland H. Jenks, "Early Phases of the Management Movement," *Administrative Science Quarterly* 5 (December 1960): 424, 424, 439, and 421–47 passim; on Jenks, see the finding aid to the Leland H. Jenks Papers housed at Mudd Manuscript Library at Princeton University and described at http://diglib.princeton.edu/ead/getEad?eadid=MC213&;kw=.

9. Jenks, "Phases of the Management Movement," 425, 426, 422, and 421–47.

10. See esp. Nelson, *Managers and Workers*; Samuel Haber, *Efficiency and Uplift* (Chicago: University of Chicago Press, 1964); David Noble, *America by Design: Science, Technology, and the Rise of Corporate Capitalism* (New York: Knopf, 1977), 57–59.

11. Harry Braverman, *Labor and Monopoly Capital*; Noble, *America by Design*, 310–12.

12. Joan Hoff Wilson, *Herbert Hoover: Forgotten Progressive* (Prospect Heights, IL: Waveland Press, 1992, originally 1975); Jeremy Mouat and Ian Phimester, "The Engineering of Herbert Hoover," *Pacific Historical Review* 77 (November 2008): 553–84; Federated American Engineering Societies, *The Twelve-Hour Shift in Industry* (New York: E. P. Dutton, 1922), 47, 106, 288, and passim; Robert K. Murray, "Herbert Hoover and the Harding Cabinet," in Ellis Wayne Hawley, ed., *Herbert Hoover as Secretary of Commerce, 1921–1928: Studies in New Era Thought and Practice* (Iowa City: University of Iowa Press, 1981), 27–29.

13. Jenks, "Early Phases of the Management Movement," 436; see also Haber, *Efficiency and Uplift*, 12.

14. Frank J. Weed, "The Sociological Department at the Colorado Fuel and Iron Company, 1901–1907: Scientific Paternalism and Industrial Control," *Journal of the History of the Behavioral Sciences* 41 (Summer 2005): 269, n.1 and 269–84. For works that consider immigrant workers, race, and paternalism at Ford see Stephen Meyer, III, *The Five Dollar Day: Labor Management and Social Control in the Ford Motor Company, 1908–1921* (Albany: SUNY Press, 1981); August Meier and Elliott Rudwick, *Black Detroit and the Rise of the UAW* (New York: Oxford University Press, 1979); John Brueggemann, "The Power and Collapse of Paternalism: The Ford Motor Company and Black Workers, 1937–1941," *Social Problems* 47, no. 2 (May 2000), 220–40; and Jeffrey Eugenides's novel *Middlesex* (New York: Farrar, Straus and Giroux, 2002), which includes a spectacular re-creation and invocation of the melting pot pageant at Ford and its meaning for forging white Americans at 79–105.

15. For the "smaller caliber" quotation, see Milton J. Nadworny, *Scientific Management and the Unions, 1900–1932* (Cambridge, MA: Harvard University Press, 1955), 156, n. 12.

16. Upton Sinclair, *King Coal: A Novel* (New York: Macmillan, 1917), 64–67; William Attaway, *Blood on the Forge* (New York:, Monthly Review Press, 1987, originally 1961), 122–23. See also chapter 6.

17. Braverman, *Labor and Monopoly Capital*; Frederick Winslow Taylor, *The Principles of Scientific Management* (London: Routledge, 1911), 91–92 and 103–4; Robert Kanigel, *The One Best Way: Frederick Winslow Taylor and the Enigma of Efficiency* (New York: Viking, 1997), 330–33.

18. On Commons and Taylor, see Chris Nyland, "Taylorism, John R. Commons, and the Hoxie Report," *Journal of Economic Issues* 30 (December 1996): 985–1016.

19. Taylor, *Principles of Scientific Management*, 40–61 and 147 ("Hungarians"); Kanigel, *One Best Way*, 319 and 316–22 with blaming the Hungarians at 322; Haber, *Efficiency and Uplift*, 23 and 23, n. 12 on "Patrick" and on "racehorses." On fabricated and embellished aspects of the Schmidt story, see Judith Merkle, *Management and Ideology: The Legacy of the International Scientific Management Movement* (Berkeley: University of California Press, 1980), 28–29.

20. George Preston, "Scientific Management (From the Standpoint of a Trade Unionist)" (March?, 1911) in Taylor Papers at http://stevens.cdmhost. com/cdm4/document.php?CISOROOT=/p4100coll1&CISOPTR=442 &;REC=1; see Carol Carlson Dean, "*Primer of Scientific Management*: by Frank B. Gilbreth: A Response to the Publication of Taylor's *Principles* in *The American Magazine*," in Michael C. Wood and John C. Wood, eds., *Frank and Lillian Gilbreth: Critical Evaluations in Business and Management*, vol. 1 (London: Routledge, 2003), 114–15, both on Preston and quoting Sears.

21. Haber, *Efficiency and Uplift*, 23, n. 12; H. D. Minich, "The Value of Time Study," *100%: The Practical Magazine of Efficient Management* 1 (November 1913): 6. See also Bill Schwarz, "Rationalism, Irrationalism and Taylorism," *Science as Culture* 1 (1990): 154 on the congressional committee testimony by Taylor, and Bernard Doray, *From Taylorism to Fordism: A Rational Madness* (London: Free Association Books, 1988), 84.

22. W. E. B. Du Bois, *The Philadelphia Negro: A Social Study*, E. Digby Baltzell, ed. (New York: Schocken Books, 1967, originally 1899), 129, xxxvii–xxxviii, and 129–31. Taylor, "Answer to Criticism of Mr. Upton Sinclair (1911?)" in the Frederick Winslow Taylor Papers at Stevens Institute of Technology Archives in Hoboken, New Jersey [hereafter Taylor Papers], and online at http://stevens.cdmhost.com/cdm4/document. php?CISOROOT=/p4100coll1&CISOPTR=262&REC=20 for Taylor on drinking and ethnicity at Midvale, see "Taylor to Willard Price" (September 17, 1914) in Taylor Papers and at http://stevens.cdmhost.com/ cdm4/document.php?CISROOT=/p41000coll1&CISOPTR=1245&;R EC=3 and Richard T. Nalle, *Midvale and Its Pioneers* (New York: Newcomen Society of England, 1948), 15–16. On Midvale, Du Bois, and Taylor,

see Jacqueline Jones, "'Lifework' and Its Limits: The Problem of Labor in *The Philadelphia Negro*," in Michael B. Katz and Thomas J. Sugrue, eds., *W. E. B. Du Bois, Race, and the City: The Philadelphia Negro and Its Legacy* (Philadelphia: University of Pennsylvania Press, 1998), esp. 108–9 and Walter Licht, *Getting Work: Philadelphia, 1840–1950* (Philadelphia: University of Pennsylvania Press, 2000), 46–47. For a different account of the timing of the coming of the black labor force to Midvale, see Lorenzo J. Greene and Carter G. Woodson, *The Negro Wage Earner* (Washington, DC: The Association for the Study of Negro Life and History, 1930), 139–40. Howell Harris, *Bloodless Victories: The Rise and Fall of the Open Shop in the Philadelphia Metal Trades, 1890–1940* (Cambridge: Cambridge University Press, 2000), 19–20 does not identify Taylor as the innovator in his account of integration at Midvale.

23. For a particularly vivid example of Taylor undermining the foremen's day-to-day control over individual workers, see "Taylor to Charles Morse" (May 20, 1907) in http://stevens.cdmhost.com/cdm4/document.php?CISOROOT=/p4100coll1&CISOPTR=1547&REC=2in which he valorizes having an individual worker "taught" by eight different foremen, and Loren Baritz, *The Servants of Power: A History of the Use of Social Science in American Industry* (New York: John Wiley and Sons, 1965), 21–41.

24. David W. Southern, *The Progressive Era and Race: Reaction and Reform, 1900–1917* (Wheeling, WV: Harlan Davidson, 2005).

25. Harry Franklin Porter, "When Foremen Make Managers," *Factory: The Magazine of Management* 13 (September, 1914): 174; Willard C. Brinton, "Graphic Methods of Presenting Data," *Engineering Magazine* 47 (September 1914): 823, figure 28. Generally, see John Higham, *Strangers in the Land: Patterns of American Nativism* (New Brunswick, NJ: Rutgers University Press, 1955), and David Roediger, *Working toward Whiteness: How America's Immigrants Became White* (New York: Basic, 2005), esp. 3–130.

26. Albert Williams, Jr., "Racial Traits in Machine Designing," *Engineering Magazine* 10 (October 1895): 93, 94, 95, and 97.

27. Casper L. Redfield, "Industrial Ascendancy of the Anglo-American Peoples," *Engineering Magazine* 20 (February 1901): 850–51 and 849 on brain size. See also Casper L. Redfield, *Dynamic Evolution: A Study of The Causes of Evolution and Degeneracy* (New York: G. Putnam's Sons, 1914).

28. Rick Halpern, *Down on the Killing Floor: Black and White Workers in Chicago's Packinghouses, 1904–54* (Urbana: University of Illinois Press, 1997), 23 and 24 (on "divide and rule," including Armour). For the context of Commons' remarks, and an apt discussion of the labor process in packing, see James R. Barrett, "Immigrant Workers in Early Mass Production Industry: Work Rationalization and Job Control Conflicts in Chicago's Packinghouses, 1900–1904," in Hartmut Keil and John B. Jentz, eds., *German Workers in Industrial Chicago* (Dekalb: Northern Illinois University Press, 1983), 106 and 105–9.

29. Barrett, "Immigrant Workers," 105–9; on potential and actual competition, see Susan Olzak, *The Dynamics of Ethnic Competition and Conflict* (Stanford, CA: Stanford University Press, 1992), 116.

30. David Brody, *Steelworkers in America: The Nonunion Era* (Cambridge, MA: Harvard University Press, 1960), 20. For Carnegie, see John Hinshaw, *Steel and Steelworkers: Race and Class Struggle in Twentieth Century Pittsburgh* (Albany: State University of New York Press, 2002), 28; James Howard Bridge, *The Inside History of the Carnegie Steel Company: A Romance of the Millions* (New York: Aldine,1903), 81, with thanks to Robert Zeidel; Jeffrey Haydu, *Between Craft and Class: Skilled Workers and Factory Politics in the United States and Britain, 1890–1922* (Berkeley: University of California Press, 1988), 114 ("to quietly pit").

31. Unsigned, "The Green Branch," *Factory: The Magazine of Management* 13 (August 1914): 83. On "rivalry" and "brawny foreigners," see also L. DeG. Moss, "Iron and Steel Making in America: Its Fundamentals and Its Future," *Engineering Magazine* 46 (February 1914): 688.

32. Michael Nash, *Conflict and Accommodation: Coal Miners, Steel Workers, and Socialism, 1890–1920* (Westport, CT: Greenwood, 1982), 96.

33. W. J. Lauck, "Recent Immigration: Its Significant Aspects to the Iron and Steel Industry," *Iron Age* 87 (April 13, 1911): 898; Brody, *Steelworkers in America*, 99 and 98–101; Unsigned, "Strong Support for Selective Immigration," *Iron Age* 111 (January 11, 1923): 163; Roediger, *Working toward Whiteness*, 74; Charles Rumford Walker, *Steel: The Diary of a Furnace Worker* (Boston: Atlantic Monthly Press, 1922), 107 ("too damn dirty").

34. Brody, *Steelworkers in America*, 101 and 102; Roediger, *Working toward Whiteness*, 74 and 43–45; Crystal Eastman, *Work Accidents and the Law* (New York: Russell Sage Foundation, 1910), 13–14.

35. Halpern, *Down on the Killing Floor*, 89.

36. David Montgomery, *The Fall of the House of Labor: The Workplace, the State, and American Labor Activism, 1865–1925* (Cambridge: Cambridge University Press, 1987), 242–43; for all quotes. See also Sanford M. Jacoby, "A Century of Human Resource Management," in Bruce E. Kaufman, Richard A. Beaumont, and Roy B. Helfgott, eds., *Industrial Relations to Human Resources and Beyond: The Evolving Process of Employee Relations Management* (Armonk, NY: M. E. Sharpe, 2003), 148–50. David Noble, *America by Design: Science, Technology, and the Rise of Corporate Capitalism* (New York: Knopf, 1977), 306.

37. John M. Williams, "An Actual Account of What We Have Done to Reduce Our Labor Turnover," *Annals of the American Academy* 71 (May 1917): 64; Eliott Frost, "What Industry Does and Does Not Want from the Psychologist," *Journal of Applied Psychology* 4 (March 1920): 21–22; Roediger, *Working toward Whiteness*, 72 and 73–78; William Leiserson, *Adjusting Immigrant and Industry* (New York: 1924), 92–93. For the 1911 report and "hunky," see Edward Slavishak, *Bodies of Work: Civic Display*

and Labor in Industrial Pittsburgh (Durham, NC: Duke University Press, 2008), 56 and 55. More typically on women's labor and management without a "race" dimension, see the extended series during World War I in *Factory*, all titled "Handling Women Workers." Consisting mostly of short vignettes signed only with initials, these appear in 1918 for example in the August (pp. 352–54), September (pp. 576–84), October (pp. 701–10), and December (pp. 1116–26) issues. See also, Unsigned, "The Iron Industry's Labor Supply," *Iron Age* 96 (July 8, 1915): 91.

38. Roediger, *Working toward Whiteness*, 75–77; for the Iron Range, "Industrial Progress and Efficiency," in vol. 16, part 18, "Iron Ore Mining," in "Reports of the Immigration Commission, Immigrants in Industries": Senate Documents, 61st Congress, 2nd Session 1909–1910, vol. 78 (Washington, DC: Government Printing Office, 1911), 339–41, with thanks to Thomas Mackaman; Lauck, "Recent Immigration," 899. For Commons blithe ranking of European immigrants, in part based on their class consciousness, see his "The Sweating System in the Clothing Trade," in John R. Commons, ed., *Trade Unionism and Labor Problems* (Boston: Ginn and Company, 1905), 332–33. On the use of "race" to refer to European groups later thought of as "ethnic," see Victoria Hattam, *In the Shadow of Race: Jews, Latinos, and Immigrant Politics in the United States* (Chicago: University of Chicago Press, 2007).

39. Dwight Thompson Farnam, "Negroes as a Source of Industrial Labor," *Industrial Management* (August 1918): 123–29; on climate, geography, and racial theory, see Daniel E. Bender, *American Abyss: Savagery and Civilization in the Age of Industry* (Ithaca, NY: Cornell University Press, 2009); on humidity and heat, see also Griffith Taylor, "The Distribution of Future White Settlement: A World Survey Based on Physiographic Data," *Geographical Review* 12 (July 1922): 375–402. Research on race chronically assumes categories it also investigates but even in the period under consideration much more vigorously empirical work, allowing for insights into the possibility that "work curves" were fundamentally not "racial," was produced by educational investigators. See, e.g., Thomas R. Garth, "Racial Differences in Mental Fatigue," *Journal of Applied Psychology* 4 (June–September 1920): 235–44 and Garth, "White, Indian and Negro Work Curves," *Journal of Applied Psychology* 5 (March 1921): 14–25, esp. 23–25.

40. Farnam, "Negroes as a Source of Industrial Labor," 123–29. See also William P. Jones, *The Tribe of the Black Ulysses: African American Lumber Workers in the Jim Crow South* (Urbana: University of Illinois Press, 2005).

41. John Bodnar, Roger Simon, and Michael Weber, *Lives of Their Own: Blacks, Italians, and Poles in Pittsburgh, 1900–1960* (Urbana: University of Illinois Press, 1983), 240 reprints the chart.

42. Hugh Reid, "Why Bar the Door to Labor?," *Nation's Business* 9 (January 1921): 31; Luther D. Burlingame, "Americanizing a Thousand Men,"

Industrial Management 53 (June 1917): 385–92; Unsigned, "The Southern Negro in Cleveland Industries," *Monthly Labor Review* [*MLR*] 19 (July 1924): 41–44; Unsigned, "Negro Labor During and After the War," *MLR* 12 (April 1921): 853–58; Unsigned, "Working and Living Conditions of Negroes in West Virginia," *MLR* 21 (August 1925): 256–59 and esp. Unsigned, "Industrial Employment of the Negro in Pennsylvania," *MLR* 22 (June 1926): 48–51; Ross as quoted in Stanley Lieberson, *A Piece of the Pie: Black and White Immigrants since 1880* (Berkeley: University of California Press, 1980), 25; Roediger, *Working toward Whiteness*, 54. Commons is quoted from his "Social and Industrial Problems," *Chautauquan* 39 (March 1904): 18 and 13–22; Yngve Ramstad and James L. Starkey, "The Racial Theories of John R. Commons," *Research in the History of Economic Thought and Methodology* 13 (1195): esp. 16–17 and 63–64 and, for the context, Bari Jane Watkins, "The Professors and the Unions: Academic Social Thought and Labor Reform, 1883–1915" (PhD diss., Yale University, 1976); on Russians, see Jerome Davis, *The Russian Immigrant* (New York: Macmillan, 1922), esp. 23–25.

43. Hugo Münsterberg, *Psychology and Industrial Efficiency* (Boston: Houghton Mifflin, 1913), 50, 27–28, and 69. On the origins of industrial psychology, see Loren Baritz, *The Servants of Power: A History of the Use of Social Science in American Industry* (New York: John Wiley, 1965), 21–41.

44. Münsterberg, *Psychology and Industrial Efficiency*, 129–31.

45. Farnam, "Negroes as a Source of Industrial Labor," 128; Eliott Frost, "What Industry Does and Does Not Want From the Psychologist," *Journal of Applied Psychology* 4 (1920), 21–22; the handbook is Leon Pratt Alford, ed. *Management's Handbook*, first familiar to us through Zach Sell's extraordinary " 'A Jungle to Work In': Race and the Social Terrain of Foundry Production" (Senior thesis, University of Wisconsin-Milwaukee, 2009). See Alford, ed., *Management's Handbook: By a Staff of Specialists* (New York: Ronald Press, 1924), 1462–63.

46. Ordway Tead, *Instincts in Industry: A Study in Working-Class Psychology* (Boston: Houghton Mifflin, 1918), 13, 89–90, and 143; the "map" is reproduced in Bruce E. Kaufman's excellent *The Origins & Evolution of the Field of Industrial Relations in the United States* (Ithaca, NY: ILR Press, 1993), 14–17. See also 19–63 for an account of the early evolution of industrial relations in which race and ethnicity are absent. See also Ordway Tead and Henry C. Metcalf, *Personnel Administration: Its Principles and Practice* (New York: McGraw-Hill, 1926, originally 1920), 48.

47. Everett Cherrington Hughes and Helen Macgill Hughes, *Where Peoples Meet:: Ethnic and Racial Frontiers* (Glencoe, IL: Free Press, 1952), 67; T. J. Woofter, Jr., *Races and Ethnic Groups in American Life* (New York: McGraw-Hill, 1933), 144; Reinhard Bendix, *Work and Authority in Industry: Ideologies of Management in the Course of Industrialization*

(Edison, NJ: Transaction, 2001, originally 1974), 273 and 278; Nyland, "Taylorism, John R. Commons, and the Hoxie Report," 986. See also Nelson, *Managers and Workers*, 80–83. For Taylor, see *Principles of Scientific Management*, 212.

48. See chapter 6 and, for the *Iron Age* quotation and its context, Unsigned, "Iron Industry's Labor Supply," 91 and Slavishak, *Bodies of Work*, 55.

49. Brody, *Steelworkers in America*, 107; Katherine Stone, "The Origins of Job Structures in the Steel Industry," in Richard C. Edwards, Michael Reich, and David M. Gordon, eds., *Labor Market Segmentation* (Lexington, MA: D.C. Heath, 1975), 49 ("job ladders"); Jacobson, *Barbarian Virtues*, 65, quoting Commons. For Worman and broad insights, see Montgomery, *Fall of the House of Labor*, 115.

50. Slavishak, *Bodies of Work*, 55, 54–59, and on the body as displayed commodity, esp. 245; see also Williams, "Labor Turnover," 60–61.

51. Katherine Blackford and Arthur Newcomb, *The Job, the Man, the Boss* (New York: Doubleday, Page, 1919); Blackford, *Reading Character at Sight*, Lesson Six (New York: Independent Corporation, 1918), 5; "Learn How to Read These Faces," advertisement, *American Magazine* 7 (January 1915): 80. We are much in the debt of the important article on Blackford by Zachary Sell, " 'These Modern Necromancers': Character Analysis, Race, and the Spaces of Capitalist Production" (Unpublished paper in the possession of the authors, University of Illinois, 2010). On Blackford's theories and character analysis in general, see also Elspeth Brown, *The Corporate Eye: Photography and the Rationalization of American Commercial Culture, 1884–1929* (Baltimore, MD: Johns Hopkins, 2005), 25–56.

52. William Judson Kibby, "How Character Analysis Solves the Man Problem," *Transactions of the American Foundrymen's Association: Proceedings of the Twenty-Second Annual Meeting*, A. O. Backert, ed. (Cleveland, OH: American Foundrymen's Association, 1918), 172; Sell, "These Modern Necromancers," 3; Blackford and Newcomb, *The Job, the Man, the Boss*, 123; Williams, "Labor Turnover," 63.

53. On Cartwright, see chapter 2; Blackford and Newcomb, *The Job, the Man, the Boss*, 123; Harry Balkin, *The New Science of Analyzing Character* (Boston: Four Seas), 171–72; Sell, "These Modern Necromancers," 13–20; Glen V. Cleeton "Validity of Character Judgments Based on External Criteria," *Journal of Applied Psychology* 8 (June 1924): 215–31.

54. Nelson, *Managers and Workers*, 35–78; Montgomery, *Fall of the House of Labor*, 115 (including Worman); Sumner H. Slichter, *The Turnover of Labor* (New York: D. Appleton, 1919), 375 and passim; Jacoby, "Century of Human Resource Management," 154 and 148–55; in packing, see the acute remarks on the resilient "foreman's empire" in Halpern, *Down on the Killing Floor*, 89–90.

55. For Fitch, see Nelson, *Managers and Workers*, 44.

56. Frank H. Rindge, "From Boss to Fore-Man," *Industrial Management* 53 (July 1917): 508, 509, and 511–12. See also Frederic R. Coburn, "A Foreman's Responsibility and Authority," *Industrial Management* 53 (June 1917): 349; M. Turner, "A Foreman's Opinion of the Employment Department," *Industrial Management* 53 (June 1917): 446.

57. Meyer Bloomfield, "Relations of Foremen to the Working Force," *Industrial Management* 53 (June 1917): 343 and 341–42.

58. Harry Franklin Porter, "Showing Unskilled Labor How," *Factory: The Magazine of Management* 13 (October 1914): 268.

59. Unsigned, "What's New in Personnel and Industrial Relations?," *Personnel* 7 (November 1930): 69; Roediger, *Working toward Whiteness*, 75; Roger Horowitz, *Negro and White, Unite and Fight: A Social History of Industrial Unionism in Meatpacking, 1930–1990* (Urbana: University of Illinois Press, 1997), 90; John Bodnar, *Workers' World: Kinship, Community, and Protest in an Industrial Society, 1900–1940* (Baltimore, MD: Johns Hopkins University Press, 1982), 93; Herman Feldman, *Racial Factors in American Industry* (New York: Harper and Bros., 1931), 147; Louis Adamic, *What's Your Name?* (New York: Harper and Bros., 1942), 96–97; Niles Carpenter, *Nationality, Color, and Economic Opportunity in the City of Buffalo* (Westport, CT: Negro Universities Press, 1970), 118–30.

60. Doray, *From Taylorism to Fordism*, 83–84 and Braverman, *Labor and Monopoly Capital*, 104–23.

61. John R. Commons et al., *History of the Labour Movement in the United States*, 4 vols. (New York: Macmillan, 1918–1935), 3: xxv and 322–33, esp. 328 for Don D. Lescohier's section on personnel management; Ramstad and Starkey, "Racial Theories of John R. Commons," 16–18, quote Commons on the "competition of races." Their study is as acute on his antiblack racism as it is obtuse on his racial nativism. See also John R. Commons, "Industry," *Chautauquan* 38 (February 1904): 533–43 and Commons, "Social and Industrial Problems," 19 ("physical exertion") and 17–22; Harold M. Baron, *The Demand for Black Labor: Historical Notes on the Political Economy of Racism* (Somerville, MA: New England Free Press, 1971). Barrett, "Immigrant Workers," 106 and 105–9; see also Halpern, *Down on the Killing Floor*, 23–24 and 89–90. See also James R. Barrett, *Work and Community in the Jungle: Chicago's Packinghouse Workers, 1894–1922* (Urbana: University of Illinois Press, 1987) on the industry and its workers.

62. Farnam, "Negroes as a Source of Industrial Labor," 123, 125, and 127–28; Fred H. Rindge, Jr., "From Boss to Fore-Man," *Industrial Management* 53 (July 1917): 511–12; Kaufman, *Origins & Evolution of the Field of Industrial Relations*, 15 and 17 and Tead and Metcalf, *Personnel Administration*, 48.

63. Doray, *From Taylorism to Fordism*, title page and 83–84.

Chapter 6

1. Upton Sinclair, *The Jungle* (New York: Doubleday, Page, 1906), 44, 204, 362, and 347.

2. John R. Commons, *Races and Immigrants in America* (New York: Macmillan, 1907), 150.

3. Upton Sinclair, *The Flivver King: A Story of Ford-America* (Detroit, MI: United Automobile Workers of America, 1937).

4. Ibid; cf. Alexander Saxton, "In Dubious Battle," *Pacific Historical Review* 73 (May 2004): 249–62.

5. Clara Weatherwax, *Marching! Marching!* (Detroit, MI: Omnigraphics, 1990, originally 1935), 113–14; for a brilliant contextualization of the novel, see William Scott, *Troublemakers: Power, Representation, and the Fiction of the Mass Worker* (New Brunswick, NJ: Rutgers University Press, 2011).

6. William Attaway, *Blood on the Forge* (New York: Monthly Review Press, 1987, originally 1941), 122–23.

7. John R. Commons, "Introduction to the Edition of 1920," in his *Races and Immigrants in America* (New York: Macmillan, 1920), xix; for much more sweeping overstatement, see Loren Baritz, *The Servants of Power: A History of the Use of Social Science in American Industry* (New York: John Wiley and Sons, 1965), 13; Chad Pearson, " 'Organize and Fight': Communities, Employers, and Open-Shop Movements, 1890–1920" (PhD diss., University of Albany, 2008), 254 ("spirited"); Sanford M. Jacoby, "A Century of Human Resource Management," in Bruce E. Kaufman, Richard A. Beaumont, and Roy B. Helfgott, eds., *Industrial Relations to Human Resources and Beyond: The Evolving Process of Employee Relations Management* (Armonk, NY: M.E. Sharpe, 2003), 149, 154, and 148–55; David R. Roediger, *Working toward Whiteness: How America's Immigrants Became White* (New York: Basic, 2005), 76 and 216–20.

8. Laura J. Owen, "Worker Turnover in the 1920s: What Labor-Supply Arguments Don't Tell Us," *Journal of Economic History* 55 (December 1995): 822–41 with the figures on 822; the classic account of turnover and of the need for critique of the "drive" system, Sumner H. Slichter, *The Turnover of Factory Labor* (New York: Appleton, 1919) appeared after the war but deliberately used prewar data so as to root its case in making general arguments rather than taking the easy route provided by wartime labor shortages. See esp. vii, 203, and 424–29. See also Unsigned, "How Other Men Manage," *Factory* 21 (July 1918): 118; David Brody, *Workers in Industrial America: Essays on the Twentieth Century Struggle* (New York: Oxford University Press, 1993, originally 1980), 48–81; on the limits of liberalism and the absence of turnover as an ongoing concern, see Sanford M. Jacoby, *Employing Bureaucracy: Managers, Unions, and the Transformation of Work in the 20th Century* (Mahwah, NJ: Lawrence Erlbaum Associates, 2004), 124–53 and 206, esp. 125, 127 ("buyer's" market) and 132; Bruce E. Kaufman, *Hired Hands or Human Resources? Case Studies of HRM*

Programs and Practices in Early American Industry (Ithaca, NY: Cornell University Press, 2010), 97–98. On job ladders, see Katherine Stone, "The Origins of Job Structures in the Steel Industry," in Richard C. Edwards, Michael Reich, and David M. Gordon, eds. *Labor Market Segmentation* (Lexington, MA: D.C. Heath, 1975), 49.

9. Matthew Jacobson, *Whiteness of a Different Color: European Immigration and the Alchemy of Race* (Cambridge, MA: Harvard University Press, 1998), 92–102; cf. Nathan Glazer, "Is Assimilation Dead?" in Peter Kivisto, ed., *Incorporating Diversity: Rethinking Assimilation in a Multicultural Age* (Boulder, CO: Paradigm, 2005), 118 and 119, where Glazer writes that experts on assimilation in the early 1920s were "unconsciousness of the fact that race might include other than Europeans" in a language that would have had fully different meaning "had it been used 20 years later."

10. Frederick Winslow Taylor, *Principles of Scientific Management* (New York: Harper and Bros., 1913), 40; Eugene O'Neill, *The Hairy Ape, Anna Christie, The First Man* (New York: Boni and Liveright, 1922); on *The Hairy Ape*, race, and labor see David Roediger, "White Looks: Hairy Apes, True Stories, and Limbaugh's Laughs," *Minnesota Review* 47 (1996): 37–48; David Brody, *Steelworkers in America: The Nonunion Era* (Cambridge, MA: Harvard University Press, 1960), 33 ("gorilla men"). See also Reinhard Bendix, *Work and Authority in Industry: Ideologies of Management in the Course of Industrialization* (New York: John Wiley and Sons, 1956), 308–31 and Ordway Tead, "The Problem of Incentive and Output," *Annals of the American Academy of Political and Social Science* 89 (May 1920): 173 ("bellowing- bull").

11. John Higham, *Strangers in the Land: Patterns of American Nativism, 1860–1925* (New York: Atheneum, 1966, originally 1955), 315; Roediger, *Working toward Whiteness*, 214–23.

12. Unsigned, "The Americanization of Our Alien Workmen: Report of the Chamber's Committee on Immigration," *Nation's Business* 4 (February 1916): 71 and 83.

13. David Montgomery, *The Fall of the House of Labor: The Workplace, the State, and American Labor Activism, 1865–1925* (Cambridge: Cambridge University Press, 1987), 388–94; David R. Roediger and Philip S. Foner, *Our Own Time: A History of American Labor and the Working Day* (New York: Verso, 1990), 212–31.

14. W. J. Lauck, "Recent Immigration: Its Significant Aspects to the Iron and Steel Industry," *Iron Age* 87 (April 13, 1911): 898; James Howard Bridge, *The Inside History of the Carnegie Steel Company: A Romance of the Millions* (New York: Aldine, 1903), 81.

15. David G. Saposs, "The Mind of Immigrant Communities in the Pittsburgh District" in *Public Opinion and the Steel Strike: Supplementary Reports of Investigators to the Commission of Inquiry, Interchurch World Movement* (New York: Harcourt, Brace, 1921), 239–40 ("immigrant

rebellion"). On the steel strike see David Brody, *Labor in Crisis: The Steel Strike of 1919* (Urbana: University of Illinois Press, 1987).

16. The graphic is reproduced in William Z. Foster, *The Great Steel Strike and Its Lessons* (New York: Huebsch, 1920), unnumbered page following 188 and originally in the *Pittsburgh Chronicle-Telegraph*, October 6, 1919.

17. Unsigned, "The Test of Citizenship," *Workers' World*, November 21, 1919, 4. On sabotage, see Salvatore Salerno, ed., *Direct Action & Sabotage: Three Classic IWW Pamphlets* (Chicago: Charles H. Kerr, 1991); Joyce Kornbluh, ed., *Rebel Voices: An I.W.W. Anthology* (Ann Arbor: University of Michigan Press, 1972), 51–63; Mike Davis, "The Stop Watch and the Wooden Shoe: Scientific Management and the Industrial Workers of the World," *Radical America* 9 (January/February 1975): 69–95; Jules Witcover, *Sabotage at Black Tom: Imperial Germany's Secret War in America, 1914–1917* (Chapel Hill, NC: Algonquin Books, 1989); Stephen Meyer, III, *The Five-Dollar Day: Labor Management and Social Control in the Ford Motor Company, 1908–1921* (Albany: SUNY Press, 1981), 169–94, esp. 176–77. See also Luther D. Burlingame, "Americanizing a Thousand Men," *Industrial Management* 53 (June 1917), for an on-the-ground account of the naturalization campaign at Brown & Sharpe in Providence reflecting early wartime patterns of optimism and urgency in addressing the problem as "recent floods of immigration composed of races that have not as yet been assimilated," 385 and 385–92.

18. Frances Kellor, "Chambers of Commerce and Alien Workmen," *Nation's Business* 3 (December 1915): 19 and 18; On Ford English School, see Daniel M.G. Graff, "Ford Welfare Capitalism in Its Economic Context," in Sanford G. Jacoby, ed., *Masters to Managers: Historical and Comparative Perspectives on American Employers* (New York: Columbia University Press, 1991), 98 and (for the quote) 99. For "hunkie" (or "hunky"), see Roediger, *Working toward Whiteness*, 37–45. On the melting pot and Ford, see Elizabeth Esch, "Fordtown: Managing Race and Nation in the American Empire, 1925–1945" (PhD diss., New York University, 2004).

19. Kellor, "Chambers of Commerce and Alien Workmen," esp. 18; Edward George Hartmann, *The Movement to Americanize the Immigrant* (New York, AMS Press, 1967, originally 1948), 130, 131, and 149; on Kellor's ties to business and government elites and her evolution, see Higham, *Strangers in the Land*, 239–41, 243–44, and 257–58; Unsigned, "A Good Point in Handling Aliens," *Factory* 18 (April 1917): 612; G. F. H., H. M. J., and N. C., "Hire-and-Keep Employment Plans," *Factory* 21 (December 1918): 1074–80; Unsigned, "How Other Men Manage," *Factory* 21 (September 1918): 430.

20. Frances Kellor, "Immigration and the Future," *Annals of the American Academy of Political and Social Science* 93 (January 1921): 201, 203, 205, 206, and 201–11; Scovill Manufacturing Company records, ca. 1790–1956 (inclusive) at Baker Library Historical Collections, Harvard Business

School in carton 33, folders 26, 33, and 34. In 33, folder 26, "Memoran-
dum of Board of Governors Committee," 3 (May 7, 1920) calls for figures
of strikebreaking/loyalty to strike by nationality. These documents are
online at http://pds.lib.harvard.edu/pds/view/5383723?n=78&imagesize=1
200&jp2Res=.25&;printThumbnails=no and http://pds.lib.harvard.edu/
pds/view/5383723?n=87&imagesize=1200&;jp2Res=.25. See also Unsigned,
"The Bolsheviki in America: How the Foes of Society Seek to Gain Their
Ends," *Personnel* 1 (November 1919): 1–3 and Unsigned, "The European
Economic Situation," *Personnel* 1 (December 1919): 13.

21. Unsigned, "Making Americans," *Personnel* 1 (March 1919): 1; G. J. Soderberg,
"Building Up Good Will of Industrial Workers to Increase Production,"
Personnel 3 (February 1921): 1; Unsigned, "What Americanization Means,"
Personnel 1 (August 1919): 8. Goodwin, "A Test for Fair-Mindedness," *Indus-
trial Psychology* 2 (February 1927): 84–92.

22. Unsigned, "Immigration and Unskilled Labor," *Barron's*, November 20,
1922, 9; see also Hugh Reid, "Why Bar the Door to Labor? War-time
Drains Have Not Yet Been Made Up and Those Who Speak Fearfully
of 'Immigrant Hordes' Have Failed to Examine Carefully Both Sides of
the Ledger," *Nation's Business* 9 (January 1921): 29–31; J. P. Austin, M.D.,
"Why Physical Examination?," *Personnel* 3 (February 1921): 5; Boxed in-
sert, "The Americanization of the Foreign-Born in Relation to Industrial
Management," *Personnel* 1 (April 1919): 4; Clarence Herr, "EXAMINA-
TION: A New Method of Increasing the Supply of Available Labor for
Industry," *Personnel* 2 (August 1920): 1 and 7–8.

23. Unsigned, "Selective Immigration," *Iron Age* 3 (January 18, 1923): 235;
Unsigned, "Labor Relief Not Probable," *Iron Age* 3 (February 1, 1923):
357; Unsigned, "No Relief in Sight," *Iron Age* 3 (March 1, 1923): 602, Unsigned, "Strong Support for Selective Immigration," *Iron Age* 3 (January
11, 1923): 163–64.

24. Higham, *Strangers in the Land*, 315–17; Thomas Mackaman, "The Foreign
Element: New Immigrants and American Industry, 1914–1924" (PhD
diss., University of Illinois, 2009), 136–271. See esp. 242 and 265–66.

25. Alan Dawley, *Changing the World: American Progressives in War and
Revolution* (Princeton, NJ: Princeton University Press, 2003), 291; Calvin
Coolidge, "Whose Country Is This?" *Good Housekeeping* 72 (February
1921): 13–14.

26. Mae Ngai, *Impossible Subjects: Illegal Aliens and the Making of Modern
America* (Princeton, NJ: Princeton University Press, 2004), 34–35; Abraham Hoffman, *Unwanted Mexican Americans in the Great Depression:
Repatriation Pressures, 1929–1939* (Tucson: University of Arizona Press,
1974), 39; Herbert Hoover, "State of the Union Address, 1931" (Washington, DC, December 8, 1931), archived at http://stateoftheunionaddress.
org/1931-herbert-hoover. The Hoover correspondence is in the secretary
of commerce period section of the archives of the Hoover Presidential

Library in West Branch, Iowa. See box 289 and especially "Hoover to Hon. John Baker" (February 13 and 19, 1924); "Hoover to My Dear [Secretary of Labor James J.] Davis" (November 21, 1923) and the letter from C. S. Ching to Hoover (October 31, 1923) urging "greater consideration of our labor needs" for the rubber industry.

27. Dawley, *Changing the World*, 287–88; Elizabeth G. Messina, "Perversions of Knowledge: Confronting Racist Ideologies behind Intelligence Testing" in William J. Connell and Fred Gardaphé, eds., *Anti-Italianism: Essays on a Prejudice* (New York: Palgrave Macmillan, 2010), 45 ("tennis") and 44–52.

28. Messina, "Perversions of Knowledge," 44–52; Leon J. Kamin, *The Science and Politics of I.Q.* (Potomac, MD: Lawrence Erlbaum, 1974), esp. 20.

29. Messina, "Perversions of Knowledge," 52 for Young's quotations and "union card."

30. Kamin, *Science and Politics of I.Q.*, 27 and 18–29; Messina, "Perversions of Knowledge," 52 and passim.

31. Baritz, *Servants of Power*, 1965), 61; Elspeth Brown, *The Corporate Eye: Photography and the Rationalization of American Commercial Culture: 1884–1929* (Baltimore, MD: Johns Hopkins, 2005), 119–20, on Lewis Hine. See also H. D. Harman, *Industrial Psychology and the Production of Wealth* (New York: Dodd, Mead, 1925), 46 and Stephen Jay Gould, *The Mismeasure of Man* (New York: Norton, 1996, originally 1981), 264–85.

32. Messina, "Perversions of Knowledge," 49, including the quote from the expert.

33. Young as quoted in Messina, "Perversions of Knowledge?" 49; James S. Hunter, "Can Psychology Offset Restricted Immigration?," *Industrial Psychology* 1 (February 1926): 105 and 106–7. On the sharp rise in immigration from Canada in the '20s and the skepticism of a prominent industrial psychologist, see Alan Dawley, *Struggles for Justice: Social Responsibility and the Liberal State* (Cambridge, MA: Harvard University Press, 1991), 291.

34. Katherine Murdoch, "Racial Differences Found in Two American Cities," *Industrial Psychology* 1 (February 1926): 99–104, highlights Hawaii to get at differences among people of color in "moral traits" (as measured largely by professors' opinions) and intelligence; Marjorie E. W. Smith, "Racial Tastes," *Industrial Psychology* 1 (February 1926): 118–20 sought to study "aesthetic preferences" by race and nationality reaching the not unexpected conclusion (120) that in cultural production "Northwestern Europeans" were "more adventurous" and "more inventive." For honesty, see C. H. Twitchell, "What Kind of Men Are Honest?," *Industrial Psychology Magazine: The Magazine of Manpower* 3 (October 1928): 439.

35. Florence M. Teagarden, "Are We a Nation of Morons?" *Industrial Psychology* 1 (August 1926): 535–43; H. A. Worman, *How to Get Workmen*

(Chicago: A. W. Shaw, 1913), 16 had "at least" four-fifths of job-seekers in large cities labeled as "undesirable."

36. Untitled filler, *Industrial Psychology* 1 (February 1926): 82; Baritz, *Servants of Power*, 65 and 128; Roy Willmarth Kelly, "Hiring the Worker," *Industrial Management* 53 (April 1917): 14–15; C. Stanley Raymond, "Industrial Possibilities of the Feeble-Minded," *Industrial Psychology* 2 (September 1927): 473–78; Charles Bernstein, "How Small-Town Industry Makes Use of the Feeble-Minded," *Industrial Psychology* 2 (June 1927): 305–10; Emily Burr, "Adapting the Feeble-Minded to Industry," *Industrial Psychology* 2 (March 1927): 132–38; Arthur W. Kornhauser, "Intelligence Test Ratings of Occupational Groups," *American Economic Review* 15 (March 1925): 190–96. On disability and immigration restriction generally, see Douglas Baynton, "Defectives in the Land: Disability and American Immigration Policy, 1882–1924," *Journal of American Ethnic History* 24 (Spring 2005): 31–44.

37. Henry Pratt Fairchild, "The Making of Americans" [taken from *The Melting-Pot Mistake*], *Industrial Psychology* 1 (February 1926): 123, 127–28, and 121–31.

38. M. R. Trabue, "A Demonstration of Character Reading," *Industrial Psychology* 1 (August 1926): 521–24; W. E. B. Du Bois, "Race Intelligence," *Crisis* 20 (July 1920): 118–19.

39. Carl C. Brigham, "Validity of Tests in Examination of Immigrants," *Industrial Psychology* 1 (June 1926): 417 and 413–17; Kamin, *Science and Politics of I.Q.*, 21 and 20–23.

40. F. H. Hankins, "Racial Differences and Industrial Welfare," *Industrial Psychology* 1 (February 1926): 94, 96, 97–98 and passim.

41. Kimball Young, "The New Immigrant and American Industrial Society," *Industrial Psychology* 1 (February 1926): 134, 135, 136, 141–42 and continued in the March 1926 issue under the same title at 191–92, 194, 195, and 201.

42. Unsigned, "A Study of Natio-Racial Mental Differences," *Industrial Psychology* 2 (March 1927): 163–64.

43. David Colcord, "A Beast That Nurtures Children," *Nation's Business* 18 (November 1930): 32–34 and 170–71.

44. Dwight Thompson Farnam, "Negroes as a Source of Industrial Labor," *Industrial Management*, August 1918, 123–29.

45. Farnam, "Negroes as a Source of Industrial Labor," 123–29, esp. 123 for headnote and 125 on the Irish. On humidity and heat, see also Griffith Taylor, "The Distribution of Future White Settlement: A World Survey Based on Physiographic Data," *Geographical Review* 12 (July 1922): 375–402; Daniel E. Bender, *American Abyss: Savagery and Civilization in an Age of Innocence* (Ithaca, NY: Cornell University Press, 2009). No substantial body of management theory produced the searching questioning of racial assumptions that occurred in Franz Boas's anthropology or W. E. B. Du Bois's sociology but some recognition that social

structures produced racial difference was present did at time occur. See, e.g., Thomas R. Garth, "Racial Differences in Mental Fatigue," *Journal of Applied Psychology* 4 (June–September 1920), 235–44, and Garth, "White, Indian and Negro Work Curves," *Journal of Applied Psychology* 5 (March 1921): 14–25, esp. 23–25.

46. Farnam, "Negroes as a Source of Industrial Labor," esp. 125–28 and, on crime, 124. See also William P. Jones, *The Tribe of the Black Ulysses: African American Lumber Workers in the Jim Crow South* (Urbana: University of Illinois Press, 2005), 72–74.

47. Unsigned, "Negro Labor During and After the War," *MLR* 12 (April 1924): 140, 141, and 137–42; Unsigned, "Working and Living Conditions of Negroes in West Virginia," *MLR* 21 (August 1925): 10–13; Unsigned, "The Southern Negro in Cleveland Industries," *MLR* 19 (July 1924): 42, 44, and 41–44; Unsigned, "Industrial Employment of the Negro in Pennsylvania," *MLR Review* 22 (June 1926): 48–51, provides especially glowing accounts for steel. See also Charles H. Wesley, *Negro Labor in the United States, 1850–1925: A Study in American Economic History* (New York: Vanguard Press, 1927), 296–97 on enthusiasm for black labor in war production in shipbuilding.

48. David Montgomery, "Empire, Race, and Working Class Mobilizations," in Peter Alexander and Rick Halpern, eds., *Racializing Class, Classifying Race: Labour and Difference in Britain, The U.S.A., and Africa* (Basingstoke, UK: Macmillan, 1999), 16; Kimberly L. Phillips: *Alabama North: African—American Community, and Working-Class Activism in Cleveland, 1915–45* (Urbana: University of Illinois Press, 1999), 235–37.

49. Quoted in Paul Street, "The Logic and Limits of Plant Loyalty: Black Workers, White Labor, and Corporate Labor Paternalism in Chicago's Stockyards, 1916–1940," *Journal of Social History* 29 (Spring 1996): 661–62; for the question on loyalty, see Unsigned, "Practical Questions," *Industrial Psychology* 1 (February 1926): 83. For "adjustable," see Harold M. Baron, "The Demand for Black Labor: Historical Notes on the Political Economy of Racism," in James Green, ed., *Workers' Struggles, Past and Present: A "Radical America" Reader* (Philadelphia, PA: Temple University Press, 1983), 42.

50. Paul S. Taylor, *Mexican Labor in the United States*, 2 vols. (New York: Arno Press, 1970, originally 1930 and 1932 respectively), 2: 93; John Hinshaw, *Steel and Steelworkers: Race and Class Struggle in Twentieth Century Pittsburgh* (Albany: State University of New York Press, 2002), 43; on race and strikebreaking the most acute treatment remains Warren C. Whatley, "African-American Strikebreaking from the Civil War to the New Deal," *Social Science History* 17 (Winter 1993): 525–58; see also Eric Arnesen, "Specter of the Black Strikebreaker: Race, Employment and Labor Activism in the Industrial Era," *Labor History* 44 (Winter 2003): 319–35.

51. Street, "Logic and Limits of Plant Loyalty," 664; William M. Tuttle, Jr., *Race Riot: Chicago in the Red Summer of 1919* (Urbana: University of Illinois Press, 1996, originally 1970), viii, 108, 152, and 108–56.

52. Lorenzo J. Greene and Carter G. Woodson, *The Negro Wage Earner* (Washington, DC: The Association for the Study of Negro Life and History, 1930), 253 and 140–41; Lloyd H. Bailer, "The Negro Automobile Worker," *Journal of Political Economy* 51 (October 1943): 417, 419, and 415–28; see also T. J. Woofter, "The Negro and Industrial Peace," *Survey* 45 (December 18, 1920): 420–21. See also Herbert R. Northrup, *Organized Labor and the Negro Worker* (New York: Harper and Bros., 1944), 187–92.

53. Zachary Sell, " 'Home Sweet Home': Work, Race, and the Making of Black Beloit" (Senior thesis, Department of History, University of Wisconsin-Milwaukee, 2008), 25; Joe William Trotter, Jr., *Coal, Class, and Color: Blacks in Southern West Virginia, 1915–1932* (Urbana: University of Illinois Press, 1990), 106, 107, and 109.

54. Dennis C. Dickerson, *Out of This Crucible: Black Steelworkers in Western Pennsylvania, 1875–1980* (Albany: State University of New York Press, 1986), 60–61; on skill and danger, see Bailer, "Negro Automobile Worker," 417, with the further observation that there were some skilled jobs in the foundry as well; on steel in the same regard, see Northrup, *Organized Labor and the Negro Worker*, 176–77; for "white men won't do," see Baron, "Demand for Black Labor," 43.

55. Daniel DeNoyelles, "The Negro as Laborer," *Industrial Psychology* 1 (February 1926): 91 and 92.

56. Ibid., 93.

57. Dickerson, *Out of This Crucible*, 105 and 122–23; Trotter, Jr., *Coal, Class, and Color*, 107; Hinshaw, *Steel and Steelworkers*, 42.

58. Charles S. Johnson, "How the Negro Fits in Northern Industries," *Industrial Psychology* 1 (June 1926): 408. Thanks to Zachary Sell for directing us to Johnson's article.

59. Matthew Ward, *Indignant Heart* (New York: New Books, 1952), 29–30; Hinshaw, *Steel and Steelworkers*, 42.

60. Katherine Benton-Cohen, "Other Immigrants: Mexicans and the Dillingham Commission of 1907–1911," *Journal of American Ethnic History* 30 (Winter 2011): 33, 38, and 33–57.

61. Benton-Cohen, "Other Immigrants," 39, 40, and 33–57.

62. Emilio Zamora, *The World of the Mexican Worker in Texas* (College Station: Texas A&M University Press, 1993), 32 and 300–333; Taylor, *Mexican Labor in the United States*, 1: 335; David Montejano, *Anglos and Mexicans in the Making of Texas, 1836–1986* (Austin: University of Texas Press, 1987), 161–259; Devra Weber, *Dark Sweat, White Gold: California Farm Workers, Cotton, and the New Deal* (Berkeley: University of California Press, 1994), 35 ("pigeon").

63. Mae Ngai, "The Architecture of Race in American Immigration Law: A Reexamination of the Immigration Act of 1924," *Journal of American History* 86 (June 1999): 91–92 and *Impossible Subjects*, 7–8. Benton-Cohen, "Other Immigrants," 40; Roediger, *Working toward Whiteness*, 154–55; Montejano, *Anglos and Mexicans*, 61–259.

64. Paul S. Taylor, "Some Aspects of Mexican Immigration," *Journal of Political Economy* 38 (October 1930): 614; on Chicago as a borderlands city, see Nicholas De Genova, *Working the Boundaries: Race, Space, and "Illegality" in Mexican Chicago* (Durham, NC: Duke University Press, 2005).

65. Dionicio Nodín Valdés, *Barrios Norteños: St. Paul and Midwestern Mexican Communities in the Twentieth Century* (Austin: University of Texas Press, 2000), esp. 43 and 103, and Valdés, *Al Norte: Agricultural Workers in the Great Lakes Region, 1917–1970* (Austin: University of Texas Press, 1991), esp. 25 and 59; Taylor, "Some Aspects of Mexican Immigration," 611 and *Mexican Labor in the United States*, passim.

66. See chapter 4. See also Ngai, *Impossible Subjects*, 106.

67. Charles Teague, "A Statement on Mexican Immigration," *Saturday Evening Post* 200 (March 10, 1928): 169–70; on Teague, see the biographical materials in "Guide to the Charles Collins Teague Papers," housed in the Bancroft Library, University of California, online at http://cdn.calisphere. org/data/13030/5h/tf4g5004sh/files/tf4g5004sh.pdf; Kathleen Mapes, *Sweet Tyranny: Migrant Labor, Industiral Agriculture, and Imperial Politics* (Urbana: University of Illinois Press, 2009), 147.

68. Abraham Hoffman, *Unwanted Mexican Americans in the Great Depression: Repatriation Pressures, 1929–1939* (Tucson: University of Arizona Press, 1974), 10 quotes Clements; Karl De Laittre, "The Mexican Laborer and You," *Nation's Business* 18 (November 1930): 107, 44, and 104–6. See also Teague, "Statement on Mexican Immigration," 169–70 and Weber, *Dark Sweat, White Gold*, 35 ("totally dependent").

69. Hoffman, *Unwanted Mexican Americans in the Great Depression*, 16–17 and 182, n. 5; on a relative lack of "independence," see Adrian Cruz, "Racialized Fields: Asians, Mexicans and the Farm Labor Struggle in California" (PhD diss., University of Illinois, 2009), 32; Taylor, *Mexican Labor in the United States*, 2: 92.

70. Montejano, *Anglos and Mexicans*, 218; José M. Alamillo, *Making Lemons Out of Lemonade: Mexican American Labor and Leisure in a California Town, 1880–1960* (Urbana: University of Illinois Press, 2006), 139–40; Francisco Arturo Rosales, *Chicano! The History of the Mexican American Civil Rights Movement* (Houston, TX: Arte Publico Press, 1997), 117–19; Taylor, *Mexican Labor in the United States*, 1: 45–54, 158, 211, 330, and 351; Varden Fuller, *Hired Hands in California's Farm Fields* (n.p.: Giannini Foundation Special Reports, 1991), 156.

71. *Report of Governor C. C. Young's Mexican Fact-Finding Committee* (San Francisco, CA: R and E Research Associates, 1970, originally 1930), 162;

Emory S. Bogardus, *The Mexican in the United States* (Los Angeles: University of Southern California Press, 1934), 40–41.

72. Taylor, *Mexican Labor in the United States*, 1: 8, 9, and 11–12.

73. Taylor, *Mexican Labor in the United States*, 1: 130, 148–49, 160, and 130–61; Fuller, *Hired Hands in California's Farm Fields*, 156.

74. Taylor, *Mexican Labor in the United States*, 1: 41 and 330.

75. *Report of Governor C. C. Young's Mexican Fact-Finding Committee*, 90–91, 163, and 170; Cruz, "Racialized Fields," 32, including quote from Fisher; Unsigned "The Filipino Problem in California," *Monthly Labor Review* 30 (June 1930): 73 and 72–74.

76. Glenn E. Hoover, "Our Mexican Immigrants," *Foreign Affairs* 8 (October 1929): 99, 100, 101, 102, 103, and 104.

77. T. N. Carver, "Where Peril Lurks in Immigration," *Nation's Business* 18 (June 1930): 40–42 and 138–40; the insert is at 42 and is titled "A Business View of Immigration" by F. Stuart Fitzpatrick, of the Chamber's Civic Development Department; F. H. Hankins, "Racial Differences and Industrial Welfare," *Industrial Psychology* 1 (February 1926): 98 and passim. On Carver, see Higham, *Strangers in the Land*, 77–78.

78. Benton-Cohen, "Other Immigrants," 44; Taylor, "Some Aspects of Mexican Immigration," 611–14; for the desire of preeminent steel industry leader to bring in "Oriental labor" in this period, see Brody, *Steelworkers in America*, 187.

79. Taylor, *Mexican Labor in the United States*, 2: 1, 56–57, 4, 13, and 1–57 passim; Unsigned, "Selective Immigration," *Iron Age* 3 (January 18, 1923): 235; Wyndham Lewis, *Paleface: The Philosophy of the " Melting-Pot"* (London: Chatto and Windus, 1929), 262–63 similarly speaks of "white men as a class."

80. Taylor, *Mexican Labor in the United States*, 2: 10, 14, and 13.

81. Gabriela F. Arredondo, *Mexican Chicago: Race, Identity and Nation, 1916–1939* (Urbana: University of Illinois Press, 2008), 62.

82. *Report of Governor C.C. Young's Mexican Fact-Finding Committee*, 90, 92, 93; Zaragosa Vargas, *Proletarians of the North: Mexican Industrial Workers in Detroit and the Midwest, 1917–1933* (Berkeley: University of California Press, 1999), 102; Taylor, *Mexican Labor in the United States*, 2: 80 ("no Mexicans" and "intelligent labor"), 82, 83, 88, 89, and 92; Arredondo, *Mexican Chicago*, 62 ("suave"). See also Valdés, *Al Norte*, 46.

83. Arredondo, *Mexican Chicago*, 64.

84. Ibid., 60 and 59–62; Taylor, *Mexican Labor in the United States*, 1: 151–52.

85. Arredondo, *Mexican Chicago*, 62–63; Taylor, *Mexican Labor in the United States*, 2: 86, 87, and 89.

86. Taylor, *Mexican Labor in the United States*, 2: 81, 82, 85, 86, 90, 91, 93, 94.

87. Ibid., 1: 153 and 155; see also 150; Arredondo, *Mexican Chicago*, 57, 58–59, 63–64 (Wisconsin Steel), and 134; Charles S. Johnson, *The Negro in American Civilization: A Study in Negro Life and Race Relations in the Light of Social Research* (New York: Henry Holt, 1930), 37.

88. Zaragosa Vargas, *Proletarians of the North: Mexican Industrial Workers in Detroit and the Midwest, 1917–1933* (Berkeley: University of California Press, 1999), 102 ("hot dirty jobs").
89. Taylor, *Mexican Labor in the United States*, 2: 82–83, 87 ("adept"), 88, 90–91.
90. Ibid., 2: 93–94.

Afterword

1. On uses of "discriminating," "racial discrimination," and their variants, we have used the University of Michigan Library's massive Making of America database at http://quod.lib.umich.edu/m/moagrp/. The paragraph specifically refers to George White, "Yankee Lewis' Famous Hostelry in the Wilderness," in Michigan Pioneer and Historical Society, *Historical Collections*, vol. 26 (Lansing: Robert Smith, 1896), 305; "Inaugural Address of Robert Rutter, President," General Society of Mechanics and Tradesmen of the City of New York, *One Hundred and Third Annual Report* (New York: J. J. Little, 1889), 18; W. C. Brownell, "The Painting of George Butler," *Scribner's Magazine* 26 (September 1899): 302; Hinton Rowan Helper, *Compendium of the Impending Crisis of the South* (New York: A. B. Burdick, 1860), 41; True Worthy Hoit, *The Right of American Slavery* (St. Louis, MO: L. Bushnell, 1860), 10 ("savagism"); Rev. Samuel Seabury, *American Slavery Distinguished from the Slavery of English Theorists, and Justified by the Law of Nature* (New York: Mason Brothers, 1861), 190 and 277 ("slave-labor").
2. See, e.g., Carol P. Harvey and M. June Allard, *Understanding and Managing Diversity* (Boston: Prentice-Hall, 2008); Norma Carr-Ruffino, *Managing Diversity* (Boston: Pearson, 2009); for a historical account too unproblematically valorizing the role of corporate management in promoting diversity, particularly regarding inclusion of black workers, see Jennifer Delton, *Racial Integration in Corporate America, 1940–1990* (Cambridge: Cambridge University Press, 2009).
3. Grace Hong, *The Ruptures of American Capital: Women of Color Feminism and The Culture of Immigrant Labor* (Minneapolis: University of Minnesota Press, 2006) and Roderick Ferguson, *The Reorder of Things: On the Institutionalization of Difference* (forthcoming from University of Minnesota Press) eloquently show the many different ways in which capital has not merely accommodated diversity but has learned to use it over the last four decades, though some of the dynamics involved may not be entirely peculiar to that period.
4. David R. Roediger, *Working toward Whiteness: How America's Immigrants Became White* (New York: Basic, 2005), 200–240.
5. See Dan Georgakas and Martin Surkin, "Niggermation in Auto Company Policy and Rise of Black Caucuses in Detroit," *Radical America* 9 (January/February 1975): 31–57; Bernard Maegi, "Dangerous Persons, Delayed Pilgrims: Baltic Displaced Petrsons and the Making of the Cold

War" (PhD diss., University of Minnesota, 2009); Deborah Cohen, *Braceros: Mexican Citizens and Transnational Subjects in the Postwar United States and Mexico* (Chapel Hill: University of North Carolina Press, 2011).

6. On the Middle East, see Nigel Harris, *The New Untouchables: Immigration and the New World Worker* (London: Penguin, 1995, 58 and 59–62) and, for background, Robert Vitalis, *America's Kingdom: Mythmaking on the Saudi Oil Frontier* (Stanford, CA: Stanford University Press, 2007); see also Jackson Allers and Simba Russeau, "The Sleeping Giant: Foreign Workers in Dubai," *Menasset*, June 6, 2008, at http://www.menassat. com/?q=en/news-articles/3877-sleeping-giant-foreign-workers-dubai; Ben Bland, "Singapore Pulls the Welcome Mat for Foreign Workers," *Asia Sentinel*, February 5, 2010, at http://www.asiasentinel.com/index. php?option=com_content&task=view&id=2285&;Itemid=195.

7. Ariana Eunjung Cha, "Underclass of Workers Created in Iraq," *Washington Post*, July 1, 2004, A1; Naomi Klein, *The Shock Doctrine: The Rise of Disaster Capitalism* (New York: Picador, 2007), 368–69 and 448–53; Lourdes Garcia-Navarro, "Trafficking of Foreign Workers Flourishes in Iraq," NPR, April 6, 2009, at http://www.npr.org/templates/story/story. php?storyId=102705618; T. Christiann Miller, "War Contractors: The Numbers on American vs. Foreign Workers in Iraq and Afghanistan" ProPublica, June 19, 2009, at http://www.propublica.org/feature/war-contractors-the-numbers-on-american-vs.-foreign-workers-619; Emir Imamovic, "Bosnian Brothels Flourish," Institute for War & Peace Reporting, September 6, 2005, at http://www.iwpr.net/report-news/bosnian-brothels-flourish.

8. Catherine Ceniza Choy, *Empire of Care: Nursing and Migration in Filipino American History* (Durham, NC: Duke University Press, 2003); Victor Devinatz, *High-Tech Betrayal: Working and Organizing on the Shop Floor* (East Lansing: Michigan State University Press, 1999); Rhacel Salazar Parreñas, *Servants of Globalization: Women, Migration, and Domestic Work* (Stanford, CA: Stanford University Press, 2001); Susan Chandler and Jill B. Jones, *Casino Women: Courage in Unexpected Places* (Ithaca, NY: Cornell University Press, 2011).

9. Faranak Miraftab, "Rapid Racial and Cultural Change in Two Former Sundown Towns" *Sundown Town News* 3 (2009): 1–7 at http://sundown. afro.illinois.edu/newsletters/sundownnewletter09-09.pdf; S. Lynn Walker, "Beardstown: Reflection of a Changing America," *Springfield State Journal-Register*, November 9, 2003, for the quotations; Karen Fitzgerald, "Welcome to America," *Illinois Times*, June 29, 2006, at http://www. illinoistimes.com/Springfield/article-3191-welcome-to-america.html.

10. Miraftab, "Racial and Cultural Change," 1-7; Bob Burgdorfer, "Immigration Officials Arrest 62 at Pork Plant," Reuters, April 4, 2007, at %3Ca href= http://www.reuters.com/article/domesticNews/idUSN0435166620070404? pageNumber=2&;virtualBrandChannel = 0. On sundown towns see James

Loewen, *Sundown Towns: A Hidden Dimension of American Racism* (New York: New Press, 2005).

11. Marx, *Grundrisse: Foundations of the Critique of Political Economy*, translated by Martin Nicolaus (Harmondsworth, UK: Penguin 1973), 296–98.

12. See sources in notes 8 and 9 and conversations with Faranak Miraftab; Eileen Diaz McConnell and Faranak Miraftab, "Sundown Town to 'Little Mexico': Old-Timers and Newcomers in an American Small Town" forthcoming in *Rural Sociology*; Libby Sander, "Immigration Raid Yields 62 Arrests," *New York Times*, April 5, 2007; Jennifer Lundeen, "Meat Processors Look to Puerto Rico for Workers," NPR, December 6, 2007, at http://www.npr.org/templates/story/story.php?storyId=16962455.

13. See also Nicholas De Genova, *Working the Boundaries; Race, Space and "Illegality" in Mexican Chicago* (Durham, NC: Duke University Press, 2005); De Genova, "The Management of 'Quality': Class Decomposition and Racial Formation in a Chicago Factory," *Dialectical Anthropology* 34 (June, 2010): 249–72; David Roediger, "Comment on De Genova's 'Management of Quality," in the same issue, 273–76; Unsigned, "Anheuser-Busch InBev Who's Who," at http://www.ab-inbev.com/go/investors/overview/who_is_who.cfm (consulted August 18, 2011).

14. Peter Rachleff, "Immigrant Rights Are Labor Rights," *MRzine*, August 19, 2008, at http://www.monthlyreview.org/mrzine/rachleff190808.html; Rachleff, "A Union of Immigrants Wins Minneapolis Hotel Strike," *Labor Notes* 257 (August 2000); David Bacon, "Unions Come to Smithfield," *American Prospect*, December 17, 2008, at http://www.prospect.org/cs/articles?article=unions_come_to_smithfield.

15. Joseph Nevins, *Dying to Live: A Story of US Immigration in an Age of Global Apartheid* (San Francisco, CA: City Lights, 2008); Julia Preston, "Foreign Students in Work Visa Program Stage Walkout at Plant," *New York Times*, August 17, 2011, at http://www.nytimes.com/2011/08/18/us/18immig.html?_r=1&pagewanted=all&src=ISMR_HP_LO_MST_FB; on educational exchanges and the value of diversity, see also Roderick Ferguson, *Reorder of Things*, forthcoming.

16. See James Lamont and Joe Leahy, "US Matches India Outsourcing Costs," *Financial Times*, August 17, 2010, at http://www.ft.com/cms/s/2/0f6d8f76-aa29-11df-9367-00144feabdc0.html#axzz1VM2qzJuX; Carolyn Beeler, "Outsourced Call Centers Return, to US Homes," NPR, August 25, 2010, at http://www.npr.org/templates/story/story.php?storyId=129406588 (with graph on efficiency inside and outside the United States); Mehui Srivastava, "Philippine Call Centers Overtake India," *Bloomberg Businessweek*, December 2, 2010, at http://www.businessweek.com/magazine/content/10_50/b4207017538393.htm; Juan Gonzales, "Verizon Workers, Management Dig in for Decisive Labor Battle," *New York Daily News*, August 17, 2011, at http://www.nydailynews.com/ny_local/2011/08/17/2011-08-17_verizon_workers_management_dig_in_for_decisive_labor_battle_this_is_no_

ordinary_.html; Jefferson R. Cowie, *Capital Moves: RCA's 70-Year Quest for Cheap Labor* (New York: New Press, 2001), esp. 100–127 and 152–79.

17. On the *Wards Cove* case and its continuing influence despite 1991 legislation partly contravening it, see Amos N. Jones and D. Alexander Ewing, "The Ghost of *Wards Cove*: The Supreme Court, The Bush Administration and Ideology Undermining Title VII," *Harvard Blackletter Law Journal* 21 (2005): 165–84. For the logic of the changes wrought by the decision in the case, see especially Justice John Paul Stevens's minority opinion in *Wards Cove Packing Co. v. Atonio*, 490 U.S. (1989) at http://www.law.cornell.edu/supct/html/historics/USSC_CR_0490_0642_ZD1.html, esp. 662–72 and n. 4 and 24. The majority opinion is at http://www.law.cornell.edu/supct/html/historics/USSC_CR_0490_0642_ZO.html.

18. Nicholas De Genova, "The Queer Politics of Migration: Reflections on 'Illegality' and Incorrigibilty," *Studies in Social Justice* 4 (2010): 101–26.

INDEX